3 9158 00250824 1

DATE DUE

D1452317

A PICTORIAL HISTORY OF AUSTRALIA

REX & THEA RIENITS

A PICTORIAL HISTORY OF AUSTRALIA

REX & THEA RIENITS

Paul Hamlyn
London/New York/Sydney/Toronto

Authors' Note

The illustrations in this book come from many sources, and the authors wish to record their sincere thanks to all who have contributed them. In particular they express their gratitude to Mr Rex de C. Nan Kivell, who allowed them unlimited access to his unrivalled collection of Australiana; Mr H. L. White and the staff of the National Library, Canberra; Mr G. D. Richardson and the staff of the Mitchell Library, Sydney; Mr W. Thorn and the staff of the Library, Australia House, London; Mr H. J. Murphy and the staff of the Australian News and Information Bureau, London; Mr W. R. Lancaster and the staff of the Australian War Memorial, Canberra; Mr D. Simpson, librarian of the Royal Commonwealth Society; and the National Bank of Australasia Ltd.

Published by The Hamlyn Publishing Group Ltd
Hamlyn House · The Centre · Feltham · Middlesex

SBN 6000 3125 X

Filmset in Great Britain by Filmtype Services
Printed in Hong Kong by Lee Fung

Contents

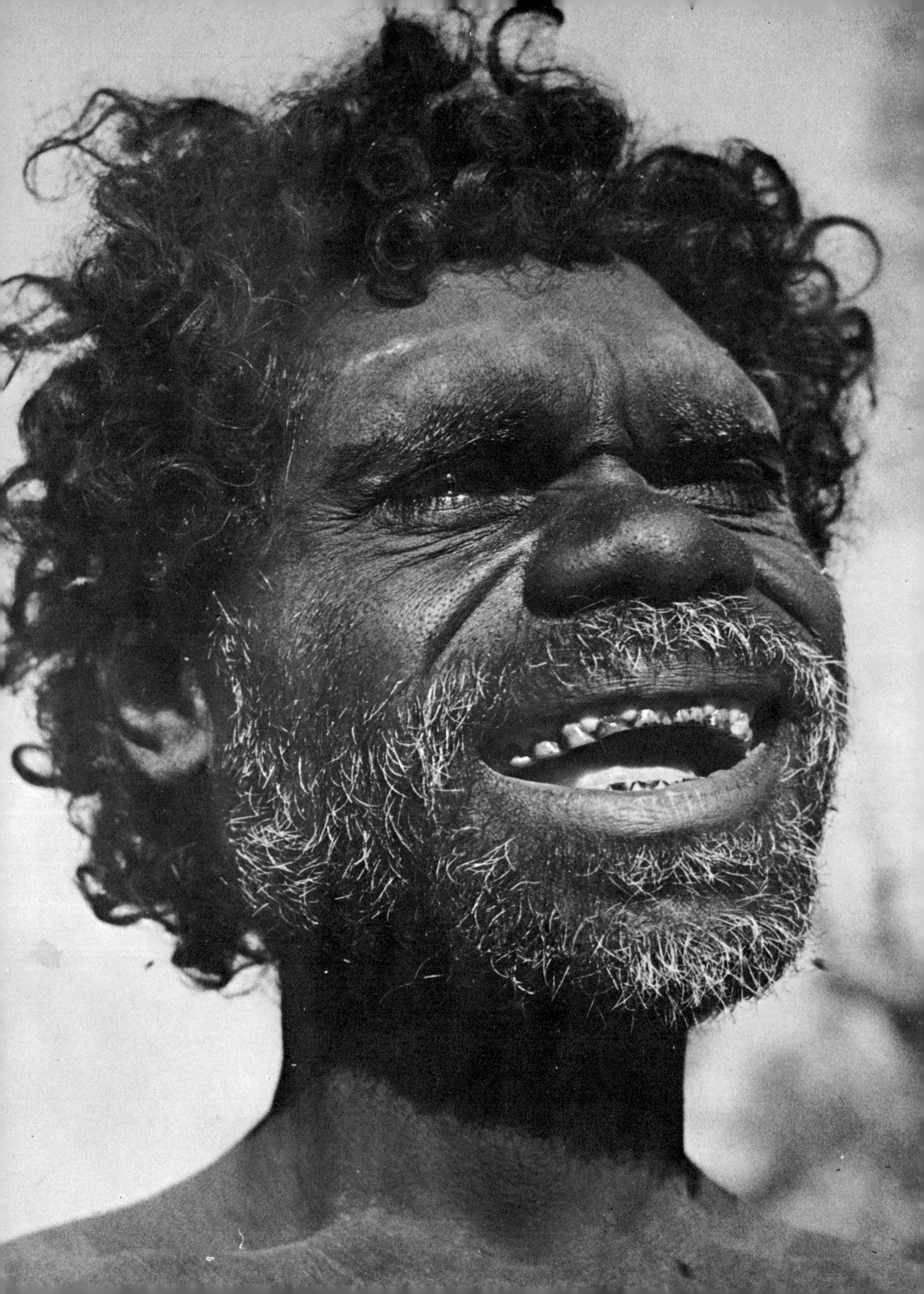

1 Before the White Man

Australia is the fifth and smallest of the continents, three-quarters the size of Europe, a quarter the size of Africa and a sixth the size of Asia or the Americas. On the other hand, it is by far the largest island in the world with a coastline of 12,210 miles and an overall area of almost three million square miles, which makes it slightly smaller than the United States and about twenty-four times the size of the British Isles.

Geologically Australia dates back at least 2,000 million years, and the poet who described it as 'a land as old as time' was not far wrong. Some people believe it was once part of the Antarctic continent and that it reached its present site by a process of gradual drift. There is a wider theory that until a few million years ago it was part of a great land mass which reached north to the Asian mainland and east as far as New Zealand, Tonga, Fiji, the New Hebrides and New Caledonia. When Captain James Cook discovered New Caledonia in 1774 he noted that parts of it looked remarkably like Australia and this remains obvious today even to the most casual, unscientific eye.

Skeletal remains and fossils indicate that at one time Australia was inhabited by giant land fauna which included a wombat called *Diprotodon australis* as large as a present-day rhinoceros, kangaroos and emus up to three times their present size, and lizards up to twenty feet long. There was also a small marsupial lion, probably carnivorous, which would have made him almost unique in a land of herbivores. The country's vegetation in those days was very much as it is now.

In its present shape, which will no doubt change greatly in the next few million years, well over a third of Australia lies within the tropics. Cape York, its northern tip, is in a roughly equivalent latitude to Costa Rica, Gambia, Somaliland, the far south of India and the central islands of the Philippines. The southern tip of Tasmania has its approximate northern equivalents in Portland (Maine), Toulon,

Left A man of northern Australia.

Right Karri trees in the south-west of Western Australia. They grow to 300 feet and are the world's tallest hardwoods.

Above Giant anthills – more correctly nests of the magnetic termite – up to twelve feet high are a feature of northern Australia.

Australian fauna. *Far left* A venomous tiger snake rearing to strike. *Left* The cuscus, a member of the possum family, mostly found in northern Queensland. *Lower left* A monitor lizard or goanna. This specimen is about nine feet long. *Near left* The ever-popular koala.

Top right Grose Valley in the once impenetrable Blue Mountains west of Sydney.

Right An old watercourse cutting through eroded hills in central Australia.

Perugia, the Black Sea and Vladivostock. This wide geographical spread makes for much variety in physical character and climate, ranging from jungle to desert to alps. It is a comparatively flat country with inconsiderable mountain ranges near the eastern seaboard of which the highest peak, Mount Kosciusko, reaches a mere 7,316 feet, roughly a quarter the height of Mount Everest. Much of its interior is barren and almost rainless, and as a result the very great bulk of its people live on or within reach of its generally fertile east and south-east coasts. Despite huge conurbations such as Sydney and Melbourne its overall population is sparse in relation to its size. Its present average of four people to the square mile compares with, for instance, well over 750 to the square mile in England and Wales.

No one quite knows when it first became inhabited by humans but modern archaeologists, using radio-carbon dating techniques, think it was probably 15,000 years ago or even more. Nor can anyone be

Above right Except for the ostrich the Australian emu is the world's largest bird. It stands up to six feet and although flightless is exceptionally fleet of foot.

Two species of Australian fauna now extinct, drawn by a French artist, E. Lesueur, in 1803. The short-legged cassowary and (*right*) the banded kangaroo.

sure whence came its first inhabitants, or how. The earliest immigrants appear to have been the Tasmanian Aborigines, a people of negroid characteristics. Some think they made drift voyages in canoes and rafts from New Guinea and other Melanesian areas but the more popular theory is that they arrived when the sea level was still low enough to allow access from Asia. The Tasmanoids were followed much later by waves of Australoids, who probably originated somewhere in south Asia. These newcomers assimilated or destroyed some of the Tasmanoids and drove the remnants down into the south-east corner, where in time the flooding of what is now Bass Strait effectively isolated them from further attack. Thus when the first white man appeared less than four centuries ago there were two distinct races, those of the mainland and those of the island of Tasmania. Cook was the first to come in contact with both races and the first to record their physical differences. The impact of the white

Above right Kangaroos grazing. Since the conquest of the rabbit pest wild kangaroos have multiplied greatly.

intruders was fatal. The last Tasmanian died almost a century ago after a mere seventy years of contact with 'civilization'; and the mainland Aborigines seemed equally doomed until a belated stirring of conscience during the present century checked the rate of their annihilation and offered them some hope of a future.

The first European settlers in Australia saw the Aborigines as primitive survivors of the Stone Age, uncouth, unintelligent and of such a low cultural status as to be barely human. In this they echoed the judgment of the English seaman William Dampier, who in 1688 met some Aborigines on the north-west coast. In his best-selling book *A New Voyage Round the World* Dampier wrote: 'The inhabitants of this country are the miserablest people in the world . . . setting aside their human shape they differ but little from brutes.' Cook, who met them a century later on the east coast, saw them through more charitable eyes. 'These people may appear to some to be the most wretched on earth', he wrote, 'but in reality they are far happier than we Europeans. They live in a tranquility which is not disturbed by inequality of condition, the earth and sea furnish them with all things necessary for life, they covet not magnificent houses and they sleep as sound in a small hovel or even in the open

Top left Among Australia's unique flora is the yacca, a species of *Xanthorrhoea*, popularly known as 'Blackboy'.

Below left Snow country, in the Snowy Mountains, south-eastern Australia.

Right Tribal Aborigines of the Rawlinson Ranges in the far north-west.

Below Rock painting in the Wellington Range, Arnhem Land, showing male and female spirit beings.

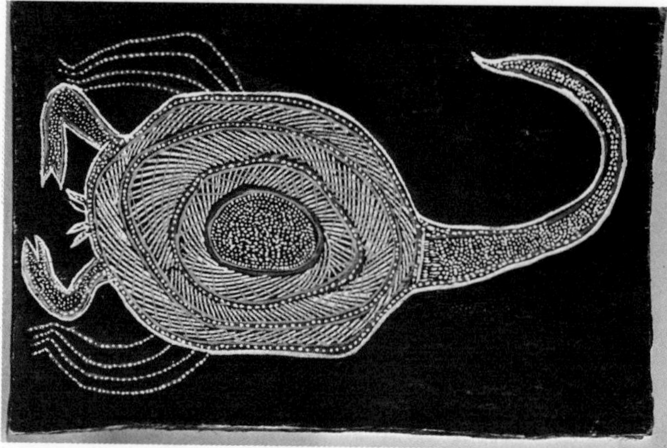

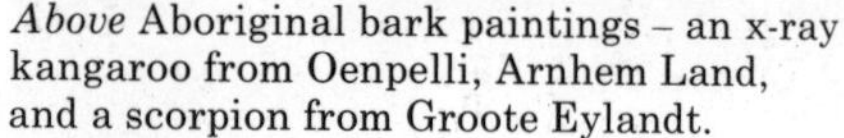

Above Aboriginal bark paintings – an x-ray kangaroo from Oenpelli, Arnhem Land, and a scorpion from Groote Eylandt.

Below Aborigines during a corroboree.

Top right A didgeridoo-player provides music for a corroboree.

Below right An artist at work on a bark painting.

as the king in his palace on a bed of down.'

As the Aborigines had no knowledge of metal-working their culture was indeed of the Stone Age, but in all other respects the assessments of the early settlers were wide of the mark. Far from being unintelligent they had come to terms with their generally harsh environment in a way that no white man could hope to do, and in a sense they had become as much a part of that environment as the animals they hunted and the bush in which they lived. There were perhaps 300,000 of them spread throughout the continent and they lived in tribes based broadly on family units and ruled by their male elders, to whom obedience was a prime virtue. Their social and religious disciplines were complex and strict, and transgressors were severely punished. They spoke perhaps 500 languages, but many of these so fundamentally resembled one another that communication was rarely difficult. Their country had virtually no indigenous plants that could be cultivated for crops and no animals except their own dogs that could be domesticated; so they neither grew nor bred their food but killed it and plucked it from trees and dug for it. In the interior this imposed on them a semi-nomadic way of life; in coastal areas where much of their food came from the water they were able to lead a more settled existence. Each tribe had its own recognized territory in which its people could hunt and move at will. In the interior, where food resources were scattered, this might measure some thousands of square miles; on the coast it was usually small. Because of the need to move camp from time to time it was pointless for them to build permanently or to clutter themselves with possessions. Huts which could be put up or pulled down in a few hours sheltered them adequately enough from wind and rain; pottery, woven cloth and other household goods would merely have hampered their freedom of movement. In hot weather both sexes generally went naked; in colder regions they wore cloaks of kangaroo or possum skin. They were fond of ornaments and for ceremonial occasions or for combat the men painted themselves in a wide variety of designs.

When they were on the move – on walkabout as it is nowadays known – the men went first carrying only their weapons in case they should encounter game or enemies and the women followed, burdened with their few belongings and infant children and usually carrying smouldering brands to save the tedious necessity of making fire at night. They ate whatever came their way that was edible, usually when and where they found it. Their diet was wide. It included, among living things, kangaroo, emu,

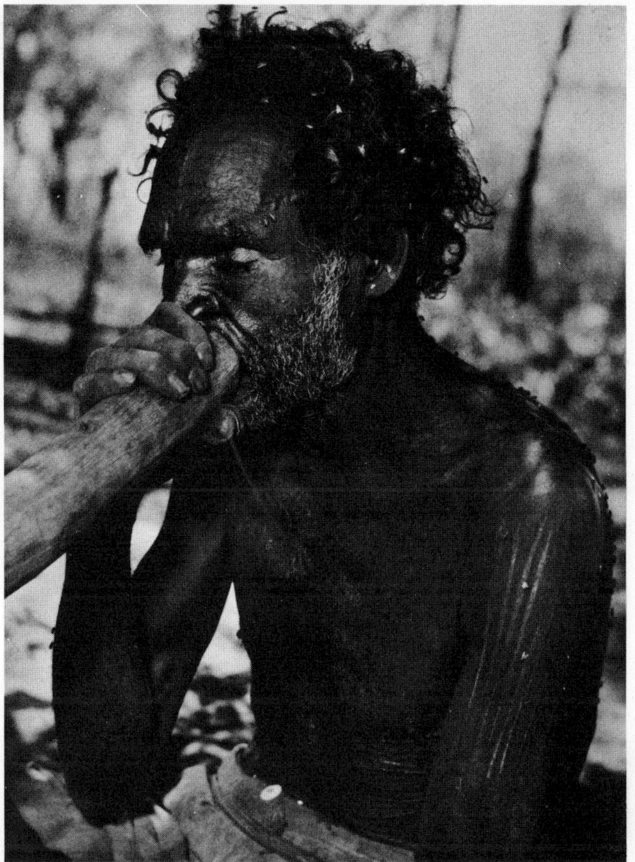

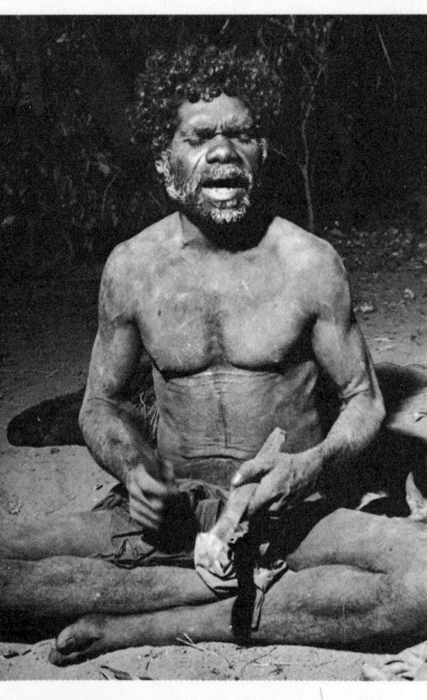

Left An attractive young girl from Yirrkalla, Arnhem Land, and an old man chanting at a night corroboree.

Below Skinning a crocodile caught in the Liverpool River, Arnhem Land.

Below right Young men taking part in a sacred ritual.

bandicoot, possum, native cat, koala, flying fox, wombat and kangaroo-rat. They ate snakes and goannas, birds of all kinds and birds' eggs, honey-ants, white-ants, locusts and many other insects, including the well-known witchety grub. Honey was their favourite delicacy. On the coast they ate fish, shell-fish, turtle, turtle-eggs, seal, whale and whatever else the sea offered. While the men hunted the women and children collected plant foods – seeds, nuts, berries, fruits, roots, tubers and palm-tree pith. When food was plentiful they gorged; when it was scarce they accepted hunger philosophically.

Their main weapons were the spear, tipped with bone or stone, barbed for hunting or warfare and multi-pronged for fishing, and its accessory, the spear-thrower or woomera, a sort of artificial extension of their throwing arm, with a hooked or notched end into which fitted the butt of the spear. With the aid of his woomera a good spearman could throw up to sixty yards with great accuracy and could usually hit a moving target at twenty-five yards. In addition they had shields, clubs for hand-to-hand combat or for throwing, and, of course, the boomerang. Their boomerangs were of two kinds, returnable and non-returnable, and contrary to general belief the latter were by far the more important as hunting or offensive weapons. A boomerang of this type usually weighed about a pound and a half and it could maim or even kill a kangaroo, bring down a bird on the wing, or seriously injure a human adversary. The fact that non-returning boomerangs were also used in southern India is thought by some to indicate that it was here the Australians originated. But sceptics point out that the same weapon was used in ancient Egypt, too.

On the whole the Aborigines were a peaceable people. Each tribe minded its own business and conceded its neighbours the right to mind theirs. Their ambitions did not run to territorial conquest and

Left A man of northern Australia smoking his pipe.

Right Young mother and child.

they had no lust for power. When wars occurred they were usually limited affairs provoked by one tribe encroaching too blatantly on another's territory or by the need to avenge some insult or crime, and casualties rarely exceeded a few dead or wounded. They never killed for the sake of killing, nor were they in the habit of raping the women or murdering the children of their enemies. They were not given to human sacrifice, nor to enslaving or torturing their prisoners. Once honour was satisfied friendly relations were resumed. There was much intertribal contact for trade and for joint participation in various rites and ceremonies and there was a good deal of intermarriage.

The Aborigines were a deeply religious people and much of their mythology was of great poetic and imaginative beauty. Their myths described the creation, and explained away most human behaviour and activity, and they were handed down by word of mouth or expressed through the medium of song and dance. Their dances were called corroborees and they were performed to the accompaniment of percussion instruments and didgeridoos or drone-pipes, formidable instruments of about six feet made from bamboo or hollow saplings and extremely difficult to play. Corroborees were often held to persuade ancestral or other spirits to bring rain when it was needed or to ensure successful hunting. If the object was not achieved the blame was laid on some error in ritual or chanting, or on some breach of tabu, or on the desecration of a sacred place. There were also corroborees to climax the initiation of boys into manhood, to mourn death, to encourage love, or simply to entertain by miming some event such as a successful hunt or, in more recent times, the sight of an aeroplane or white men playing cricket.

The Aborigines' urge for artistic self-expression manifested itself usually in rock and cave paintings and engravings, in wood sculpture and in painting on bark. In Arnhem Land, on the north coast, much creative work of this kind reached a high standard. Most Aboriginal art was linked with religious and other rituals but sometimes it was purely secular and sometimes the artist worked for nobody's satisfaction but his own. The actual creation of a painting or carving was all that mattered; once completed it ceased to interest him and was something to be given away or just thrown away.

So for perhaps 500 generations these simple, gentle and peaceful people lived out their quiet, unchanging lives in an unchanging land. Elsewhere men were learning the use of metals and the wheel, learning to write and to build, developing the techniques of destruction. Cities appeared and nations rose and fell in a welter of blood and ruin. Secure, as it seemed, in their isolation the Australian Aborigines knew nothing of these things, and were doubtless the happier for not knowing. But their security was an illusion and like all illusions it could not last forever.

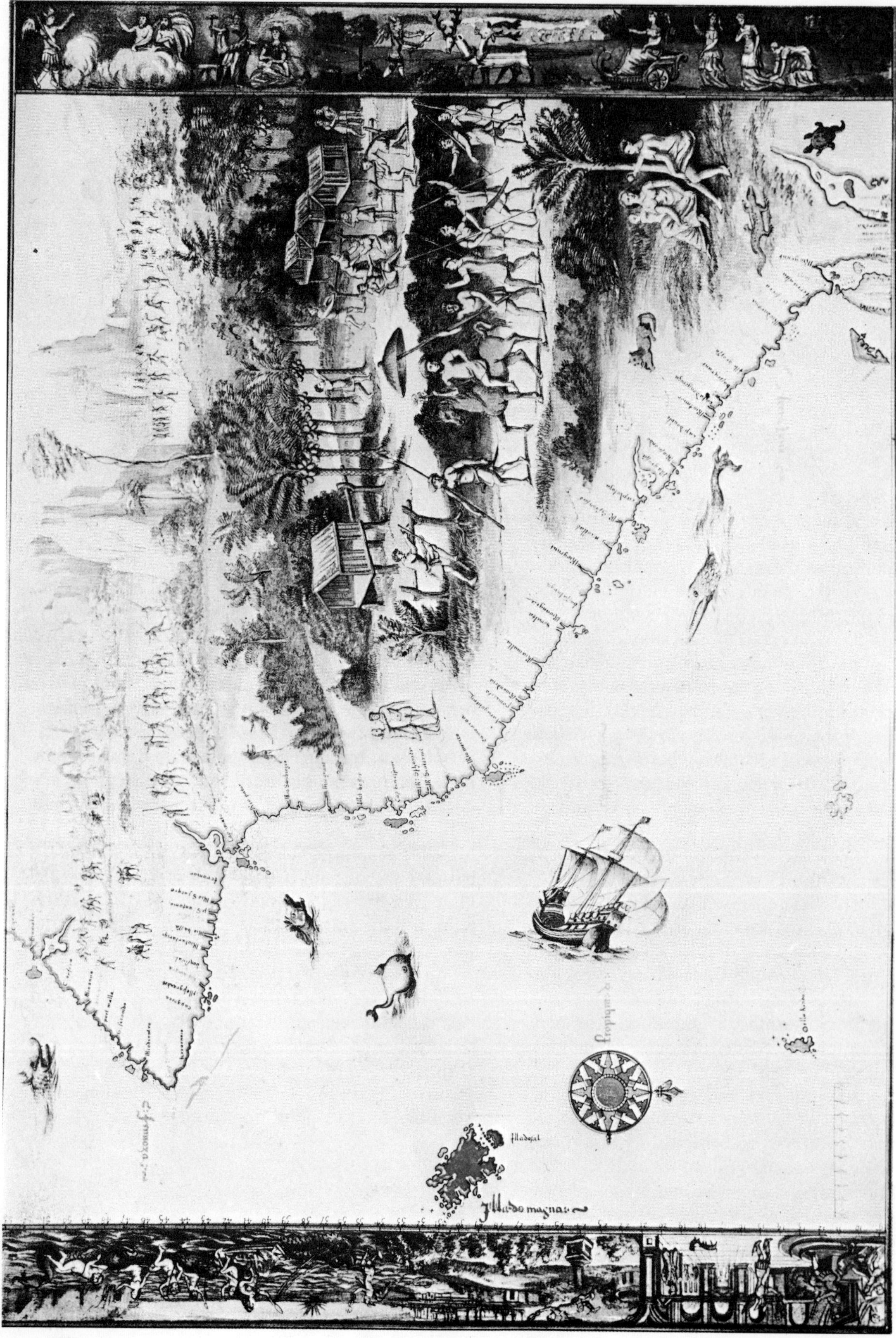

2 The Discovery of Australia

In ancient times it was assumed, except by a few scholars, that the world was flat and this belief persisted until five hundred years ago. Once the fact of its roundness was accepted old theories were revived that there must be a great southern continent on its underside to balance the land mass of the northern hemisphere and so there began to appear on maps vague outlines labelled *Terra Australis Incognita*.

For a while nobody cared much about this unknown land of the south. To Europeans it seemed much more profitable to establish a sea-route to the rich markets of the Far East as a less hazardous alternative to the existing overland caravan trails. In 1488 in search of such a route the Portuguese captain Bartholomeu Diaz reached the southern tip of Africa, which he called the Cape of Good Hope, and in 1497 Vasco da Gama continued on from there and reached India. Within a few years the Portuguese had formed highly profitable trade settlements in East Africa, Arabia, Persia and India. Pushing further on they reached and conquered the Spice Islands, now known as the Moluccas, which lie about 750 miles north of Australia.

Meanwhile a Genoese seaman, Christopher Columbus, with backing from the Spanish court had sailed west from Europe and found some islands in the West Indies which he persuaded himself were part of Japan and China. However, Spaniards who followed him soon realized the truth, and realized too that the only practical western route to China was around the southern tip of South America. Ferdinand Magellan, who set out in 1519 with five small ships, was the first to use this route. Sailing north-west across the Pacific he missed Australia but reached the Philippine Islands, where he was killed in a fight with natives. His expedition broke up but one ship continued home to Spain by way of the Cape of Good Hope and was thus the first to sail round the world.

When Spanish ships next ventured into the Pacific it was not to challenge the Portuguese but to find a continent rich in slaves and gold which according to Peruvian legends existed about 1,800 miles to the west. In 1567 in search of this mythical land Álvara de Mendaña discovered the Solomon Islands, about 1,500 miles north-east of Australia but then 'lost' them and died while trying to locate them twenty-six years later. The next to try was Pedro Fernandes de Quirós, who had been Mendaña's pilot on his second voyage. In 1605 Quirós got as far as the island of Espiritu Santo in the New Hebrides, about 1,200 miles east of Australia and was sure he had found the elusive continent. But his lieutenant Luis Vaez de Torres thought otherwise. He sailed round the

Left The first known attempt to portray an imaginary Terra Australis, from Nicholas Vallard's Atlas, 1547.

Right Vasco da Gama, the Portuguese captain, whose voyage to India in 1497 opened the way to the conquest of the East Indies.

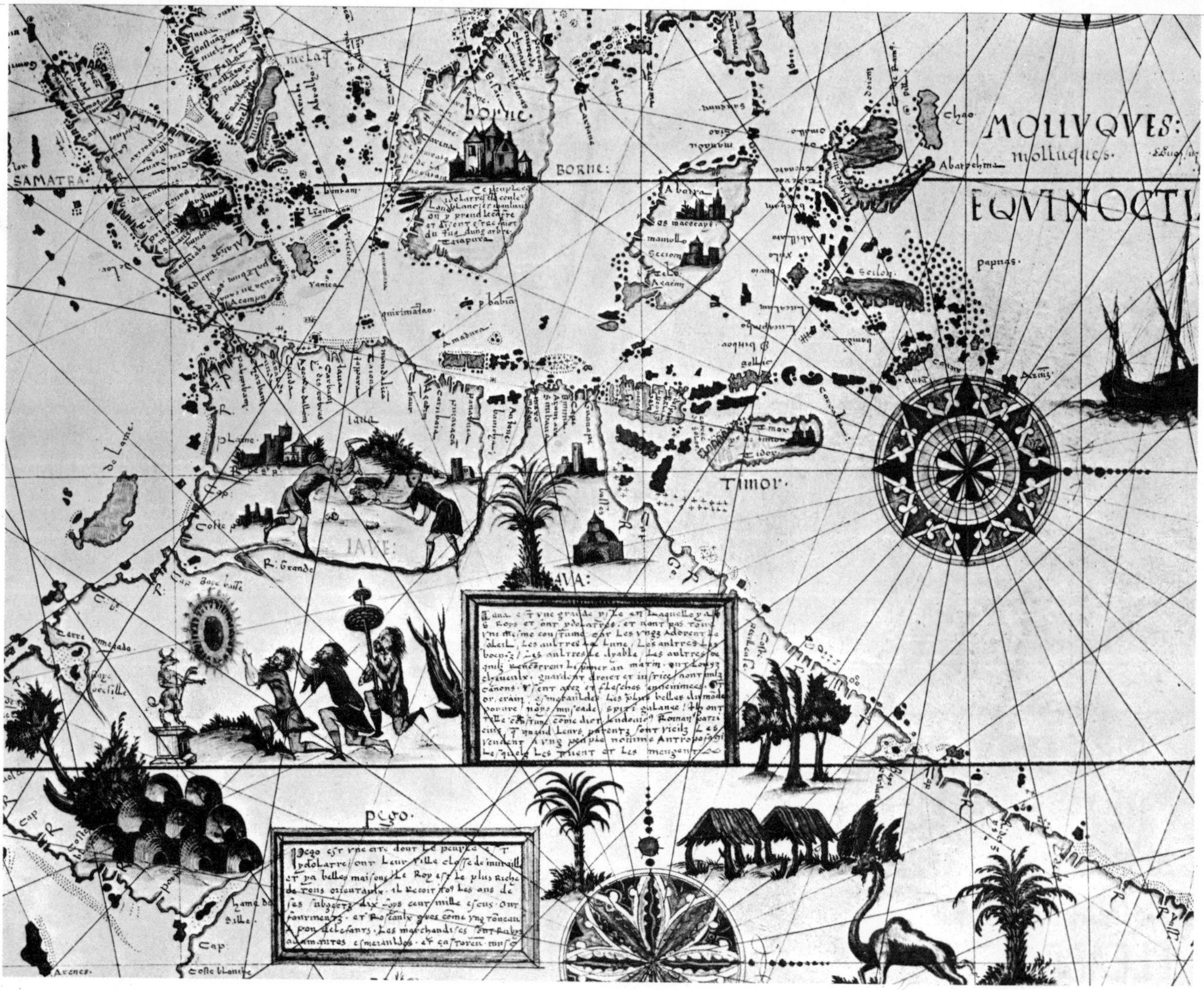

MOLLVQVES:
EQVINOCTI
BORNE:
SAMATRA
TIMOR
IAVE:
PEGO

Left Portuguese carracks of the type used in the East Indian trade during the sixteenth century.

Below left Section of a world map by Pierre Desceliers, 1550. His interpretation of Terra Australis is based on reports, reproduced in panels, by Marco Polo. An inlet on the east coast called 'Baye Verdue' could possibly represent Botany Bay, but there is no evidence to support this.

Right Section of Abraham Ortelius's global map of 1587, which shows a southern continent linking Tierra del Fuego and New Guinea.

Below Dutch shipping at Amsterdam, early seventeenth century.

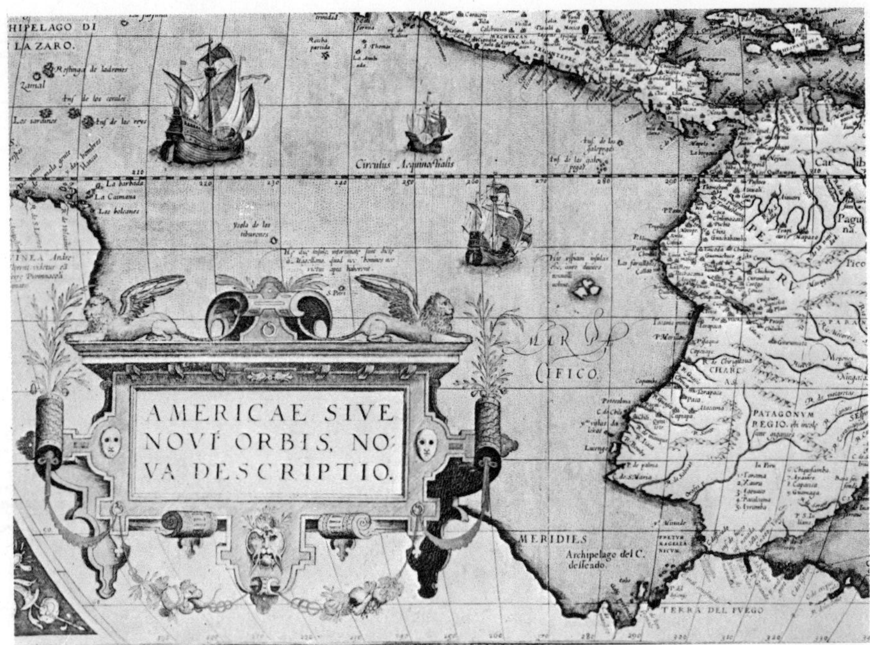

island to prove his point and then continued west and passed through the strait which separates New Guinea from Australia and which still bears his name. Torres may actually have seen the Australian mainland but in any case he would not have been the first European to do so. As far as historians have established that honour had fallen a few months earlier to Willem Jansz, a Dutchman.

While the Portuguese and Spaniards had been drawing gradually closer to Australia during the sixteenth century vital history was being made in Europe. The Dutch, who had been under the despotic rule of Philip II of Spain, rose in revolt against him and for thirty years the Netherlands were bathed in blood. The Dutch found a powerful ally in Elizabeth I of England and the seaways became opened to them when Spain's great Armada was destroyed in 1588. Seven years later some Amsterdam merchants sent four ships under Cornelis de Houtman on a trading voyage to the Spice Islands. The voyage was so successful that whole fleets followed and in a few years Portugal's monopoly was broken. The Dutch occupied the Cape of Good Hope and formed a settlement at Batavia, now known again by its old name of Jakarta, in Java. They ranged as far east as China and Japan, estab-

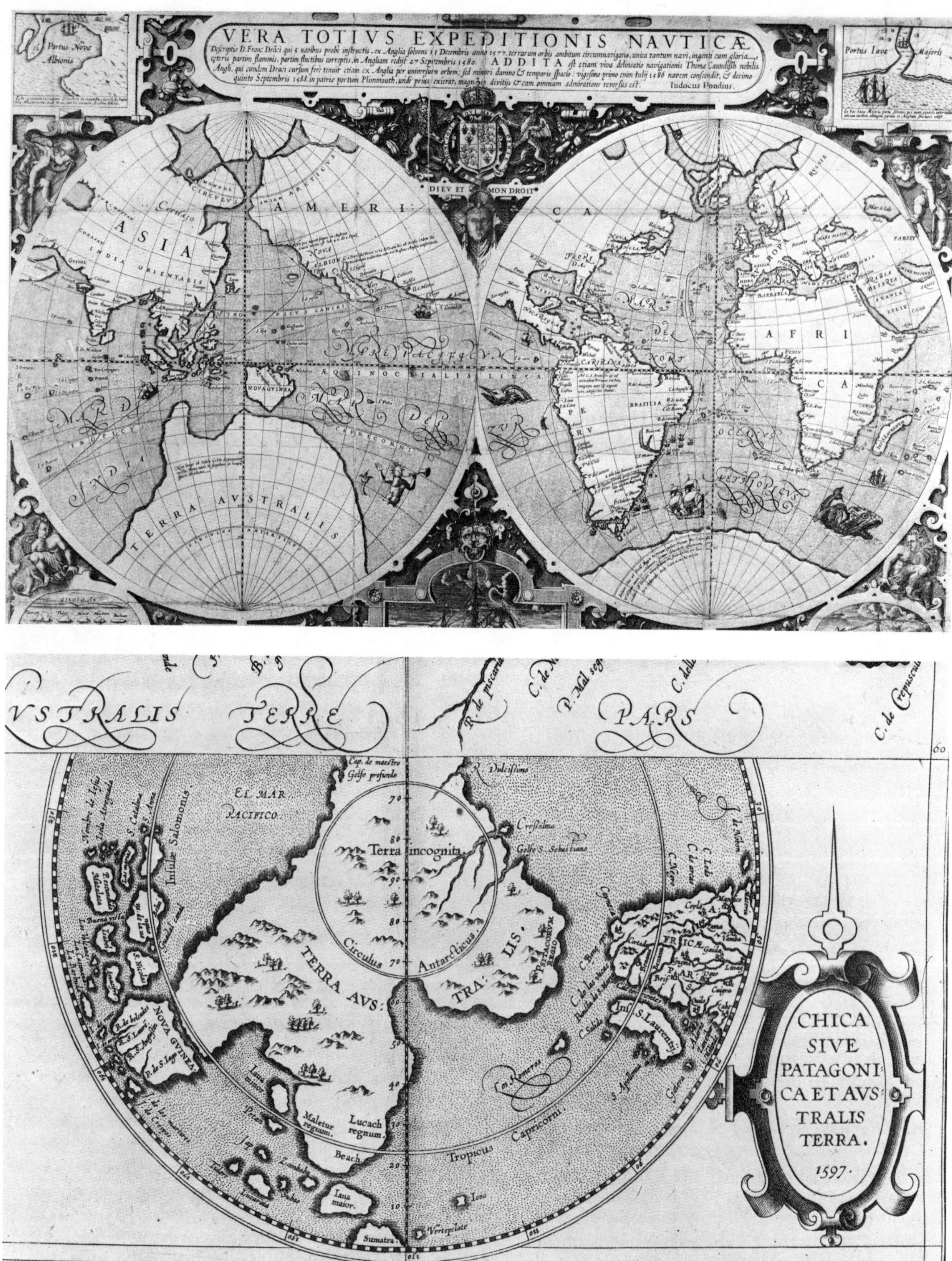
VERA TOTIVS EXPEDITIONIS NAVTICÆ
ADDITA
Iudocus Hondius.
Portus Novæ Albionis
Portus Iavæ Majoris
DIEV ET MON DROIT
ASIA
AMERI
CA
AFRI
CA
TERRA AVSTRALIS
NOVA GVINEA
EVROPA
BRASILIA
PERV
VSTRALIS TERRE PARS
EL MAR PACIFICO
Terra incognita
Circulus Antarcticus
TERRA AVS TRA LIS
Tropicus Capricorni
NOVA GVINEA
Insulæ Salomonis
Iaua minor
Iaua maior
Beach
Sumatra
Maletur regnum
Lucach regnum
Golfo S. Sebastiano
R. Dulcissimo
Ins. S. Laurentij
CHICA SIVE PATAGONICA ET AVSTRALIS TERRA. 1597.

Left The Hondius global map of 1588 showing the tracks of the English circumnavigators Drake and Cavendish. Both sailed close to Australia on their way home.

Below left Part of a map by Cornelius Wytfliet, 1597, which shows Australia and New Guinea separated by a strait. History credits the Spaniard, Luis Vaez de Torres with discovering the strait nine years later.

Right Frontispiece from the published account of the wreck of the *Batavia*. The smaller ship is the *Sardam* which rescued survivors.

Far right Francis Pelsart, captain of the *Batavia*.

Ongeluckige Voyagie,
Van't
SCHIP BATAVIA,
Nae Oost-Indien.
Uytgevaren onder den E. FRANCOIS PELSAERT:
Gebleven op de Abrolhos van Frederick Houtman, op de hooghte van 28½ graet/ by Zuyden de Linie Æquinoctiael.
Verhatende 't verongelucken des Schips/ en de grouwelijcke Moorderyen onder 't Scheeps-volck/ op 't Eylandt Bataviaes Kerckhof; nevens de straffe der handdadighers, in den Jare 1628, en 1629.
Nevens een Treur-bly-eynde Ongeluck, des Compagnies Dienaers in 't Jaer 1636. weder-varen, in 't Koninckllijcke Hof van *Siam*, in de Stadt *Iudia*, onder den E. JEREMIAS van VLIET.
En de groote Tyrannye van ABAS, Koninck van Persien/ Anno 1645. begaen aen sijn grootste Heeren des Rijcks/ in sijn Koninckllijck Hof tot *Espahan*.

t'AMSTELREDAM,
Voor Jooft Hartgerts, Boeck-verkooper in de Gasthuys-Steegh/ bezijden het Stadt-huys/ in de Boeck-winckel, 1648.

lished trading posts in India, conquered Ceylon and occupied the Spice Islands. By 1606 they were the new masters of the East and one result of this was the discovery of Australia.

In 1602 the Dutch East India Company had been formed in Holland and it was this rather than the home government which ruled Dutch possessions in the East. Generally the company frowned on any venture which risked ships and men without the promise of a rich reward. This did not, however, rule out occasional voyages to unknown parts in search of new trade sources. In November 1605 the yacht *Duyfken*, or 'little dove', was sent from Bantam in Java to see what the south coast of New Guinea had to offer. During the voyage she came to what her captain, Willem Jansz, took to be a deep bight. Without investigating it he turned south and, reaching an unbroken coastline again, continued on for about 250 miles. The country he saw was barren and inhabited by 'wild, cruel black savages', who killed some of his crew. Rather than risk more lives he returned to Bantam. What Jansz had thought to be a bight was actually the strait which divides New Guinea from Australia – the same strait through which Torres was to sail six months later – and the land he had coasted was part of the Australian continent. Jansz's report excited little enthusiasm. A barren country peopled by hostile natives offered poor prospects for trade and for the next five years the Dutch kept well away from it. It may have remained unseen for many years more had another Dutch captain not decided to try an experiment.

On their way to the East Indies the Dutch normally sailed north-west from the Cape of Good Hope across the Indian Ocean. This took them through the searing heat and doldrums of the tropics and often a captain would find his ship becalmed for weeks and his crew decimated by scurvy. In 1611 Hendrick Brouwer, who later became governor-general of the East Indies, resolved to avoid this. From the Cape he sailed due east for about 3,000 miles and then turned sharply north for Java. In this way he not only dodged the doldrums but had favourable winds all the way and reached his destination in the record time of seven months out from Holland. The company was so impressed that it instructed all captains to follow Brouwer's route.

As the Cape of Good Hope and the west coast of Australia are in the same latitude and only about 4,300 miles apart it was inevitable that sooner or later others would come in sight of the continent. The first known to have done so was Dirk Hartog in the *Eendracht*, which means 'concord'. On 25 October 1616 Hartog made landfall at what is now Shark Bay, about 450 miles north of Perth. He landed on an island which still bears his name, and there erected a post bearing a tin plate on which were engraved the details of his achievement.

Captains now had a landmark, a visible point at which to turn north, and amended orders were issued that in future they were to sail from the Cape direct to Eendrachtland, as the area was called, and then on to their destination. In the following years many Dutch ships sighted the Australian coast, some north and some well south of Hartog's landfall and a few captains bothered to explore what they saw. Chart was added to chart and from these

gradually emerged an almost continuous map of the south, west and north coasts of what became known as New Holland. In general it appeared an arid, unpromising land and the Dutch were content to record its existence without troubling to claim it.

It was a treacherous coast and wrecks were frequent. One which has passed into history because of its bizarre sequel was the wreck of the *Batavia,* commanded by Francis Pelsart. On the night of 4 June 1629, outward bound from Holland with many passengers including women and children, the *Batavia* ran aground on a reef which was part of a complex of small islands discovered by Frederick Houtman and known as the Abrolhos, a Portuguese word which means 'keep your eyes open'. At daybreak the passengers and some of the crew went ashore on to two nearby islands. As no water could be found Pelsart took other members of the crew and rowed in an open boat to the mainland twenty-four miles away. He spent almost a fortnight in futile search for water and then decided to make for Batavia. After a long and perilous journey he got there and was given a yacht, the *Sardam,* in which to return and rescue any survivors. In fact water had been found soon after Pelsart's departure, there was adequate food and it was neither thirst nor

Above This pictorial account of the wreck of the *Batavia* is a forerunner of the modern strip cartoon. It tells the whole story of the incident from the ship's approach to the reef to the torture and execution of the mutineers.

Left Antony van Diemen, Governor-General of the Dutch East Indies, who sponsored the historic voyages of Abel Janszoon Tasman.

hunger which destroyed many of the survivors but the evil genius of Pelsart's supercargo, Jeronimus Cornelisz. Under his persuasion some of the crew chose women for themselves from among the passengers and then murdered most of the rest and some other seamen who opposed them. By the time the slaughter had ended 125 people were dead. When the *Sardam* arrived Cornelisz and his gang planned to seize her and murder those aboard but Pelsart was warned by a loyal survivor of the crew. He struck first and the mutineers were routed. Cornelisz and several others had their right hands cut off and were then hanged, and two were marooned on the mainland.

In 1636 Anthony van Diemen became Governor-General of the Dutch East Indies. He was a man of great curiosity who believed that discovery for its own sake was worthwhile. He wondered, for instance, whether the Gulf of Carpentaria might be the northern end of a sea which divided New Holland into two, and he sent one of his captains to investigate. The expedition was a failure and van Diemen realized that if a voyage of exploration was to succeed it must be led by the right man. In time he appeared. His name was Abel Janszoon Tasman.

Tasman was born obscurely in 1603 at Lutjegast, a village in Friesland, northern Holland. It is known that he married twice while still young; otherwise his early history is obscure. He was, however, a man of great ability and within two years of joining the Dutch East India Company as a seaman he had become a captain. In the East Indies he soon won fame as a navigator, and when in 1642 van Diemen decided to equip an exploratory expedition Tasman was chosen as captain. The voyage had been planned by Franz Jacobszoon Visscher, a noted pilot, and its object was to find a more convenient route than was then known between the East Indies and South America. But Visscher also dreamed of sailing right around the world in high southern latitudes and of finding the great unknown continent.

The expedition, comprising the ships *Heemskirk* and *Zeehaen,* set out on 14 August 1642. Tasman was nominally in charge but according to Dutch custom he was authorized to make major decisions only in council with his officers. After a stay at Mauritius for stores the ships sailed south into the 'roaring forties' and then turned east, gradually easing north into warmer seas. On 24 November land was seen, which Tasman later named Van Diemen's Land. A week later the ships had rounded its south coast and were at anchor in what is now Blackman Bay. A party sent ashore for wood and water heard voices but failed to see any natives. Next day, in rough

Left From Tasman's journal, showing his ships at anchor off the east coast of Van Diemen's Land. It was here that a carpenter swam ashore and planted the Dutch flag.

Right Tasman with his second wife and daughter. Portrait by Jacob Gerritsz Cuyp.

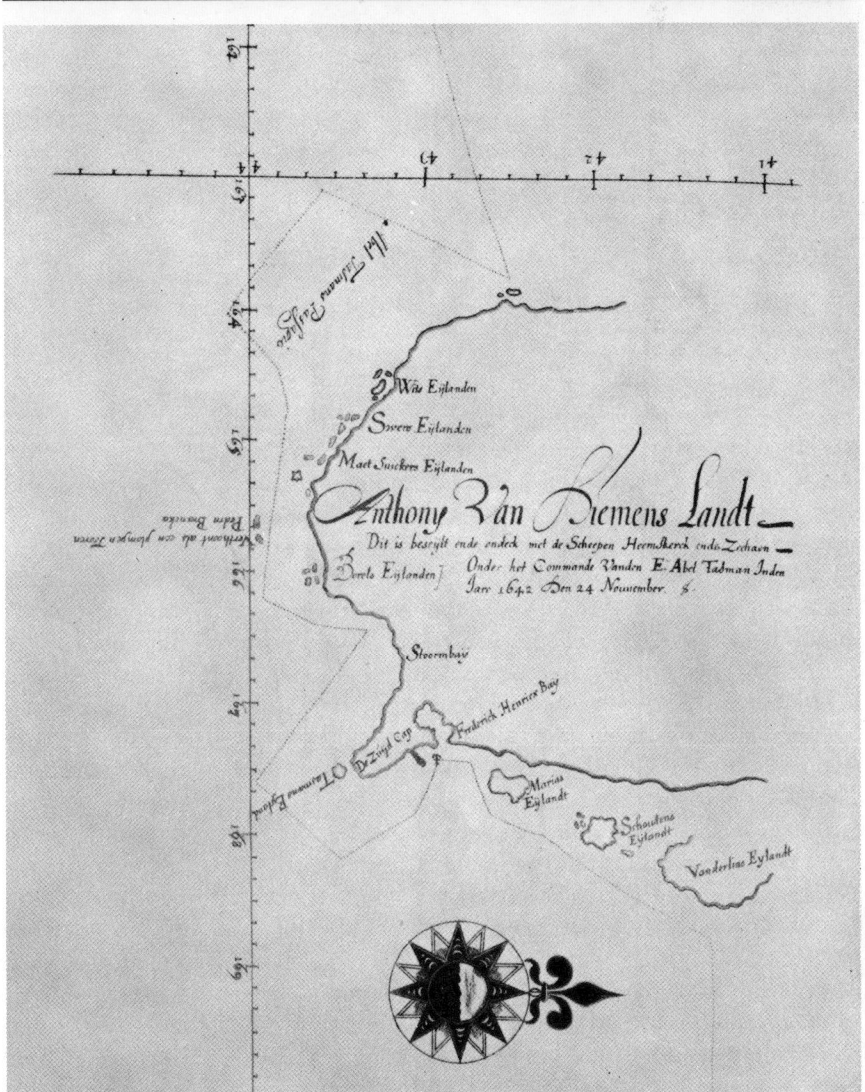

Right Tasman's chart of Van Diemen's Land.

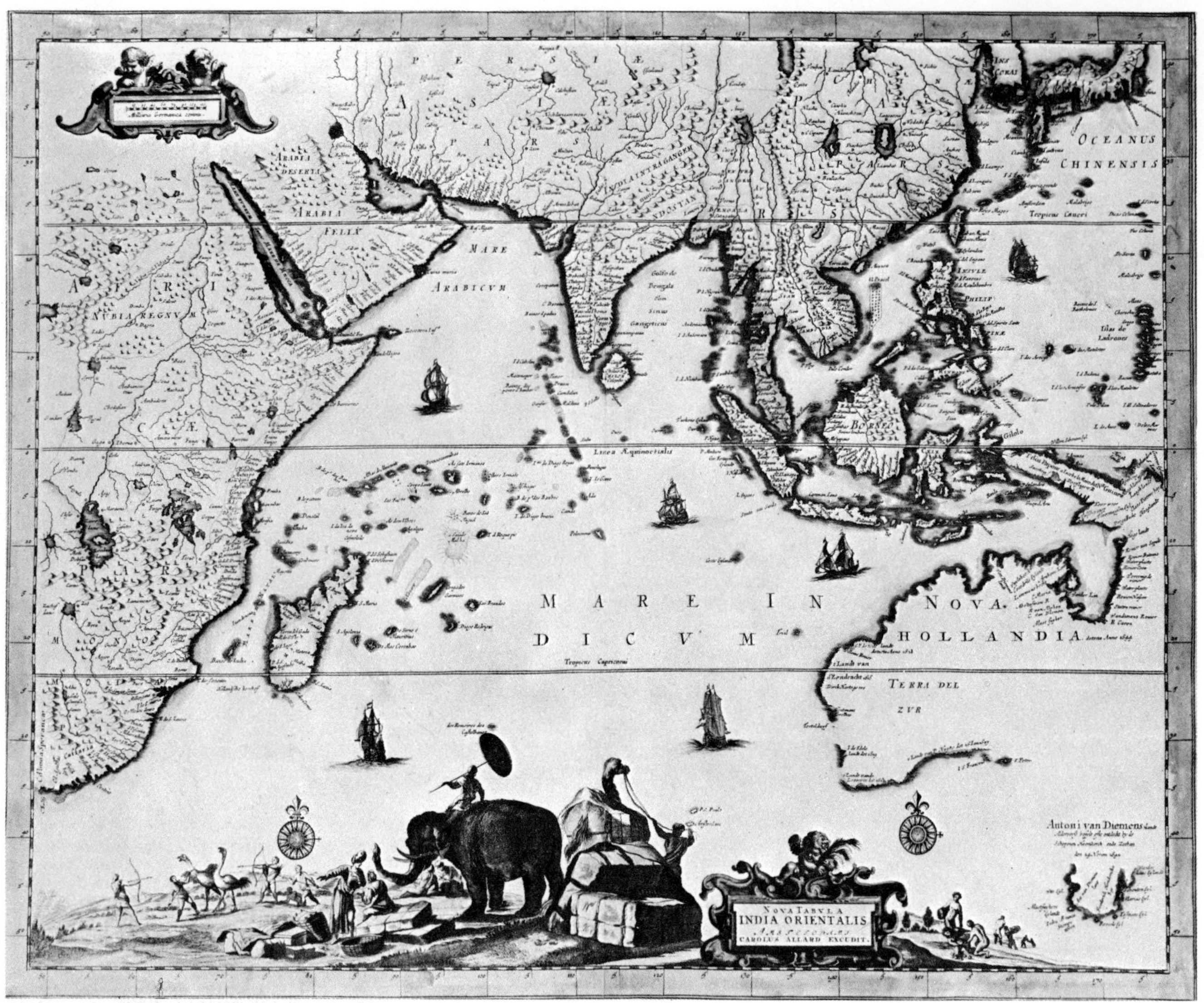

weather, Tasman tried and failed to land at another spot and eventually a ship's carpenter swam ashore through the surf and planted the Dutch flag on what is now Tasmanian soil.

Continuing on the two ships came in sight of land again after nine days, on the west coast of the south island of New Zealand. In a bay where they hoped to replenish stores they were surrounded by warlike Maoris in canoes. Four men were killed and others had to swim for their lives. Shocked by this unprovoked assault Tasman raised anchor and fled, calling the spot Murderers' Bay. He passed what he took to be a deep bight but is in fact Cook Strait which separates the two main islands, coasted up the north island to its furthermost point and then turned north-west into the open Pacific in search of Mendaña's missing Solomon Islands. Instead he found a group which were to become known later as the Friendly Islands and later still as Tonga. From here he sailed north and thence along the north coast of New Guinea to Batavia, which he reached on 15 June 1643.

The company was not pleased. The voyage had cost good money, and although Tasman had discovered two new and apparently fertile countries he had learned little about them. Nevertheless, van Diemen retained faith in him and the following year he persuaded the company to support a second voyage. This time Tasman's orders were to search for a strait between New Guinea and New Holland and if it existed to go through it and then sail south to Van Diemen's Land. Had he done so the east coast of Australia would have been discovered a century and a quarter earlier than it actually was. As the only surviving record of this voyage is Tasman's own map one can only assume what happened. It seems fairly sure, however, that he searched for and failed to find a strait and then decided instead to make a thorough survey of the north and north-west coasts of New Holland. In

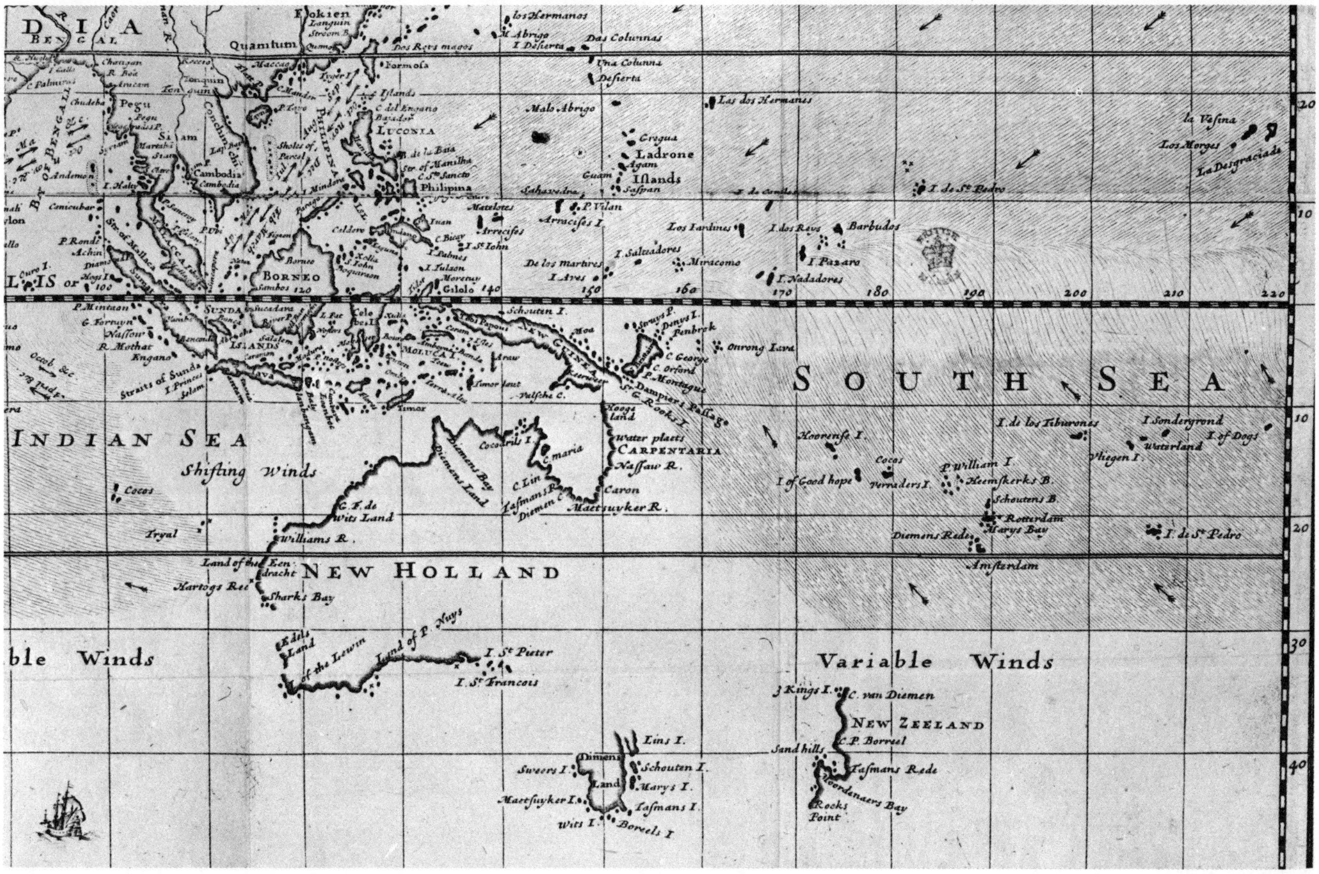

Left What was then known of Australia, or New Holland as it was called, is fairly accurately shown in this map by Carolus Allard of about 1650.

Above Discoveries by Tasman, Dampier and others are incorporated in this section of a world map, published by John Harris in 1705.

Below The English buccaneer, explorer and best-selling author, William Dampier.

doing so he added greatly to geographical knowledge and disproved the theory that the continent might be bisected by an inland sea. But this achievement brought no dividends to the company and a reprimand was on its way from Holland to van Diemen when he died about a year later. Eventually Tasman became a successful merchant in Batavia and he too died there in 1659.

At this time there lived in East Coker, Somerset, a boy of eight named William Dampier, whose great ambition was to go to sea. He served briefly in the Navy, then for several years roamed around the West Indies. In 1679 he turned pirate, and he and his companions harried Spanish shipping and settlements in the Panama area. Dampier claimed that he had no great liking for 'the trade' and followed it more to satisfy his curiosity than to gain wealth. In 1686 he transferred his activities to the North Pacific as a crew member of the *Cygnet*. The ship ranged as far south as the Spice Islands, to the

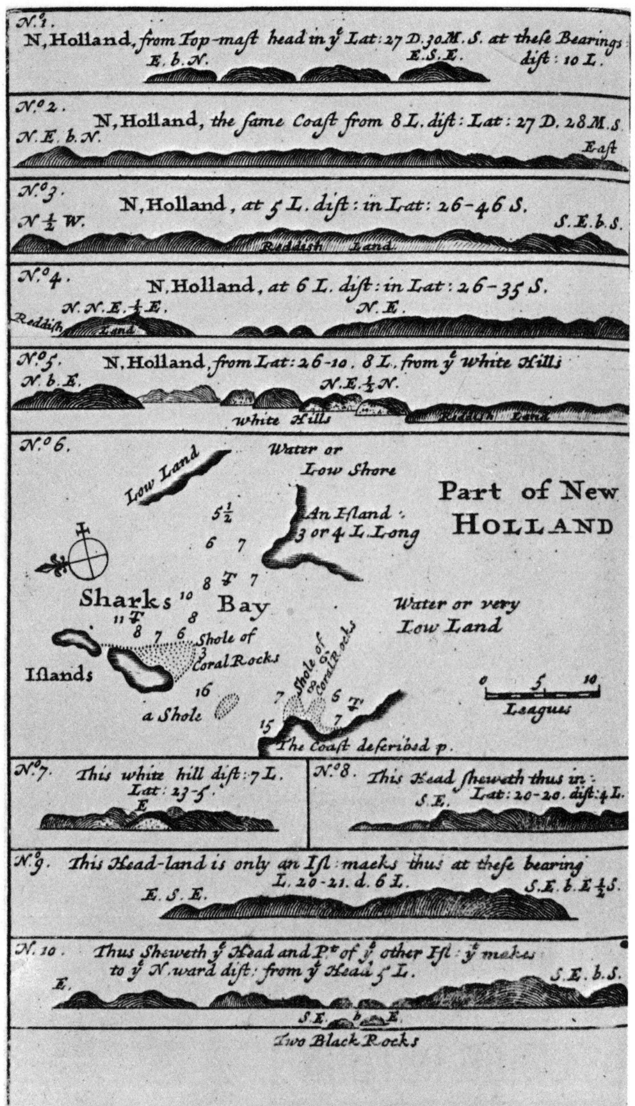

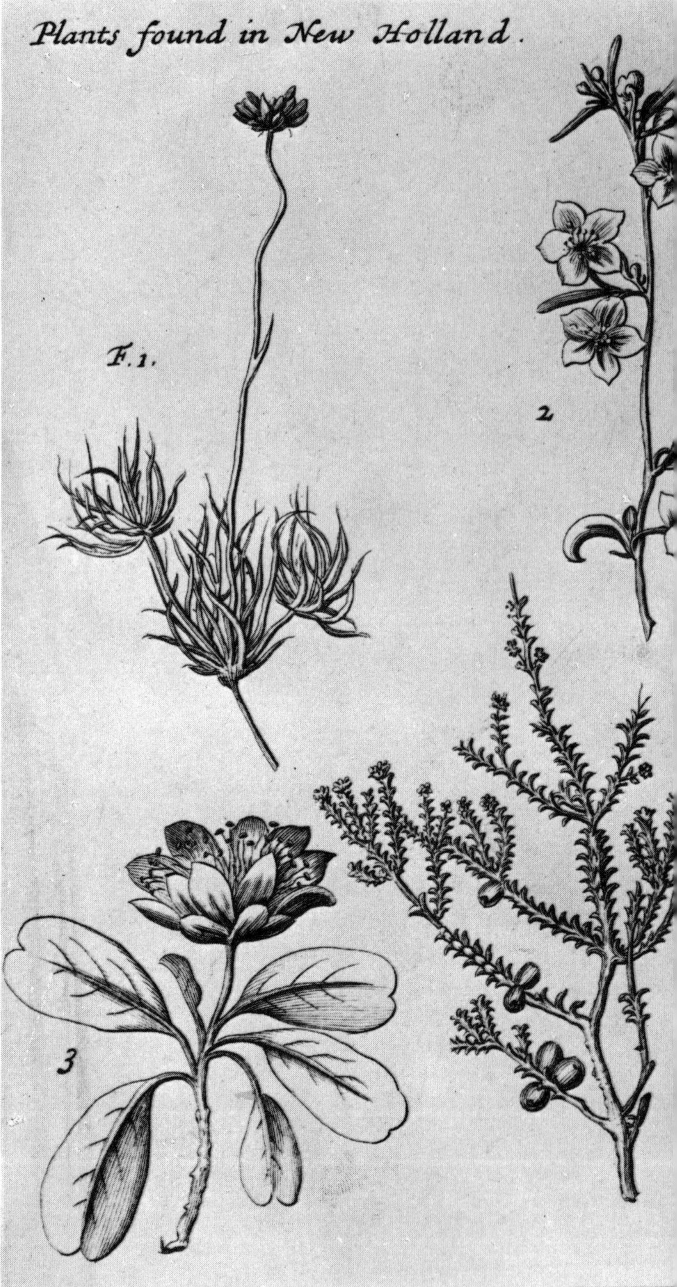

annoyance of the Dutch; then, perhaps feeling it safer to disappear for a while, her captain took her further south. Early in 1688 she reached the north-west coast of New Holland near some islands which later became known as the Buccaneer Archipelago. The ship was careened and for some time Dampier was able to indulge his curiosity ashore. He was not impressed. The land, he declared, was 'a dry and dusty soil . . . destitute of water unless you make wells' and devoid of food. His low opinion of the local Aborigines has already been quoted. The area was, of course, already well-known to the Dutch; but even so the *Cygnet's* appearance has some historic importance for Dampier and his companions were the first Englishmen known to have set foot on Australian soil. After various adventures which included a brief marooning on one of the Nicobar Islands Dampier returned to England in 1691. He wrote a long account of his travels and when it appeared in 1697 its success was immediate and Dampier found himself a national hero.

Meanwhile the Dutch continued resolutely to ignore New Holland. Then in 1696 Willem de Vlamingh, in search of a ship lost some years earlier, reached the coast at Rottnest Island, opposite the mouth of what is now the Swan River.

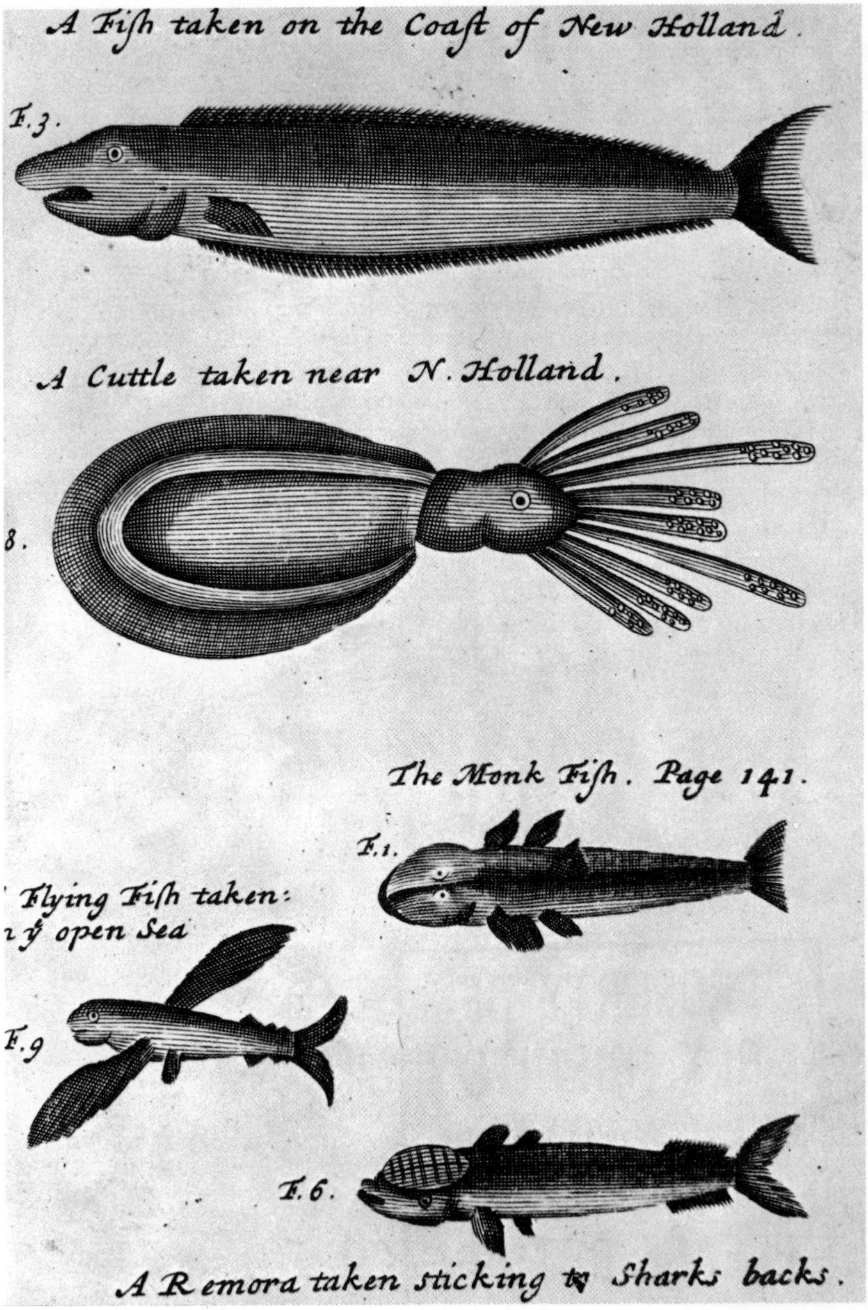

A Fish taken on the Coast of New Holland.

F.3.

A Cuttle taken near N. Holland.

The Monk Fish. Page 141.

F.1.

F.9

F.6.

A Remora taken sticking to Sharks backs.

Illustrations from Dampier's account of his voyage to north-western Australia. *From left* Coastal profiles and a chart of Shark's Bay; plants collected by Dampier and taken home to England; fishes, including a Spanish mackerel, caught off the coast; and some sea-birds of New Holland.

During a brief stay Vlamingh rowed upstream about forty-two miles, which would have taken him past the site of Perth. He caught some black swans which he took alive to Batavia and no doubt he reported on the fertility of the area he had seen. But the Dutch were not interested in settlement and nothing was done to follow up his discovery.

Back in England Dampier's eyes turned seaward again. With support from the Royal Society he persuaded the government to outfit an expedition to explore the east coast of New Holland, and in 1699 he sailed in the *Roebuck,* a sloop of twelve guns with a crew of fifty. Sailing by way of the Cape of Good Hope he reached the continent at the same point Hartog had and it was he who called it Shark Bay. It was midwinter and the crew had no liking for cold seas, so Dampier turned north instead of south and for four months he cruised slowly along the west and north-west coasts. All hope of accomplishing his main mission gradually receded. His crew were insubordinate and scurvy-ridden, provisions were low and his ship was in urgent need of repair. Dampier took her to Timor where shipwrights patched her up and from there he cruised for a while north of New Guinea, making a few minor discoveries. On the way home, at Ascension Island in the South Atlantic, the ship finally crumbled and sank. Dampier and his crew got ashore without loss and were eventually picked up and taken home by two British warships. This time there was no hero's welcome. He had achieved little and his reputation was further tarnished by dismissal from the Navy. Although he made other voyages he was a forgotten man when he died in 1715, aged sixty-three.

In the next seventy years only one man got near the still unexplored east coast of New Holland. This was Louis Antoine de Bougainville, a brilliant French soldier, who entered the Pacific in 1678 in quest of colonies for France. He called at Tahiti, to find that the English had forestalled him by a few months; discovered the Samoan islands which he called the Navigator Group; cursorily re-examined the New Hebrides; and then sailed west towards New Holland. His course would have taken him to what is now northern Queensland but he found himself involved in such a maze of coral reefs that he decided it was impossible to get through and turned away. He was then a mere hundred miles from the mainland, and had he found a passage there is little doubt that he would have annexed at least the eastern half of the continent for France. Instead it was left to an Englishman to do the same thing for England a year later.

At 6 a.m. on Thursday, 19 April 1770, Lieutenant Zachary Hicks, of His Majesty's bark *Endeavour,* nineteen days out from New Zealand, saw land ahead and reported to his captain, Lieutant James Cook. It was part of the south-east mainland coast of Australia and as far as is known those on the *Endeavour* were the first Europeans ever to see it. Cook called the spot Point Hicks but this name has disappeared and it is now thought to be identical with the present Cape Everard.

Like Tasman and Dampier, Cook was of humble birth. His father was a Scottish farm-labourer who had migrated to Yorkshire and Cook was born at

Left The Frenchman Louis Antoine de Bougainville, who narrowly missed discovering the east coast of Australia in 1769.

Above Cook's companion, Joseph Banks. A little-known portrait by Henry Edridge, A.R.A.

Above right Captain James Cook, one of several portraits by John Webber.

Right Cook's *Endeavour* in a rough sea. Sketch by Sydney Parkinson.

Marton, a village in the Cleveland district, on 27 October 1728. He showed great ability at school but had to leave early to work as a farm-boy. A period as assistant to a grocer and draper in the coastal town of Staithes gave him a taste for the sea and at eighteen he was apprenticed in the coal-shipping trade in the Yorkshire port of Whitby. For nine years he sailed in colliers, studying mathematics and navigation in his spare time; and in 1755 when war broke out with France he refused his employer's offer of a captaincy and joined the Navy as an ordinary seaman. Within a month he was a master's mate and three years later he went to Canada as master of HMS *Pembroke*. The part he played in sounding the St Lawrence River contributed materially to General Wolfe's victory over the French at Quebec; and in the next few years his charting of the coasts of Newfoundland and Labrador established his reputation as the best map-maker in the Navy.

In 1768, urged by the Royal Society, the government decided to send an expedition to the newly-found island of Tahiti to observe a transit of the planet Venus across the sun, a phenomenon which, it was thought, would help astronomers to calculate the sun's distance from the earth and which would not occur again for more than a century. The Society wanted the expedition to be led by Alexander Dalrymple, a noted geographer but the Navy insisted on appointing a regular officer and Cook was promoted lieutenant and given the job. He was then aged thirty-nine and for a farm-boy to reach commissioned rank was in those days almost unprecedented.

The ship chosen for the voyage, obviously on Cook's advice, was a Whitby collier, the *Earl of Pembroke,* renamed *Endeavour*. She was a small, snub-nosed vessel of 366 tons, a mere 105 feet long; a slowish sailer but easy to handle and, because of her shallow draught, able to work fairly close inshore. Cook's crew of eighty-four included his wife's cousin, Isaac Smith, a boy of sixteen. In addition he had to find room for a wealthy young squire from Lincolnshire named Joseph Banks and his entourage. At twenty-five Banks was already a Fellow of the Royal Society and a skilled naturalist and this chance to travel the world was too tempting to miss. With him were two Swedish naturalists, Dr Daniel Solander and Herman Spöring; two artists, Sydney Parkinson and Alexander Buchan; and four servants, of whom two were Negroes.

Observing the transit of Venus was to be only one of Cook's tasks. After that he was to sail south to latitude 40° in search of a southern continent and if he failed to find one he was to examine Tasman's New Zealand and then return to England by whatever route he thought best.

The *Endeavour* sailed quietly from Plymouth on 26 August 1768. There were brief stops at Madeira and Rio de Janeiro and by mid-January 1769 she was off the island of Terra del Fuego at the southern tip of South America. Banks led a party inland to do some botanizing and the result was disastrous. Buchan had an epileptic fit and during an all-night ordeal in a blizzard Banks's two Negro servants froze to death after having drunk most of the rum supply.

Tahiti was reached without further incident and the *Endeavour* dropped anchor in Matavai Bay on 13 April. Until this time scurvy had been the great scourge of long-distance voyagers but Cook had devised methods to combat it including a regular issue to all hands of sauerkraut, and at Tahiti he was able to write with pride that after eleven months at sea his people were still as fit as when they had set out.

Left Ant-house, one of many exotic plants found in tropical Australia by Joseph Banks. Drawing by Parkinson.

Below left Australian Aborigines advancing to combat. Engraved from a drawing by Sydney Parkinson.

Right Aborigines opposing Cook's landing at Botany Bay.

Below right A more sophisticated version of the same incident, by E. Phillips Fox.

Buchan died soon after arrival but it was impossible to stay gloomy for long on such a beautiful island and among such happy and friendly people. A fort was built ashore, there were some minor clashes caused by the thievery of the natives, Banks found many new plants and wrote copiously about the Tahitians and their customs, and on 3 June the transit of Venus was observed from three points. Despite ideal weather conditions the timings differed greatly, and for reasons which the Royal Society should have foreseen the whole operation was a failure.

When the *Endeavour* sailed from Tahiti she had on board a priest named Tupia, with a boy servant, and Cook hoped they would help to make friendly contact with natives elsewhere. Some weeks were spent exploring other nearby islands which Cook called the Society Group. Then he turned south. During several storm-wracked weeks he satisfied himself there was no continent where Dalrymple and others had said he would find one; and then he headed towards where New Zealand lay on Tasman's chart.

Land was sighted on 7 October 1769. Three days later the *Endeavour* anchored in a sheltered bay and Cook tried to make contact with the local natives. But though Tupia was able to talk to them freely they remained implacably hostile and several were killed in skirmishes. Cook named the place Poverty Bay, 'because it afforded us no one thing we wanted', and the unfortunate name has stuck. In the next five months Cook completely circumnavigated New Zealand, proving that it was no part of a continent but two large islands separated by a narrow strait; and except for a couple of major errors the chart he made of them was remarkably accurate.

From New Zealand Cook would have liked to sail home in high southern latitudes by way of Cape Horn to search again for a continent but with winter coming on this was not practical. Instead, after conferring with his officers, he decided to head for the east coast of New Holland and thence to return home through the East Indies and around the Cape of Good Hope.

Southerly gales drove the *Endeavour* north of the route Cook had chosen and when she made landfall she had missed both Van Diemen's Land and what is now Bass Strait. Cook's first sight of the mainland coast revealed undulating, well wooded and apparently fertile land and smoke from numerous fires showed that it was well populated. Keeping close inshore Cook turned north, looking for a harbour and charting and naming as he went. Cape Howe was rounded; then came Mount Dromedary, Cape Dromedary, Bateman's Bay, Point Upright and Pigeon House Hill. Beyond Cape St George Cook could see what is now Jervis Bay but though it answered his purpose well the wind was unfavourable and he did not try to enter. Next day off what is now the Illawarra coast some natives were seen on a beach, and Cook, Banks, Solander and Tupia tried to go ashore in the ship's yawl but the natives fled and the surf was too rough for a landing.

At daybreak on 29 April the *Endeavour* was opposite the entrance to a large, well-sheltered bay. As she sailed in natives were seen on both headlands but it was not possible to tell whether they were friendly or hostile. About 2 p.m. anchor was dropped off the south shore, near a village of six or eight primitive huts. The few Aborigines in sight appeared to take little interest in the newcomers; but when two boats put off a young man and an older one came down to the water's edge armed with spears. 'resolv'd to dispute our landing to the utmost', as Cook wrote admiringly. The boats lay to while Tupia

tried to talk to them but he could not understand their language. Proffered gifts were ignored and a musket fired over their heads had little effect. Then a charge of small shot slightly wounded the older man and he ran back to the huts. While he was away the boats pulled in to shore and according to tradition the first to land was young Isaac Smith. The older man now reappeared carrying a shield. He and his companions threw several spears which fell among Cook's party but did no harm and it took two more rounds of small shot to chase them off. Although no adult Aborigines were now in sight a few terrified children were found in the huts and Cook left some beads with them as a peace offering.

Next day Cook rowed around the bay, sounding and exploring. The few natives he saw fled as he approached. Several ventured to within a hundred yards of a watering party but though signs of peace were made and presents offered they would come no closer and, as Cook wrote ruefully, 'all they seem'd to want was for us to be gone'. Next day Cook walked towards a group of them but though he was unarmed and alone they would not allow him near. Gifts of cloth, looking-glasses, combs, beads and nails left in their empty huts remained untouched.

The natives' shyness made it impossible to gain more than a superficial impression of them. They were not numerous and apparently lived in small groups rather than as a single community. They were about as tall as Europeans, Cook noted, with dark brown skin and lank, black hair. None were seen wearing clothing or ornaments and nothing of this kind was found around their huts. Their canoes were of bark and as primitive as their huts. Their chief weapons appeared to be spears, clubs and curved pieces of wood called by Banks 'scymatars', which were almost certainly boomerangs. Their main food seemed to be fish and shellfish.

On 1 May Cook recorded the death of Forby Sutherland, a seaman. He was buried ashore and

Aerial view of Cook's landing place at Kurnell, Botany Bay. Obelisk marks the exact spot.

Cook named the south headland of the bay in his memory. Today a thriving town of the same name exists a few miles away.

Cook found the land around the bay 'deversified, with Woods, Lawns (i.e. grassland) and Marshes', and because of the lack of undergrowth he thought much of it could be cultivated 'without being oblig'd to cut down a single tree'. At what he called the head of the inlet there were areas of deep black soil which seemed capable of producing any kind of grain. 'At present it produceth besides timber as fine meadow as ever was seen', he wrote. Many have wondered how Cook, himself a farm-boy, could have been so wrong about the agricultural potentialities of the bay, which in fact hardly exist. It is generally thought that what he called the head of the inlet was actually the present George's River and that he went up this to about as far as Sans Souci, where there is some good soil.

Fish were plentiful and almost every netting yielded enough to feed the whole company. The hauls included a number of stingrays, some of which weighed 300 lb. For a while Cook thought of calling the place Stingrays Harbour but Banks and Solander had collected so many unique plants that he changed his mind. He rejected Botanists' Harbour and finally chose the name which was to become famous in history and by which it is still known – Botany Bay.

On 6 May the *Endeavour* put to sea again. At noon, about nine miles north of Botany Bay and three miles offshore she was, as Cook wrote, 'abreast of a Bay or Harbour wherein there appear'd to be safe anchorage'. He called it Port Jackson after George Jackson, second secretary to the Admiralty, whose family he had known since childhood. He could not guess that he was passing perhaps the world's safest harbour, on the shores of which was to rise the city of Sydney.

Broken Bay and Cape Three Points were passed and named and on 10 May the *Endeavour* was opposite 'a small round rock or Island laying close under the land'. This is now Nobby's Head at the mouth of the Hunter River and beyond it lies the city of Newcastle. In the next few days came Port Stephens, Cape Hawke, the Three Brothers (contiguous hills near the present town of Taree), Smoky Cape, Solitary Island, Cape Byron, Mount Warning and Point Danger, on the present Queensland border. Cook was greatly impressed by most of the country, which he found 'diversified with an agreeable variety of hills, ridges, valleys and large plains, all clothed in wood', with 'some pretty high hills' beyond.

A wide, open bay was passed on 17 May. As the water was paler than usual some on board thought that a large river must flow into it. Cook named it Morton Bay, after Lord Morton, President of the Royal Society, and on its river now stands the city of Brisbane. In an edited account of Cook's voyage the word was misspelt Moreton and so it has remained.

As the *Endeavour* continued north Double Island, Indian Head, Sandy Cape, Hervey Bay and Bustard Bay appeared on Cook's chart. Cape Capricorn marked their entry into the tropics; then came Keppel Bay, Cape Manifold and Cape Townshend. The ship was now inside the Great Barrier Reef, though Cook was not to know this. Other features were passed and named and on Whitsunday, 4 June, the *Endeavour* entered the passage to which Cook gave that name and which he found to be 'one continued safe harbour'. With unflagging zeal and invention the names continued to appear until the ship reached Cape Tribulation, beyond the present town of Cairns. 'Here began all our troubles', Cook wrote; but in fact he had been in trouble enough for the last 600 miles groping through an uncharted sea so strewn with hazards that only a superb seaman could have got through.

Left Part of Whitsunday Passage off the Queensland coast discovered by Cook. Lindeman Island is in foreground, with Seaforth Island beyond.

Above Cook's ship careened for repair in the Endeavour River. Engraved from a drawing, now lost, by Parkinson.

Right Cook's chart of the Endeavour River, showing where the ship was hauled ashore.

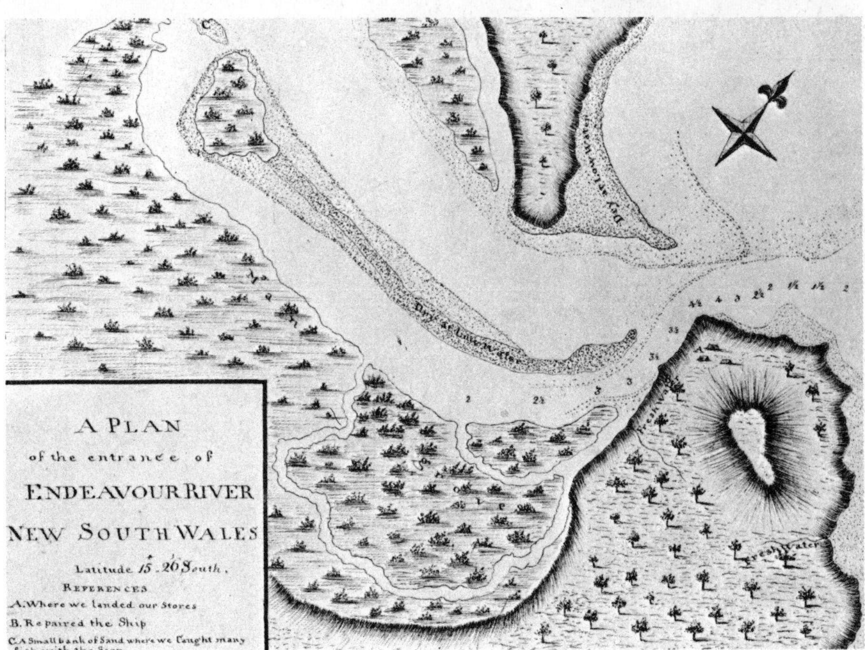

Disaster came about 11 p.m. on 11 June when, without warning, the *Endeavour* struck and was held fast on a coral reef, pounded by heavy seas from outside. As the tide fell the pounding eased but water continued to pour in below decks. Pumps were manned and to lighten ship guns, ballast and other heavy articles were thrown overboard.

The morning tide rose but it was not high enough by about eighteen inches for the ship to float clear. The water was gaining and with the mainland twenty miles away and not enough boats to hold the whole ship's company the position seemed desperate. There was no panic, however. Officers and men worked the pumps till they were exhausted then rested a while and began again. Cook knew the night tide would be higher, so more heavy articles were jettisoned and anchors were put out to heave the ship clear. About 10 p.m., with the tide at flood, the capstan and windlass were manned, the crucial effort was made and the ship was heaved clear into deep water inside the reef. Fears that she would founder at once were not realized; on the contrary she floated well and the gain of water was small. By noon she was within nine miles of the coast and as an added safety precaution Cook decided to fother the ship. Oakum and finely chopped wool were sewn

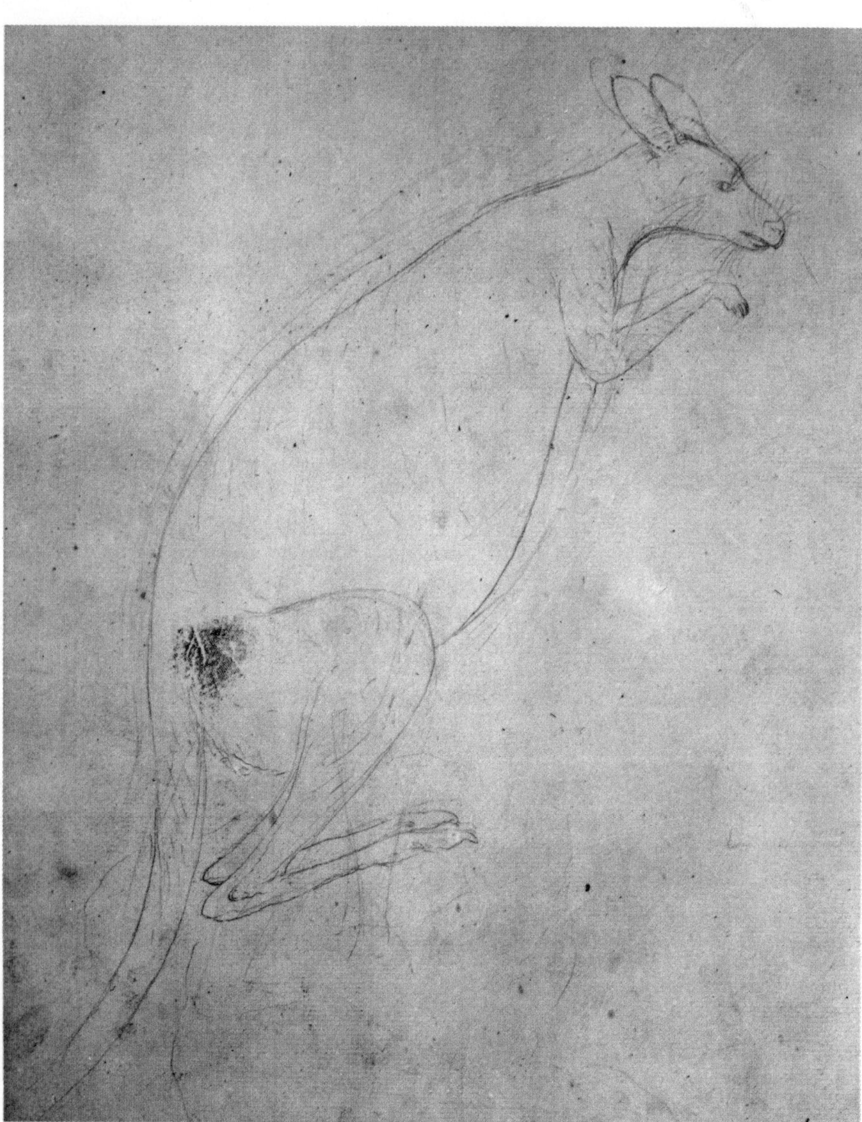

Above Slight sketch by Parkinson of a kangaroo seen at the Endeavour River.

Right Cook formally claiming possession of New South Wales for Britain. The ceremony took place on a small island off Cape York which he called Possession Island.

lightly to a sail which was then hauled under the ship's bottom. When it reached the leak water suction tore the oakum and wool free and drew it in, so that it acted as a sort of plug. From then on only one pump was needed to keep the water at bay.

A river-mouth was found a few miles north but the entrance was narrow and shallow and Cook waited three days for a favourable wind before he would risk an entry. On her way in the ship grounded twice but no damage was done and by evening she was safely inside and moored within twenty feet of the shore. Cook named the stream the Endeavour and opposite the ship's anchorage now stands the small centre of Cooktown.

Next morning she was unloaded and beached. Still wedged in the leak was found a large lump of coral and but for this partly plugging the hole she must surely have sunk. Repairs were soon made but for a month or more persistently adverse winds prevented an exit from the harbour. Banks and Solander welcomed the delay and spent a busy time gathering plants, insects, animals and birds. A strange animal was seen which the natives called a kangaroo. One was shot and they ate it and found it excellent. A sort of precarious friendship was established with the local Aborigines and although a few spe were thrown and muskets fired no harm was done on either side.

On 6 August the *Endeavour* was at sea again. With the pinnace out ahead sounding and Cook or one of his officers at the masthead she crawled for more than a week through an incredible maze of reefs, shoals and islets which Cook called The Labyrinth. He escaped from it all briefly by passing through a gap in the reef into the open sea. Then he went inside again and the ordeal was resumed. This time, however, it was brief. On 22 August the *Endeavour* reached the northern tip of the mainland, which Cook named Cape York and turned west – the first ship to pass through the strait since Torres had discovered it 164 years earlier. Cook landed on a small island, hoisted the English colours and took possession of the whole eastern coast in the name of King George III. He called it New South Wales.

The story of the rest of the voyage is tragic. Batavia, where the *Endeavour* stayed for ten weeks while Dutch shipwrights patched her rotting timbers, was at that time one of the unhealthiest places on earth, with an appalling annual deathrate from dysentery and malaria. Seven men died while she was there and another twenty-five on the long voyage home. Last of all was Zachary Hicks, the man who had first seen Australia, and it was no tropical disease that killed him but a consumption from which he had gradually weakened throughout the voyage. Cook himself contracted malaria but shook it off and Banks was desperately ill for a while.

The English coast came into sight on 10 June 1771, and three days later the *Endeavour* anchored in the Downs. After two years and nearly ten months one of the world's most historic voyages was over.

3 The First Settlement

The loss of her American colonies in 1783 faced Britain with many problems, not the least of which was what to do with her convicted criminals. It was a period of great social unrest in England. The industrial revolution and the enclosure of common lands had driven thousands of people to the cities and poverty was such that many either stole or starved. The law was savage and merciless and men, women and children were transported often for life for offences that are considered today petty misdemeanours. For more than a century about a thousand a year of these unfortunates had been shipped to America to be sold into virtual slavery to planters at up to £20 a head. With this dumping ground no longer available England's jails soon filled to overflowing. Old ships were converted into prison hulks but in time these too became overcrowded. Some hundreds of convicts were sent to Africa where tropical diseases and starvation soon killed them off and in the face of outraged public opinion the experiment was hurriedly dropped.

As far back as 1779 Joseph Banks had suggested to a House of Commons committee that Botany Bay would be an excellent site for a convict settlement and four years later James Maria Matra, who had been a midshipman on the *Endeavour,* urged the same thing in a letter to Lord Sydney, Secretary of State for the Home Department. By 1786 the situation was critical and the government decided to act. Cook's New South Wales was proclaimed a Crown colony and Captain Arthur Phillip, R.N., was appointed its first Governor with orders to form a penal settlement at Botany Bay.

Phillip was aged forty-eight, the son of a German who had settled in England. He had served with the British and Portuguese navies but with no great distinction and had spent long periods ashore on half-pay farming in Hampshire. Many wondered at his appointment and it was rumoured that he had been chosen only because other more able men had turned down the job. There is no evidence to support this. On the contrary, Phillip proved not only a capable leader and administrator but a man of great vision, convinced that his real task was not merely to clear the English jails but, in his own words, 'to lay the foundation of an Empire'.

After months of organization and struggle against official parsimony what has become known as the First Fleet sailed from England on 13 May 1787. It comprised HMS *Sirius*, the armed tender *Supply,* three storeships and six transports, with food, clothing and other supplies for two years. They carried also 1,044 people bound for Botany Bay, comprising 568 male and 191 female convicts with 13 children,

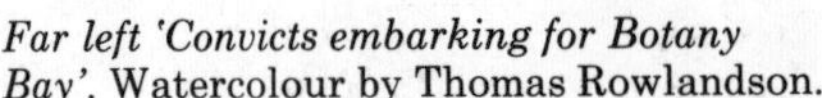

Far left 'Convicts embarking for Botany Bay'. Watercolour by Thomas Rowlandson.

Left The Sessions House, Old Bailey, London, where many convicts were sentenced to transportation.

206 marines with 27 wives and 19 children, and 20 officials. There were some who were to play notable parts in the colony's early history. Among the officers of the *Sirius* Captain John Hunter was to become its second Governor and Lieutenant Philip Gidley King its third. Among the officers of marines Captain David Collins, who filled a dual role as judge-advocate, and Lieutenant Thomas Davey were to become respectively the first and second Lieutenant-Governors of Van Diemen's Land and Lieutenant George Johnston was to have the dubious distinction of forcibly removing a later Governor from office. Hunter and Collins were to win additional fame as historians of the early settlement, and others who were to chronicle its first years were John White, surgeon-general, and Captain-Lieutenant Watkin Tench of the marines.

After stops to replenish stores, and six weeks out from the Cape, Phillip transferred to the *Supply* and with three other fast-sailing ships pressed on ahead. His aim was to have land cleared, stores disembarked and accommodation erected for the arrival of the main party but contrary winds frustrated this and when the rest of the fleet entered Botany Bay at dawn on 20 January the *Supply* had been there a mere forty hours. It had been a remarkably successful voyage. In just over eight months the fleet had

Top left Captain Arthur Phillip, founder and first Governor of N.S.W. Portrait by Francis Wheatley.

Left An English prison hulk. Watercolour by W. Bigg.

Above Captain Watkin Tench, one of several First Fleet historians.

Above right 'Fleet of Transport Under Convoy'. Satirical print by an unknown artist.

Right 'Black-eyed Sue and Sweet Poll of Plymouth taking leave of their lovers who are going to Botany Bay.'

covered 15,000 miles, yet no ship had ever lost touch with the others except by design. Despite overcrowding and the poor physical condition of many convicts when embarked only twenty men and three women died during the voyage and most landed much healthier than when they had set out.

Phillip quickly realized that Botany Bay would never serve. It was shallow and exposed to southerly winds, fresh water was inadequate, the soil was either too marshy or too sandy to grow crops or even vegetables and no sign could be found of Cook's 'fine meadow'. As a possible alternative he decided to examine Port Jackson nine miles to the north, and on 21 January he, Hunter and other officers set out in three open boats. They passed through the heads soon after noon and, as Phillip wrote, 'had the satisfaction of finding the finest harbour in the world, in which a thousand sail of the line may ride in the most perfect security'. About four miles up the harbour they found a well-wooded cove with a sizeable stream of fresh water. Phillip decided that this should be the site of settlement and he called it Sydney Cove.

On 24 January while the fleet was preparing to move two strange ships were seen outside Botany Bay, baulked from entering by an offshore wind. At first it was thought they might be Dutch warships sent to dispute the landing of the British but when they finally got in next day they were found to be French, *La Boussole* and *L'Astrolabe*. From their commander, Jean-François de Galaup, comte de la Pérouse, it was learned that they were on a voyage of discovery and that far from making any territorial claims they had merely put in to Botany Bay for wood and water. During a stay of several weeks the Frenchmen were always on friendly terms with Phillip and his officers.

Meanwhile Phillip had returned to Port Jackson in the *Supply* and in the afternoon of 26 January he led a party of officers and marines ashore in Sydney Cove. The Union Jack was hoisted, toasts were drunk and volleys fired and three cheers were given by all. Later that day the rest of the fleet arrived and next morning the work of creating a settlement began in earnest. Trees beside the freshwater stream were felled, tents were erected, livestock and stores were disembarked, land was cleared for growing grain and vegetables and Hunter began a detailed survey of the harbour. On 7 February Phillip's commission and another establishing a court of judicature were read to the assembled colonists, bond and free, a band played, a public holiday was proclaimed and Phillip entertained his officers at lunch. Next day the chaplain, the Reverend Richard Johnson, who had held his first church service

Left The First Fleet in Botany Bay.

Below left The French navigator La Perouse who appeared unexpectedly at Botany Bay soon after the arrival of the First Fleet.

Right First chaplain of the settlement, the Reverend Richard Johnson.

Below Sketch of Sydney Cove, Port Jackson, by a transported convict.

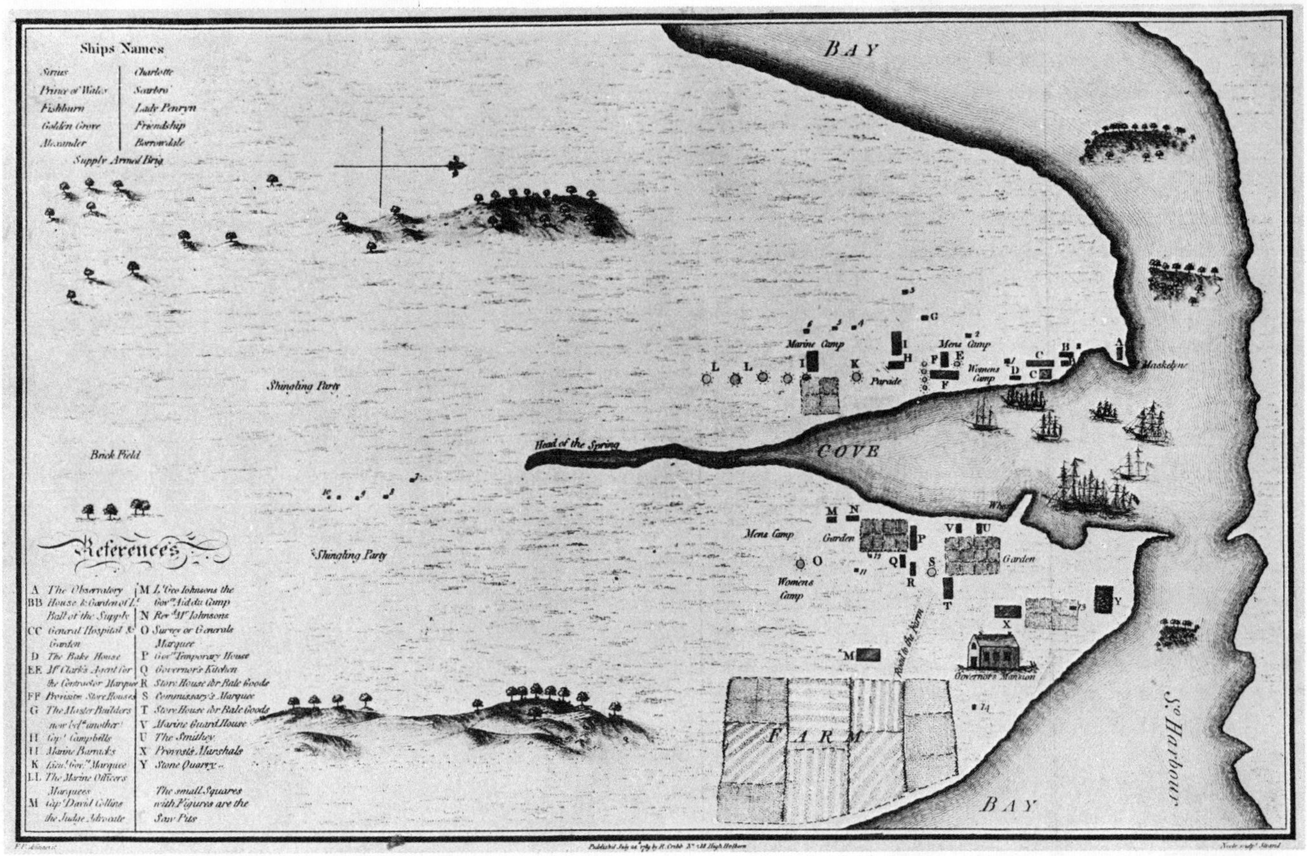

Top left Brickfield Hill, on the high road to Parramatta. Here the settlement's first bricks were made.

Centre left Sydney Cove and the settlement in August 1788. From a drawing by Captain John Hunter.

Lower left Explorers at Broken Bay try to win the friendship of an Aboriginal woman.

Above Two portraits by an unknown artist of Aborigines in Sydney. They are Abbarroo, who as a child was adopted by the chaplain, and Colbee, friend of Benelong.

Right Natives hunting kangaroos on the shore of Sydney Cove.

Preceding page
'The Founding of Australia', by Algernon Talmage, R.A. Phillip and his officers toast the new colony – Sydney Cove, 26 January 1788.

ashore under a large gum-tree on the 5th, married five convict couples. The bridegrooms included Henry Kable, who was to become a wealthy merchant and William Bryant, who three years later was to make a dramatic escape from the colony with his wife and children. Among other things Phillip had been ordered to form a subsidiary settlement on Norfolk Island, about 900 miles north-east of Sydney, mainly to prevent any other European power from occupying it. The task was entrusted to Lieutenant King and on 14 February he sailed in the *Supply* with a small party of marines and convicts.

Although order of a sort gradually emerged from the chaos of the first few weeks Phillip faced many problems and suffered many setbacks. The indiscriminate fraternizing of marines, seamen and male and female convicts, which could not be prevented, led to much drunkenness and immorality. Some convicts were lazy and had to be driven to work; others were willing enough but incapable. Thieving, of food and liquor particularly, was prevalent and floggings of up to 500 lashes and even the hanging on 6 March of James Barrett failed to check the evil. According to Tench, Barrett was 'an old and desperate offender' but seventeen seems a sad age at which to have to die even as an awful example to others. There was trouble among Phillip's officers as well. Major Robert Ross, in command of the marines, quarrelled frequently with him and refused to allow his men to superintend convict working parties. During a dinner to celebrate a royal birthday surgeon White and his first assistant, William Balmain – after whom a Sydney suburb was to be named – fought a duel with pistols but no great damage was done. Attempts to win the friendship of the local Aborigines were not notably successful and convicts who strayed in the wood were often wounded and occasionally killed. Sheep died of disease or were struck by lightning and cattle from the government's pathetically small herd strayed and were lost. Seed grain was eaten by ants and field-mice almost as soon as planted. Except in a few areas the soil around Sydney Cove was found to be unfertile and Phillip had to look further afield for land on which to grow crops. He found it eventually at the head of the harbour about fourteen miles inland and sent some of his people there to form a settlement. At first he called this Rose Hill but then changed it to its native name of Parramatta. He drew up plans that would have made Sydney a noble town with streets 200 feet wide but the wattle-and-daub huts which were now replacing the original tents continued to rise where their builders chose and the inhabitants continued to use what seemed to them the most convenient tracks through the bush. It says much for Phillip that in spite of everything he never lost heart; nor did he ever waver in his faith that the colony he was creating under such handicaps and with such unpromising human material would one day emerge as a proud nation.

By mid-1789 the Governor's overriding problem was how to continue to feed his people. Of the little left in store much had been destroyed by rats or was unfit to eat. The summer harvest had yielded only enough grain for three weeks. Rich farming land had been found on the Hawkesbury River, about thirty-five miles inland but Phillip lacked the men and resources to work it. The *Sirius,* sent to Cape Town to buy provisions, returned with only four months' supply of flour. There was little livestock left, and fish and occasional kangaroo meat barely helped to postpone the crisis. In October the already meagre ration was reduced by a third and by early 1790, as Tench wrote, 'famine was approaching with gigantic strides'. On Norfolk Island the picture was different. The land was fertile, livestock flourished and the few acres under cultivation yielded abundant crops. Phillip decided, therefore, to divide his forces and in March the *Sirius* and *Supply* sailed for the island with almost 300 people, leaving only 600 in Sydney and Parramatta. The opportunity to

Natives pursuing Kangaroos in the neighbourhood of Sydney, New South Wales.

Top The first Government House, Sydney, and the government farm at Parramatta, 1791.

Above Rescuing crew and supplies from the wrecked *Sirius,* Norfolk Island. Watercolour by George Raper.

Left Sydney Cove from the rocks on the western foreland. Wash drawing by the convict artist Thomas Watling, about 1793.

get rid of Major Ross was too good to miss and he was sent along to relieve King as commandant. The outcome was disastrous. Off the island the *Sirius* was wrecked on a reef and 500 people found themselves virtually marooned. Here they were to remain eleven months on short rations, saved from actual starvation only by slaughtering thousands of seabirds which made the island their breeding place. When the *Supply* returned to Sydney with news of the disaster Phillip sent her at once to Batavia to buy food. It was a desperate gamble, for she was his only remaining ship. Convicts began to die of sheer starvation and many became too weak to work. Phillip rationed himself as stringently as his people, and officers invited to dine at Government House were asked to bring their own bread. Supplies from England were now long overdue. 'We begin to think the mother country has entirely foresaken us', a seaman wrote despairingly. But he was wrong. The mother country had not been forgetful, merely dilatory.

Early in June a ship arrived with a cargo of women convicts and the bitter news that the storeship *Guardian,* laden with supplies for the colony, had hit an iceberg south of Cape Town and been wrecked. In the same month three more transports arrived bringing convicts and officers and men of the New South Wales Corps, a force specially recruited in England to take over guard duties from the marines. Of a thousand convicts embarked more than a quarter had died on the way out from neglect, brutality and deliberate starvation. 'The slave trade is merciful to what I have seen', one officer wrote, and it was no overstatement. Some who had lasted

Above left Two watercolours by an unknown artist – Native attacking another while asleep; and native woman curing a child's headache.

Left Wreck of the storeship *Guardian* off the Cape of Good Hope while on her way to relieve the famine in the new settlement, 24 December 1789.

out the hideous voyage died as the ships came into harbour and their naked bodies were thrown overboard. Some died as they went ashore or on the wharf and others, unable to walk, crawled on all fours or had to be carried. Surgeon White did his best but within a month another hundred were dead and many who survived were permanent invalids. What relief the food brought by the transports may have afforded had been cancelled out by the extra mouths to be fed.

On 7 December there was near-disaster of a different kind when Phillip, trying to make friends with some natives, was speared in the shoulder. Balmain extracted the barb and in six weeks the governor was up and about again.

The arrival in December of a Dutch food ship, chartered in Batavia by the captain of the *Sirius*, brought temporary relief but the position soon became critical again. Driven to desperation a number of convicts absconded, believing naïvely that they could reach China overland, and perished miserably in the bush. In March 1791 there was an escape of a different kind. William and Mary Bryant, with their two infant children and seven other convicts, stole an open boat and set out for Timor, 3,250 miles away. Although often in peril of shipwreck or starvation and harried by natives whenever they went ashore they reached Koepang in a little over two months. But the effort was in vain, for the Dutch guessed they were escaped convicts and put them in prison to await transport to England. Bryant, the two children and three others died there or on the way home and the survivors were sent to Newgate prison to complete their sentences. Mary Bryant's heriosm during her long ordeal won the admiration of James Boswell and through his influence she was released and returned to her native town of Fowey, Cornwall.

At intervals in July and August 1791 a third fleet of ten transports arrived. Of more than 2,000 convicts embarked 180 had died during the passage and many others arrived 'so emaciated,' as Phillip wrote angrily, 'so worn away by long confinement or want of food that it will be long before they recover their strength'. For many more months famine and death continued to walk hand in hand. Relief came eventually with the arrival of three storeships from England, and at long last Phillip was able to put his people back on to full rations. By this time the Governor himself was a sick man, worn out by the physical and mental strain of nearly five years in office and in December 1792 he handed control of the colony to Major Francis Grose, commanding officer of the N.S.W. Corps, and sailed for home.

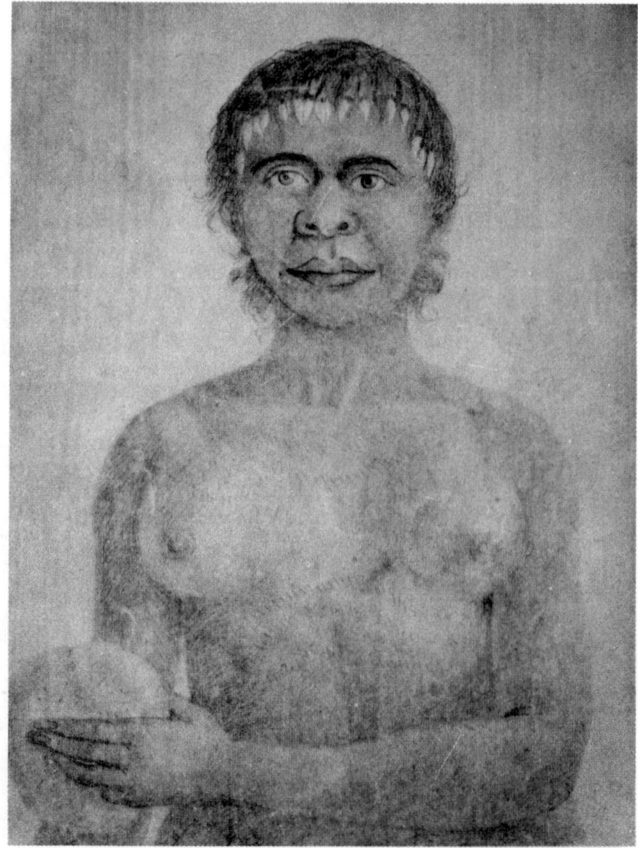

In 1793 two Spanish ships paid a friendly visit to Sydney in the course of a scientific voyage. Aboard were two artists – Fernando Brambila on the *Atrevida* and Juan Ravenet on the *Descuvierta*. The portraits of an Aboriginal man and woman (*left*) and the views of Sydney Cove (*top right*) and Parramatta (*right*) are all by Brambila.

Although about 4,650 convicts had arrived during Phillip's term the death rate, particularly among those of the second and third fleets, had been so high that when he left the total population, bond and free, was only 4,200. An overwhelming majority of the convicts were products of their times rather than vicious criminals, transported for such offences as petty larceny, burglary, stealing livestock, receiving stolen goods, prostitution, forgery, embezzlement and poaching. Although most of them lived and died in obscurity there were a few exceptions. John Irving, transported for larceny, was a surgeon who received his freedom after only two years for 'unremitting good conduct and meritorious behaviour' and practised at Norfolk Island and Parramatta. James Ruse, sentenced for burglary, received the first land grant in the colony and was a successful and prosperous farmer within eighteen months. Simeon Lord and Mary Reiby (née Haydock), whose offences were stealing some calico and a horse respectively, became wealthy and respected merchants; James Squire, also sentenced for a petty crime, became a successful farmer and the colony's first brewer. Thomas Watling, a young Scot, who chose transportation rather than face trial for forgery, was Sydney's first professional artist and left many valuable pictorial records of its early years. Molly Morgan, twice transported, once for theft and once for arson, ended her days as a wealthy landowner and a generous donor to charities. But the most famous of all in his time was George Barrington, whose elegance and wit had won him a high place in London society and who lived by picking the well-lined pockets of the gentry.

It was Barrington who, on slight evidence, was supposed to have written:

'From distant climes o'er widespread seas we come,
Though not with much eclat or beat of drum,
True patriots all; for be it understood,
We left our country for our country's good.'

One of Phillip's last acts was to give Barrington his freedom and he became chief constable of Parramatta.

Under Grose's administration the colony saw many changes, few for the better. He made generous land grants to his military and civil officers and gave them free convict labour, fed and clothed at government expense. Among those who benefited was Lieutenant John Macarthur, a man of forceful character, great vision and few scruples, who called his grant of 200 acres Elizabeth Farm after his young wife and built on it a house that still stands. Civil magistrates were dismissed and replaced by military officers. The rank and file of the N.S.W. Corps were better fed and given privileges denied to others. Roads and other public works were neglected. On the other hand, settlement was extended to the Hawkesbury, where the rich river flats were soon yielding good crops. Contrary to regulations Grose allowed his officers to engage in trade and when ships began to call with cargoes for sale they pooled their resources and claimed and exercised the right to take first pick of what was offered. In particular they bought large quantities of spirits which they sold at profits of up to 800 per cent. Soon rum became the accepted currency for buying goods, land and stock and for paying wages. The effects were demoralizing and often disastrous.

Top left A woman of N.S.W. and an officer of the N.S.W. Corps, by the Spanish artist Ravenet.

Left Simeon Lord and Mary Reiby, two emancipists who became wealthy merchants in Sydney.

Top right Frontispiece from the *Memoirs* of George Barrington, the famous pickpocket, who became chief constable of Parramatta.

Right Elizabeth Farm, Parramatta, the first home of John Macarthur and his family.

Above Elizabeth Farm today, the oldest surviving building in Australia. It is to be preserved as a museum.

Far left Captain John Hunter, second Governor of the colony. Portrait by W. M. Bennett.

Left William Skirving, one of the Scottish 'Martyrs' who were transported to the colony for their political activities.

Three other Scottish 'Martyrs'. *From left* Thomas Muir, Thomas Fyshe Palmer and Maurice Margarot.

Emancipists and the few free settlers who had arrived often worked for a week and then drank their wages in a day. Farmers sold their crops and mortgaged their land for rum. By the time Grose left at the end of 1794 his officers were on the way to becoming rich men and their vicious monopoly was complete.

Johnson, the unfortunate chaplain, who had had little encouragement from Phillip, received even less from Grose. 'No church is yet begun', he wrote despairingly to a friend. 'Most here would rather see a tavern, a playhouse, a brothel – anything sooner than a place of public worship.' In 1793 in desperation he built his own, a crude cruciform of wattle and plaster, at what is now the corner of Hunter and Castlereagh Streets in the commercial heart of Sydney. For five years it served as church and school and then it was burned down reputedly by convicts who resented being forced to attend.

However, in 1794 there arrived an assistant to share the chaplain's burden. The Reverend Samuel Marsden was everything Johnson was not – energetic, restless, shrewd and grasping, a dispenser of hell-fire from the pulpit and of savage floggings from the magistrate's bench; a man who was to leave his mark indelibly not only on the lacerated backs of his convict victims but on the history of the colony he made his home. In the same year arrived four of the so-called 'Scottish Martyrs' – Thomas Muir, Thomas Fyshe Palmer, William Skirving and Maurice Margarot – joined in 1795 by Joseph Gerrald. Their 'crime' had been to advocate at a convention in Edinburgh certain democratic reforms which every Briton accepts today as his birthright. On instructions they were treated as special prisoners, free from restraint so long as they did not indulge in political activity. Skirving and Gerrald died soon after arrival, of broken hearts it was said. Muir escaped in an American ship and died in Paris, and Palmer, having served his time, died on the way home. Of the five only Margarot ever saw England again.

In September 1795 Phillip's former colleague, Captain John Hunter, arrived in HMS *Reliance* as second Governor. Hunter was warm-hearted, honest and conscientious but it needed more than these qualities to break the power of the corrupt military clique. He did his best but it was not nearly good enough. Those who had flattered him on arrival soon became his implacable enemies and secretly and openly frustrated his every effort at reform.

In spite of this the colony progressed and expanded. Flocks and herds and the acres under cultivation increased so rapidly that the danger of

Above Tom Thumb's Lagoon, on the south coast of New South Wales, discovered and named by Bass and Flinders. It is now within the huge complex of Port Kembla iron and steel works.

Left Australia's two most noted early explorers by sea – surgeon George Bass of the *Reliance,* and Lieutenant Matthew Flinders.

famine no longer existed, except in time of drought or flood. Herds of wild cattle, descendants of the few who had strayed in 1788, were found about forty miles south-west of Sydney on rich grazing land that is still known as the Cowpastures. Captain Henry Waterhouse, of the *Reliance,* imported a few merino sheep from Cape Town, bred and sold their progeny to others, including Macarthur and so launched what was to become Australia's greatest industry. Lieutenant John Shortland discovered, about seventy miles north of Sydney, a splendid river flowing through fertile land which he named after the governor. Near its mouth were found extensive deposits of coal and Simeon Lord and other enterprising emancipists were given permission to work these. Equally rich deposits were found by some shipwrecked sailors on the Illawarra coast, south of Sydney, and by 1799 the colony was exporting coal to Bengal. In 1795 the first printing press was set up in Sydney and in the following year the first windmill was erected and the first theatre opened. The play was Edward Young's *The Revenge,* and patrons who lacked ready money could pay for admission in flour, meat (including kangaroo meat) or rum.

Most of the coastal exploration in this period was carried out by George Bass, surgeon of the *Reliance,* and Lieutenant Matthew Flinders. Both were Lincolnshire men; both were adventurous, curious, intelligent and ambitious. Flinders had learned his trade under the redoubtable William Bligh and at twenty-one was already an outstanding navigator. In 1796 in a dinghy they called *Tom Thumb* and with a boy named Martin as crew Bass and Flinders examined the coast for about fifty miles south of Sydney. They landed near a spot they called Tom Thumb's Lagoon to dry out their gunpowder and other stores, and while they did so Flinders pacified some warlike Aborigines by trimming their hair and beards with scissors. Next year in an open whaleboat with a volunteer crew Bass ventured much further south. He discovered the Shoalhaven River and Twofold Bay, sailed past Point Hicks, where Cook had first sighted the continent and continued on to a harbour which he called Western Port. Here a strong south-west swell convinced him that a strait separated the mainland from Van Diemen's Land. Hunter realized that if this were so it would save ships up to a fortnight in their passage from England and he sent Bass and Flinders in the *Norfolk,* a barely-seaworthy sloop of twenty-five tons, to make sure. They proved the point by circumnavigating Van Diemen's Land and as a reward Bass had his name given to the strait. Again in the *Norfolk* Flinders spent six weeks in 1799 examining parts of the coast of what is now Queensland as far north as Hervey Bay. A year later he was back in England but his association with Australia was by no means ended.

Meanwhile Hunter's numerous enemies had so successfully blackened his name in London that it was decided to recall him. The letter was carried by Philip Gidley King, now a post-captain, and on Whitehall's instruction it was to King as third Governor that Hunter handed over when he left in September 1800. He was a bitter and disappointed man, conscious of failure but conscious also that he had been blamed for things beyond his control; and his last few months were further soured by the too obvious eagerness of his erstwhile friend and shipmate to step into his shoes.

We are all ruin'd
Croppy lay down
Death or Liberty Major

4 Rum Rebellion

Governor King is credited with saying that when he took over the colony it comprised only two classes – those who sold rum and those who drank it. He began his government energetically, confident that he would soon break the power of the military monopolists. It was easy enough to forbid them from trading and to restrict the importation of spirits but impossible, as he found, to enforce such orders. At every turn, as he wrote bitterly to London, he found himself thwarted 'by every measure that art, cunning and fraud could suggest'. To sidestep the trading ban officers put their shops and grog shanties in the names of their convict mistresses, and when rum could not be imported legally it was smuggled in. Soon they were so openly at odds with King that many refused to attend Government House even on official occasions. King's only chance was that in time they might quarrel among themselves, and eventually this happened. Macarthur, whose arrogance had grown with his power and prosperity, had angry words with his commanding officer, Colonel Paterson, and the result was a duel in which Paterson was seriously wounded. It would have been pointless to court-martial Macarthur in the colony, for his judges would also have been his friends. Instead King sent him under arrest to England, and hoped no doubt that with the removal of the 'Botany Bay perturbator', as Macarthur came to be known, things would improve. But the officers quickly closed their ranks and remained as impregnable as ever.

In other directions King's rule was more successful. Existing roads were improved and new ones made. A granary, a church and a school were erected at the Hawkesbury; a church, a jail and a brewery at Parramatta. Wharves and bridges were built and in 1803 King launched the colony's first newspaper, the *Sydney Gazette*. He encouraged the export of coal and the manufacture of blankets and coarse linen, he greatly increased the government

Left An eye-witness's version of the clash between troops and convict rebels at Toongabbie on 5 March 1804. The mounted officers are Major George Johnston and Quartermaster Laycock. Johnston is parleying with the rebel leader, Phillip Cunningham, who is proclaiming 'Death or Liberty'. In the background Father Dixon is trying to persuade the rebels to lay down their arms.

Right Captain Philip Gidley King, third Governor of N.S.W.

flocks and herds by importing new stock, and with his wife's active help he founded a home for orphan girls.

Meanwhile in England some alarm had been caused by news that two French ships, the *Géographe* and the *Naturaliste,* commanded by Nicholas Baudin, had set out for New Holland on what was officially a scientific expedition. However, Napoleon's colonial ambitions were well-known and with much of the continent still open to anyone who cared to claim it the British government decided to take no risks. Matthew Flinders, now highly reputed as a cartographer and more restlessly ambitious than ever, was given command of HMS *Investigator* and sent off hurriedly to survey those parts of the Australian coast which still remained blank on the map and to show the British flag if need be. Among those he took with him were Robert Brown, a noted botanist; William Westall, a young landscape artist; and Ferdinand Bauer, a botanical draughtsman.

The *Investigator* reached the south-west tip of the continent at Cape Leeuwin on 6 December 1801. Four weeks were spent in King George's Sound and early in 1802 Flinders began a slow and painstaking survey of the virtually unknown south coast. Like the Dutch almost two centuries before him he found

Left 'Soldiers embarking for New South Wales, 1803'. Watercolour by Isaac Cruickshank.

Below left The 'Botany Bay Perturbator', John Macarthur with his wife Elizabeth. To their right is Captain Nicholas Baudin, leader of the French expedition which visited Sydney in 1803.

Right Sydney from the east side of the cove. Aquatint from an original by the convict artist John Eyre.

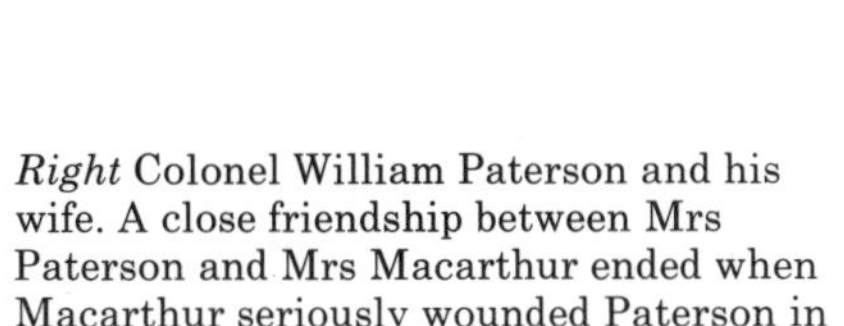

Right Colonel William Paterson and his wife. A close friendship between Mrs Paterson and Mrs Macarthur ended when Macarthur seriously wounded Paterson in a duel.

most of it barren and forbidding. However, late in February there came a dramatic change. The coastline turned sharply north and for a while Flinders believed he was on the way to discovering an inland sea or even a strait bisecting the continent. But instead it proved to be merely a deep gulf which he named for Lord Spencer of the Admiralty. Returning to the open sea he discovered a large island on which kangaroos, seals and emus 'dwelt amicably together', as he wrote, 'so unaware of human danger that they could be killed almost at will'. His company fed well on fresh meat, and he called the place Kangaroo Island. Off the mainland again he found and explored another gulf which he named for Lord St Vincent, also of the Admiralty. Nearby was to rise the city of Adelaide.

In four months Flinders had found no sign of the French expedition and could only speculate on its whereabouts. He had his answer on 8 April when a sail approaching from the east was identified as the *Géographe*. With Brown as interpreter Flinders went aboard the French ship. To his delight he learned they had achieved little in the way of exploration and had in fact just come from a long stay in Van Diemen's Land, 'picking up shells and catching butterflies' as one disgruntled officer put it.

Left The ships of Baudin's expedition, *Le Géographe* and *Le Naturaliste.*

Below left East view of Sydney, from George Barrington's *History of New South Wales.*

Above right The *Lady Nelson,* which played an important part in early coastal exploration.

Far right Colonel David Collins, first Lieutenant-Governor of Van Diemen's Land.

Below right A man and woman of Van Diemen's Land. These drawings were made by John Webber when Captain Cook visited the island during his third voyage.

The *Géographe* and *Naturaliste* had lost contact during a gale in Bass Strait and Baudin assumed that the *Naturaliste* had made her way to Sydney. As many of Baudin's own crew were down with scurvy it surprised Flinders that he had not done the same.

On 26 April as the *Investigator* coasted eastward Flinders saw and entered an extensive harbour. For a while he mistook it for Western Port, discovered by Bass, but soon realized his error and congratulated himself on having made an important new discovery. In fact, as he learned later, he had been forestalled ten weeks earlier by Lieutenant John Murray in the brig *Lady Nelson,* who had called the place Port Phillip, after the colony's first Governor. On its northern shore now stands Melbourne, the second city of Australia, and on its western shore is the thriving city of Geelong.

As Baudin had guessed the *Naturaliste* was already in Sydney when the *Investigator* arrived on 9 May. Six weeks later the *Géographe* limped in, her people so debilitated by scurvy that only four were fit for duty, and Flinders had to send a boat to tow her down the harbour. On Governor King's orders the sick were admitted to hospital and the public ration was reduced to provide them with flour and fresh meat. Unknown to Baudin one of his lieutenants, Louis de Freycinet, and a naturalist, François Péron, took advantage of their time in port to gather information about Sydney's garrison strength and inspect beaches on which invasion troops might land and later Péron submitted a report on these matters to the Governor of Mauritius, General Decaen, for transmission to Paris. As a result of this clumsy amateur spying King ordered a fort to be built on the west side of Sydney Cove and wrote to London urging the immediate formation of a settlement at Port Phillip. Soon after the French ships had left Sydney he was further alarmed to learn that some French officers had boasted that they intended to colonize Van

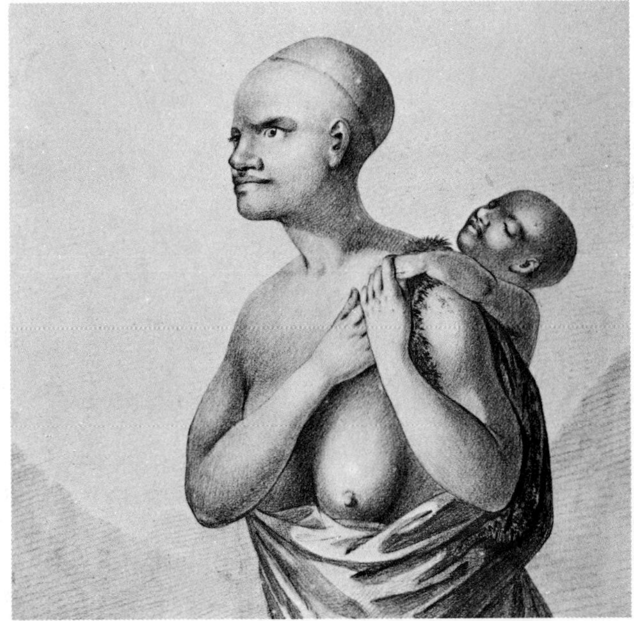

Aboriginal life in N.S.W. is vividly portrayed in these aquatints by the well-known English artist John Heaviside Clark from sketches sent from the colony. *Top left* A young warrior undergoes trial by ordeal. *Far left* Spearing birds on the wing. *Above* Climbing a tree, and smoking out a possum. *Left* Fishing with a three-pronged spear.

Diemen's Land. He promptly sent Lieutenant Charles Robbins after them with a letter warning that such an action would not be tolerated. Robbins came up with the French at King Island in Bass Strait, delivered the letter and emphasized its point by nailing the British colours to a tree. Even when Baudin sailed for Mauritius on his way home to France King remained suspicious, and in September 1803, to anticipate any possible French move, he sent Lieutenant John Bowen in the *Lady Nelson* with a small party of troops and convicts to Van Diemen's Land, where Bowen established a settlement of sorts at Risdon Cove, on the Derwent River.

Meanwhile in London King's letter recommending a settlement at Port Phillip had produced a remarkably prompt response. Within weeks of its arrival David Collins, now a lieutenant-colonel, was commissioned to organize and outfit an expedition, and within another four months it was on its way. It comprised HMS *Calcutta* and a storeship, the *Ocean,* with 300 male convicts, a guard of 50 marines and civil officers, free settlers, wives, children and servants to a total of about 470. Port Phillip was reached in October and a temporary camp was established near the harbour entrance on the site of the present town of Sorrento. Collins was not impressed and with King's approval he decided to transfer to Van Diemen's Land. Port Dalrymple, on the north coast, was examined and rejected, and early in 1804 he transferred his company in two drafts to the Derwent. Equally unimpressed by Bowen's struggling settlement at Risdon Cove Collins chose another site a few miles downstream which he called Hobart Town.

While all this was happening Flinders had pressed doggedly on with his coastal survey. Sailing north from Sydney in July 1802 he spent more than three months carefully examining the long coastline which Cook had charted thirty-two years before. By early November he had passed through Torres Strait and had begun an examination of the north

Far left Romantic version by a visiting French artist of an Aboriginal marriage ceremony.

Right and below Three paintings by William Westall, official artist aboard the *Investigator*. From top: Pobassoo's Bay, Gulf of Carpentaria, with Malayan proas at anchor; the camp on Wreck Reef, with the flag flying upside down as a distress signal; a boat's crew from the *Porpoise* picking up survivors from the *Cato* off Wreck Reef.

coast. Hitherto the luck had all been with him but now it turned. The *Investigator* began to leak badly and her timbers were found to be so rotten that it was doubtful if she would survive even a moderate gale. Despite this, however, and ignoring monsoonal rain, steaming heat, shortage of provisions, fatal clashes with Aborigines and his crew's growing discontent Flinders pressed on stubbornly for another four months. Then he gave up and sailed to Koepang in Timor where Dutch carpenters patched up his crumbling ship. The voyage back, by way of the west and south coasts of the continent, was a nightmare. Four men died, many others became seriously ill and Flinders himself could barely walk because of scorbutic sores; and within a few days of reaching Sydney there were four more deaths. Determined to obtain another ship in which to complete his survey Flinders sailed two months later for England in HMS *Porpoise,* in company with two merchantmen, the *Cato* and *Bridgewater*. At night off the Queensland coast the *Porpoise* and *Cato* ran hard on to a coral reef. The *Bridgewater,* after hovering around for a few hours sailed on and left them to their fate and it is perhaps poetic justice that some months later she disappeared and was never heard of again. Next day both ships' companies were able to land on a nearby sandbank about 300 yards long and to salvage the bulk of their stores, water, livestock and even personal possessions. With a volunteer crew Flinders set out in an open cutter for Sydney. The voyage of 750 miles, a minor epic in its way, was completed without incident in thirteen days. King sent ships to rescue those still marooned, and Flinders continued on for England in the *Cumberland,* a barely-seaworthy schooner of twenty-six tons. Only a man obsessed would have taken such a chance and the inevitable result was disaster, though not of the sort one would expect. Unaware that England and France were again at war, Flinders put in to Mauritius for supplies and refitting. Tactlessly declining an invitation to dine with Governor Decaen, Flinders found himself under arrest and six years passed before friends, including Sir Joseph Banks, were able to obtain his release. He returned to England broken in health and prematurely aged in 1810, and died on 19 July 1814, on the day of publication of his monumental work, *A Voyage to Terra Australis.*

While Flinders languished in prison in Mauritius Governor King was having troubles of his own in Sydney. Still distrustful of the French, he had sent Colonel Paterson to form a second settlement in Van Diemen's Land at Port Dalrymple. Neither this nor Collins' settlement on the Derwent was doing well. At both places convicts had absconded and were ranging the bush in armed gangs plundering outlying farms. A senseless massacre at Risdon Cove had antagonized the hitherto peaceful Aborigines and settlers who wandered too far from home were apt to get a spear in the back. Even though dwindling food supplies were being eked out by kangaroo meat both places were threatened with famine and every mail brought urgent pleas for relief. King did his best but as convicts continued to arrive the reserves in his own stores were low. The military clique continued rapacious and unamenable to discipline; and from England came the disturbing news that the court-martial of John Macarthur had been abandoned because of lack of witnesses and that Macarthur had resigned his commission and meant to return as a private citizen. If this were true, King wrote ironically, he should be sent out as Governor, 'as one half of the colony already belongs to him and it will not be long before he gets the other half'.

But perhaps King's greatest single worry at this period was the potentially explosive situation caused by the colony's large proportion of Irish convicts, many of whom had fought against the British in the bloodily-quelled rebellion of 1798. Some had been in New South Wales since 1800 and one of King's first acts had been to form volunteer defence organizations in Sydney and Parramatta in case of trouble. Among the Irish were men of character and integrity, such as 'General' Joseph Holt, who had been a noted guerrilla leader; the Reverend Henry Fulton, a Protestant clergyman who won his emancipation within a year of arrival; James Meehan, who was to become the colony's surveyor-general; and Father James Dixon, who in 1803 was allowed to celebrate the first Mass in the colony. But in spite of the considerable influence of these men the danger remained. A cache of home-made pikes was found, suspected trouble-makers were flogged and sent to Norfolk Island, and the arrival of a shipload of 'desperate and diabolical characters' from Cork further increased King's apprehension. In February 1804 reports reached him that a rising was planned by 200 convicts who worked on a government farm at Castle Hill, some miles from Parramatta, and he ordered the guard there strengthened. For a while all was quiet; then on the night of 4 March the storm broke. Led by Phillip Cunningham, a former soldier, the convicts broke out of barracks and rampaged through the district gathering recruits and arms. Houses were plundered or burned and the official flogger was dragged from under his bed and given a taste of his own medicine. News of the rising reached Sydney about midnight.

Right Floods on the Hawkesbury River in the early 1800s destroyed crops and brought the colony to the brink of famine.

Below Major George Johnston, who routed the convict rebels at Toongabbie.

Below right 'General' Joseph Holt, a hero of the Irish uprising of 1797, was sent to Norfolk Island on suspicion of having been implicated in the convict rising.

All available forces were mustered, and Major George Johnston with fifty-six men of the N.S.W. Corps marched on Parramatta, where he was joined by some armed settlers. During the morning Johnston came up with the rebels, who now totalled about 400, at Toongabbie, a few miles north of Parramatta. Father Dixon was sent to parley with them and when they refused to listen Johnston himself rode forward and ordered them to lay down their arms. When this demand was also refused Johnston gave the order to fire and almost with the first volley the rebels broke and fled, leaving about fifteen dead and many wounded. In the pursuit that followed about 200 prisoners were taken including Cunningham who was hanged at once without benefit of trial. Of many others who were court-martialled eight went to the gallows, nine received floggings of up to 500 lashes, and about fifty were sent to hard labour at the Coal River (Newcastle), where a penal station for secondary offenders had recently been formed. Although Holt had taken no part in the affair he was suspected of being implicated and was banished for a while to Norfolk Island.

As early as 1803 King had written to London asking to be relieved and by 1805, his health undermined by gout, he had had more than enough. In

Left Margaret Catchpole, the convict girl whose life formed the basis of a novel by Richard Cobbold.

Top right James Hardy Vaux, pickpocket, swindler and author, who was three times transported to N.S.W.

Right Sydney from the west side of the cove. Aquatint from a drawing by John Eyre.

June of that year Macarthur returned in triumph in his own ship, the *Argo,* bringing some prize merino sheep for breeding and an order from Earl Camden, the new Secretary of State for the Colonies, for 5,000 acres of land with the promise of another 5,000 when he had proved the commercial possibilities of the wool industry. King's disillusionment and defeat were complete and his last year in office, while he awaited a successor, must have been bitter indeed.

During King's six years in office about 2,250 convicts reached New South Wales and the overall population increased from 5,200 to about 8,500. Among the convict arrivals were several whose names have endured. William Redfern, a naval surgeon sentenced for taking the part of seamen during the mutiny of The Nore in 1797, spent his first years in the colony as assistant surgeon at Norfolk Island. He soon earned a free pardon and in time became a magistrate, a director of the first bank, a welcome guest at Government House and Sydney's most popular doctor. Less worthy but perhaps more colourful was Sir Henry Brown Hayes, a fervent Irish freemason, whose crime was to abduct a Quaker heiress and force her into a spurious marriage. During ten years in the colony Hayes was in constant trouble with authority and in addition to brief periods of exile on Norfolk Island he spent some months in the coal mines at Newcastle. Between times he built Vaucluse House, near South Head, and surrounded it with a moat of turf imported from Ireland, to keep out snakes as he explained. Oddly enough, it seemed to work. Samuel Terry, a labourer sentenced for stealing 400 pairs of stockings, had the good sense to marry a rich widow in Sydney, became the colony's wealthiest merchant and died universally known as 'The Botany Bay Rothschild'. James Hardy Vaux, first convicted for stealing a handkerchief, earned the unique distinction of being transported three times between 1801 and 1830. Although Vaux spent much of his life from choice among pimps, pickpockets and prostitutes he was a man of literary talent and his *Vocabulary of the Flash Language* and *Memoirs* throw some fascinating light on criminal life in London and convict life in Australia. Finally there was Margaret Catchpole, of Ipswich, transported in 1801 for stealing a horse to ride to the aid of her lover, a smuggler on the run from the law. A warm-hearted, intelligent woman of great integrity, Margaret became the colony's best-known midwife, and won posthumous fame as the heroine of a biographical novel by Richard Cobbold.

In August 1806 King handed over the colony to Captain William Bligh, the hero – or villain, as

Far left 'The arrest of Bligh'. A propaganda cartoon designed to present the deposed Governor as an arrant coward.

Near left Major Johnston at the entrance to Government House proclaiming the arrest of Bligh. By Raymond Lindsay.

Above Captain William Bligh, fourth Governor of N.S.W.

Left Mutiny of the *Bounty,* an earlier incident in Bligh's tempestuous life.

Above Windsor, the main settlement on the Hawkesbury River, where Bligh won his strongest support. Watercolour attributed to George William Evans.

Left Bligh's widowed daughter, Mary Putland, who defied the rebels. She remained in Sydney to marry Colonel Maurice O'Connell.

some still insist – of the famous mutiny of the *Bounty* seventeen years before. Bligh had firm orders to break the power of the military clique and he set about his task with characteristic zeal, determination and absolute lack of tact. He forbade under stringent penalties the bartering of rum for labour, land or goods; he issued new port regulations which made incoming cargoes, including spirits, available to all with the money to buy; and he clamped down hard on illicit distilling and retailing of rum. On the other hand, to distressed settlers on the Hawkesbury whose summer crops had been destroyed by heavy floods he distributed free food, clothes and farming implements, made advances against their next crop and guaranteed to buy it at a fixed and remunerative price. Inevitably he earned the gratitude of the small farmers and the hostility of the landed proprietors.

In particular John Macarthur emerged as Bligh's arch-enemy. When Macarthur's claim for extra land was angrily rejected his animosity expressed itself in a series of court actions, not important in themselves, but designed to undermine the Governor's authority. Bligh bided his time and then struck back. A convict had escaped from the colony in a schooner owned by Macarthur. Bligh demanded the forfeiture of a £900 bond and when Macarthur refused this his ship was seized. Resolved to force a showdown, Macarthur disobeyed a summons to appear before the Governor and was arrested and charged with sedition. His trial, before officers of the N.S.W. Corps who were also his friends, collapsed in chaos and stalemate. Next day he was rearrested and jailed. Major Johnston, the senior officer then in Sydney, ordered his release; and the same evening, on the flimsy pretext of preventing 'insurrection and massacre' Johnston marched on Government House at the head of his corps, with a band playing 'The British Grenadiers'. Bligh's recently-widowed daughter, Mary Putland, tried to bar his entry but was pushed aside and Bligh and his supporters were rounded up and arrested. The date was 26 January 1808, the colony's twentieth anniversary.

For the best part of a year, with Bligh under arrest, Johnston and Macarthur ran the colony to suit themselves and their friends. Rum again became the staple currency and cynical exploitation again the rule. When Johnston's senior, Colonel Joseph Foveaux, returned from long leave Bligh hoped, reasonably enough, that he would be released and restored to office. But Foveaux sided with his own people. So, a little later, did Colonel Paterson, commanding officer of the corps, when he came reluctantly from Port Dalrymple to take charge. Bligh bombarded him with demands to be reinstated and his temper and conduct became so unendurable that Paterson, a tired and sick man, wished only to get rid of him. On Bligh's undertaking to sail direct to England he was given command of HMS *Porpoise* but once on board he announced that he was not bound by a promise made to a rebel government and went instead to Hobart Town, where he hoped to win the support of Colonel Collins.

At first Collins was sympathetic but Bligh's imperious behaviour soon caused an open breach between them. Bligh was forbidden from going ashore and newly-arrived settlers from Norfolk Island who proclaimed their loyalty to him were jailed and brutally flogged. Bligh transferred his headquarters to a bay near the mouth of the Derwent where he could intercept and buy food from incoming ships and there he remained doggedly to await relief from England. In December 1809 he learned that a new Governor, Colonel Lachlan Macquarie, was on his way and may already have reached the colony; and on 2 January 1810 Bligh sailed for Sydney to vindicate himself and confound his enemies.

5 Emancipists and Exclusives

Macquarie began his government with one great advantage over his predecessors – the physical, law-enforcing presence of his own regiment, the 73rd, which he brought to the colony to replace the N.S.W. Corps. His first task was to tidy up the mess left by the deposition of Bligh and he did it briskly and firmly, ignoring all incipient opposition. All orders issued by Bligh were confirmed, all issued by the rebel government were withdrawn. Rebel appointments were nullified and rebel land-grants cancelled, though many were later reconfirmed. Those of Bligh's supporters still in jail were freed and all with official positions were restored to them. Johnston was put under open arrest and sent to England for court-martial and Macarthur and others sailed with him as his chief witnesses. When Bligh sailed soon afterwards with his own witnesses he left behind his beloved daughter Mary, who after a brief courtship had married Macquarie's aide, Lieutenant-Colonel Maurice O'Connell.

There were many other immediate problems for Macquarie. On 24 March 1810 Collins died suddenly in Hobart Town and the government was taken over by Lieutenant Edward Lord, of the marines. A bill for £700 for Collins's funeral convinced Macquarie that Lord was unfit for the job and he hurriedly sent Captain John Murray, of his own regiment, to the Derwent. In New South Wales farmers who had lost their crops and stock through flood were now losing them through drought and once more the colony was near starvation. Public buildings, long neglected, were in disrepair or ruins, roads and bridges were almost impassable. On a tour of the settled areas which had almost the flavour of a royal progress Macquarie chose sites for new towns, laid them out and ordered the erection of public buildings. As new convicts arrived they were diverted from private assignment to public works and by the end of the governor's first year progress had been considerable. A new turnpike road to Parramatta was nearing completion; new barracks, a post office and a market place had appeared in Sydney; St Phillip's Church, which had been rising desultorily for years, had been completed; Presbyterians at Ebenezer, on the Hawkesbury, had been encouraged to build their own church; and a consortium comprising D'Arcy Wentworth, the principal surgeon, and two businessmen, Garnham Blaxcell and Alexander Riley, had contracted to build in Sydney a large and handsome hospital, for which they were to receive in lieu of cash a monopolistic right to import 45,000 gallons of spirits in three years. In this way Macquarie was able to turn the rum traffic, which he could not check, to his own

Left The man who gave his name to an era – Colonel Lachlan Macquarie, fifth Governor of N.S.W.

Right 'Explorers in the Blue Mountains', by Augustus Earle. Until Macquarie's day this rugged range west of Sydney was regarded as impassable.

advantage and he was genuinely bewildered when the home government later censured the contract. By then, fortunately, the hospital had been built.

Macquarie's rule soon took on the character of a benevolent despotism. In 1811 he toured Van Diemen's Land, ordered the building of new towns and roads, designed Hobart Town very much in its present form and liberally spattered the island with names commemorating his wife, his wife's family and himself. In New South Wales he reorganized the police force, established schools, enforced laws against Sabbath-breaking, denounced cohabitation, encouraged marriage and reduced the number of public houses by two-thirds. A settler at Windsor who had publicly auctioned his wife was flogged and sentenced to hard labour in irons, the wife was sent to Newcastle and the purchaser lost his money. Macquarie frowned on pugilism, which in any case was illegal, but encouraged other sports and pastimes. The colony's first recorded horse-race took place at Parramatta in April 1810, with wheelbarrow and sack-races and a footrace for 'three vestals of the current order' on the side; and in October officers of the 73rd Regiment cleared a course and held a three-days' meeting at Hyde Park, Sydney. There were cricket matches and freak pedestrian feats. A man carrying fourteen stone

Above An early cricket match in Hyde Park, Sydney, by T. H. Lewis. Buildings on the skyline include the Supreme Court, St James' Church, Sydney Hospital and the convict barracks.

Above right Macquarie's loyal and devoted wife, Elizabeth.

Left 'Emigrants leaving England for Australia'. Watercolour by Thomas Rowlandson.

Right The Governor's friend and medical adviser Dr William Redfern, who had been transported for sympathising with mutineers at The Nore.

over fifty yards beat an opponent who covered the same distance twice, once running forward and once backward; an officer on foot outpaced another on horseback over 100 yards.

Above all Macquarie sought from the first to establish that once a man had served his time or had been pardoned he should be readmitted freely to society and set the example himself by welcoming to Government House such emancipists as William Redfern (who became his family doctor), Simeon Lord, Mary Reiby and Michael Massey Robinson, who as 'poet laureate' was paid two cows a year. This policy, which London approved in principle, was heatedly opposed by prosperous free settlers and merchants, who came to be known as 'exclusives', by many of Macquarie's own military and civil officers, and above all by the man who should have been the first to support it – the Reverend Samuel Marsden, now the colony's senior chaplain and a wealthy breeder of sheep. Indeed, relations between the two eventually became so bitter that Macquarie denounced Marsden as his 'secret enemy' and debarred him from Government House except on official duty. At least, however, Macquarie was spared the inevitable hostility on this issue of John Macarthur. In London Johnston

In 1812 encouraged by Macquarie, Absalom West, an emancipist, published Australia's first set of locally-engraved views. *Left* Port Jackson Heads; and part of Parramatta. *Below left* Native camp at Cockle Bay, now Darling Harbour. *Right* First settlement at Newcastle, with Nobby's Head, then an island. *Below* Botany Bay with a view of the heads; and Windsor from the west bank of the Hawkesbury.

Top A convict chain-gang on the way to work.

Above Colonel Thomas Davey, second Lieutenant-Governor of Van Diemen's Land.

Top right George William Evans, surveyor, artist and the colony's first major inland explorer.

Right The Three Sisters, Jamieson Valley, Blue Mountains. Once the mountain barrier had been breached the way to the west was open.

had already been cashiered for his part in deposing Bligh, and Macarthur, warned that he would be arrested should he return to the colony, had been forced into an exile that was to last seven years.

Obviously if the colony was to prosper it must expand and in 1812 George William Evans, a government surveyor, set a modest lead when he explored the rich lands of the Illawarra coast. The great barrier, however, was the Blue Mountains, a formidable range of eroded valleys and towering precipices about forty miles west of Sydney, which had defied all previous explorers. In May 1813 a party led by Gregory Blaxland, a settler, William Charles Wentworth, son of the colonial surgeon, and Lieutenant William Lawson succeeded where others had failed by advancing along the high ridges rather than through the valleys. After seventeen days of hard slogging, progressing sometimes only a mile a day, they reached a point they called Mount Blaxland and proved that a crossing was practical. Five months later Evans was sent to complete what they had begun and having penetrated almost 100 miles beyond their furthest point he returned with a glowing report of vast tracts of fertile land watered by a noble river which he tactfully called the Macquarie. Within six months William Cox, a former army officer turned settler, with a working gang of only thirty convicts had turned Evans's route into a passable road; and in April 1815 Macquarie led a triumphal progress over this and founded the present town of Bathurst. Continuing on from this point Evans discovered more good land and a second river, which he named the Lachlan, after Macquarie's infant son. Close behind the vice-regal party followed settlers with their flocks and herds, their wagons and families and servants, and Australia's great squatting era had begun.

Meanwhile Thomas Davey, another of the marine pioneers of 1788 and now a lieutenant-colonel, had been appointed to succeed Collins in Van Diemen's Land, in preference to Macquarie's own nominee, Colonel Foveaux. On his way Davey stopped at Sydney where Macquarie treated him like a junior clerk and spent weeks briefing him in his job down to the last petty detail. Macquarie deplored Davey's drinking habits and what he called his 'frivolity and low buffoonry'; and Davey, by nature informal and easy-going, found Macquarie pompous and humourless. At no time was Davey allowed any real authority and every attempt to assert any evoked Macquarie's thundering wrath. The biggest single problem Davey faced in Van Diemen's Land was also the one which finally brought their mutual antipathy to a head. When he arrived the island was infested by bushrangers, mainly a gang of

Top 'First road over the Blue Mountains'. Watercolour by the American artist Augustus Earle.

Above Earle's impression of convicts at work at the top of the steep descent at Mount York.

Top right Early settlers at Cox's River on the western side of the mountains. Lithograph from a drawing by the French artist, A. Pellion.

Right Settler's hut on the Campbell River, west of the mountains. From a drawing by John William Lewin.

convict escapees led by Michael Howe, who terrorized outlying settlements and plundered almost at will, encouraged by the fact that even if they were captured there was no local criminal court to deal effectively with them. Davey did his best to cope with the problem but it was not nearly good enough for Macquarie, who took a hand by promising to pardon all except murderers who surrendered before a stated date. In effect this was an open invitation to the bushrangers to rob with impunity for six months, and they took full advantage of it. A climax was reached when two settlers were killed in a pitched battle. Urged on by the terrified populace Davey declared martial law, several bushrangers were caught and court-martialled and four were hanged. Macquarie's reaction was predictable. He denounced Davey's action as illegal and highly derogatory to his own authority, ordered him to revoke martial law, reported the matter to London and urged his recall.

In Sydney Macquarie was facing other problems. He had already quarrelled with Ellis Bent, his judge-advocate, and when Jeffrey Hart Bent arrived in July 1814 to establish a Supreme Court and become its first judge it was understandable that he support his brother. For several months he refused to open his court because he considered the available premises inadequate and when Macquarie finally forced his hand he refused to admit emancipist attorneys to practice, even though there was only one free lawyer in the colony. Macquarie's answer to this open defiance was prompt and uncompromising. He closed the court; then he wrote to Earl Bathurst, the current Secretary of State for the

Colonies, threatening to resign if the Bents were not removed. His challenge succeeded. Bathurst dismissed both the Bents – though Ellis was dead of a long-standing illness before the letter reached him – and appointed in their stead John Wylde as judge-advocate and Barron Field as judge. Inevitably the affair had repercussions. In the colony Jeffrey Bent's stand encouraged the exclusives in their anti-emancipist campaign and on his return to London his active and unscrupulous lobbying did much to undermine Macquarie's prestige.

In the meantime the colony was growing fast. Convicts were now arriving at a rate of up to 2,000 a year, and from being short of public labour Macquarie now found himself with such an embarrassing surplus that he diverted whole shiploads to Van Diemen's Land. Despite frequent warnings from London against overexpenditure Macquarie's passion for building remained unabated and in 1814 it had been given considerable impetus by the arrival of Francis Greenway, a skilled architect under sentence of fourteen years for forgery. By 1816 Greenway was the colony's official architect and by the following year his first notable building, a lighthouse at South Head, had earned him a conditional pardon. Buildings of great simplicity and grace continued to rise – among them a barracks and compound for convicts near the Rum Hospital in Sydney and hard by it St James' church; St Matthew's church and a court-house at Windsor; St Luke's church, Liverpool; and a female 'factory' or barracks at Parramatta. All but the last have survived and are jealously protected as gems of early colonial architecture. At the same time roads and communications were greatly increased and improved, the first steam-engine was imported and operated, botanic gardens and a government domain were laid out with a harbour frontage to Farm Cove, the first bank (The Bank of New South Wales) was established against strong opposition in London

Above left Poster displayed in Van Diemen's Land to promote friendship between Aborigines and whites. The effect was negligible.

Left A French artist's impression of Government House, Parramatta. With later additions it is now part of The King's School.

Above South Head lighthouse, designed by the convict architect Francis Greenway. Lithograph from a drawing by the French artist de Sainson.

and from the exclusives, a philosophical society was founded, the first Methodist chapel was built in Sydney and Fathers Therry and Conolly arrived as official founders of the Roman Catholic church. Land-hungry settlers still poured over the Blue Mountains and the village of Bathurst became a thriving town.

In 1817 and 1818 expeditions led by the surveyor-general, John Oxley, with Evans as his second-in-command, pushed further inland from Bathurst and found new rivers and large tracts of good land, including the Liverpool Plains. The following year James Meehan, the one-time Irish exile, penetrated south to Lake Bathurst and the rich Goulburn Plains. Squatters followed close in the explorers' tracks, and soon great flocks of sheep were grazing over thousands of square miles of the newly-discovered lands. Because of the general flow of the rivers Oxley had found he assumed incorrectly that there must be an inland sea to the west, a myth which persisted for a long while. Nevertheless, his work pioneered the way for other important explorations; and his discovery of Port Macquarie, a sheltered harbour to the north of Newcastle, led to the establishment there in 1821 of a new penal station.

In 1817 Davey was succeeded in Van Diemen's Land by Lieutenant-Colonel William Sorell. Sorell, an able administrator, began with the great advantage of having Macquarie's goodwill and although theoretically restricted he was in fact given a far freer hand than his predecessor. His first and most urgent task was to end the bushranging menace. By offering big rewards and by employing Aborigines to track down the 'banditti', as they were known, he broke up the various gangs so successfully that soon only Howe himself remained at large, an almost legendary figure, long-bearded and dressed in kangaroo skins, hunted so remorselessly that he was rarely more than a few hours ahead of his pursuers. Eventually, in desperate need of food and supplies, he walked into a well-set trap and was battered to death and his decapitated head carried in triumph to Hobart Town. With law and order restored, with ample convict labour for the first time, with free settlers arriving in a growing stream, with multiplying flocks and herds, and with a vast increase in agriculture Van Diemen's Land soon began to enjoy a prosperity it had never known before.

In 1817 John Macarthur was allowed to return to New South Wales on condition that he took no part

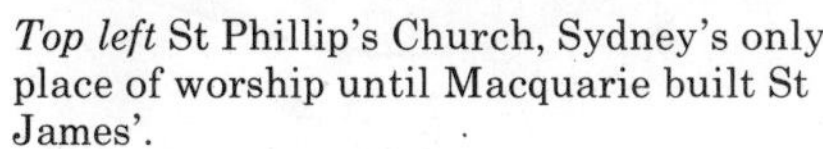

Top left St Phillip's Church, Sydney's only place of worship until Macquarie built St James'.

Left Squatters in camp on their way west to find a sheep run.

Above A squatter's first home in the bush.

Above right Squatters in search of grazing country make friends with local Aborigines. Wash drawing by Clement Hodgkinson.

Right The female 'factory' or prison at Parramatta. One of Greenway's few major buildings that has not survived.

Left Natives fishing in southern Queensland.

Below Idealized English version of a native family of Van Diemen's Land.

Right Even more idealized French engraving of a Van Diemen's Land tribe, from a drawing by de Piron.

Centre right The company of the French ship *Uranie* in camp on the coast of Western Australia.

Lower right Aborigines of southern Queensland in a tribal battle.

in public affairs. During his long absence his wife Elizabeth, leading the hard and dangerous life of a frontierswoman, had so increased and improved his flocks that their wool now equalled any in the world and sold readily and profitably on the English market. The Macquaries had befriended and greatly helped her but despite this and despite the terms of his return, Macarthur at once aligned himself with the exclusives and added his considerable influence to those in London who sought to destroy the governor's reputation and hasten his recall. Bathurst's despatches to Macquarie became increasingly critical. Macquarie's response was to offer his resignation but this was declined and instead John Thomas Bigge was sent to inquire into the state of the colony and its administration. Bigge's investigation was thorough but by no means without bias and he and the Governor were soon at odds. Above all Bigge disapproved of Macquarie's policy towards the emancipists and the breach between them became open when Macquarie appointed William Redfern a magistrate and Bigge had him removed. As an upshot Redfern and an ex-convict lawyer, Edward Eager, went to London where they pleaded the cause of their fellow-emancipists with considerable success. Bigge's voluminous report overlooked few aspects of colonial life and many of its recommendations were sound. It was marred, however, by personal animus and its attacks on Macquarie were neither subtle nor creditable to their author. Anticipating his recall the Governor offered again to resign and this time his offer was accepted. During 1821 he made a farewell tour of the settled areas and of Van

Top Attack on a settler's hut.

Above Captain John Piper's villa at Eliza Point (now Point Piper), Sydney.

Left Barron Field, Judge of the N.S.W. Supreme Court.

Above right Green Ponds, Van Diemen's Land, on the road from Hobart to Launceston.

Right Newcastle, showing the causeway to Nobby's under construction.

Diemen's Land; in November he welcomed his successor, Brigadier-General Sir Thomas Brisbane; and in February 1822 he and his family sailed for home. Sydney turned out in force to say goodbye to 'the old viceroy' and even his enemies watched him go with regret.

In a justification of his twelve years of government Macquarie wrote to Bathurst that he had found the colony 'barely emerging from infantile imbecility', its population rent by faction, many of them poverty-stricken and starving, its buildings 'mouldering to decay'. He had left it enjoying 'an enviable state of private comfort and public prosperity', its boundaries vastly increased, its population more than trebled to a total of 38,000, its agricultural land quadrupled, its sheep and cattle increased tenfold, its revenue soaring and its trade booming, its people better housed, greatly improved in morals and less given to drunkenness and crime. Obviously Macquarie made out the best possible case for himself but broadly speaking his assessment was accurate enough.

The colony which Macquarie left was, of course, still basically a penal settlement but with the vital difference that prisoners with the will to reform were now encouraged and given opportunities to do so as never before; and this surely was the real measure of his achievement. During his regime 120 transports brought to the colony a grand total of about 20,000 convicts, of whom seven-eights were males. Deducting about 2,800 who were sent on to Van Diemen's Land the net influx to New South Wales in twelve years was thus more than 17,000. Of these only a handful are remembered today. Excluding the architect Greenway perhaps the best-known is Joseph Lycett, artist, who was sent out in 1814 for forgery, and whose *Views in Australia,* published in 1824 after his return to England, although now historically important, gave an idealized impression of the colony as one vast, undulating park, replete with English trees, lawns and ornamental lakes and with vistas that may well have been created by 'Capability' Brown. Another convict artist was Richard Read, whose surviving work includes portraits of Macquarie, Mrs Macquarie, Judge Barron Field and Captain John Piper. On a different level was John Tawell, a member of the Society of Friends, whose crime was also forgery. Within a few years of his arrival in 1814 Tawell had become a wealthy chemist and general merchant. He built the first Quaker chapel in Sydney at his own expense and publicly demonstrated his worthiness by pouring 600 gallons of rum into Sydney Cove. Sad to relate, after his return to England Tawell gave his mistress a lethal dose of prussic acid and died on the gallows at the age of sixty-one. Two other convicts who prospered as merchants were Solomon Levey, transported in 1814 for complicity in the theft of a chest of tea, a charge which he denied, and Daniel Cooper, who arrived two years later under a life sentence for theft. By 1821 both had received absolute pardons and four years later they went into partnership each investing £30,000, as importers, exporters, woolbuyers and ship-owners, with extensive whaling and sealing interests. In time both returned to England, where they died wealthy and respected. Levey's younger brother Barnett, who arrived in 1821, had the double distinction of being the colony's first free Jewish settler and its first theatrical entrepreneur. After two false starts in improvized premises he built Sydney's first real theatre, the Theatre Royal, which opened in October 1833. The venture failed financially, and when Levey died in 1837 at the age of forty he left a poverty-stricken widow and four small children.

Do you wish to go to Hell
or Botany-bay's-Sir
I wonts to go to Bottomybay
like to see the Naughty Place
better than any thing

6 The Twilight of Autocracy

Sir Thomas Brisbane's passion was astronomy and because he won a gold medal and received honorary degrees from Edinburgh, Oxford and Cambridge it has often been said that he was a better astronomer than Governor. This may have been true but the implication that he was therefore a bad Governor by no means follows. Certainly his way of governing differed greatly from Macquarie's. Macquarie had been a sort of universal father who knew all his people and was passionately involved in their daily lives and affairs; Brisbane was aloof from them and spent much time in the rural calm of Parramatta with his telescopes, his wife and his infant family. Nothing had been too minor to engage Macquarie's personal attention; Brisbane confined himself to broad issues and left the details of government to his subordinates. This was a mistake, for some were incompetent and others, such as his Colonial Secretary, Frederick Goulburn, were so hand in glove with the exclusives that they often deliberately thwarted his intentions; but it certainly did not justify the persistent claims of his critics that he was lazy and disinterested. On the contrary, so many far-reaching changes occurred during his four years in the colony that he spoke the simple truth when he wrote that if Macquarie were to return 'he would not recognize the place'.

Partly on his own initiative and partly on orders from London Brisbane regularized and speeded up the survey of existing land-grants, limited the size of new grants and made them only to those willing and with the capital to use them productively. He obliged grantees to employ and maintain one convict for each 100 acres; and considerably helped the revenue both by hiring out surplus labour to settlers to clear land and by selling Crown land to approved buyers at 5/– an acre. He was the first to make government-run farms pay their way; he experimented, though with no great success, in growing tobacco, cotton, coffee, sugar and flax; he established an agricultural training college; and he encouraged the formation and became the first patron of both the N.S.W. Agricultural Society and the Sydney Turf Club, the first body in the colony to put horse-racing on an organized basis.

In religious matters he was devout and unusually broadminded. He encouraged the Wesleyans so actively that by the time he left they had eleven chapels in New South Wales; he encouraged Bible and tract societies; and he gave financial help to Father Therry to complete a Roman Catholic church in Sydney and to build schools in Sydney and Parramatta. However, he refused the same kind of help to the Presbyterians because of what he con-

Left 'A Startling Interrogation', an English satirist's view of emigration to Australia during the 1820s.

Right Native about to throw spear at kangaroos.

Left Irrawang vineyard and pottery on the Hunter River, established by James King. The best Hunter River wines now enjoy a high international reputation.

Below Two views of Sydney in the early 1820s by Major James Taylor, 48th Regiment.

Right William Charles Wentworth, explorer and statesman.

Far right Sir Thomas Brisbane, sixth governor of New South Wales.

sidered the excessive demands of the Reverend John Dunmore Lang, who reached the colony in 1823, and as a result Scots Church, completed in 1826, was built entirely by private funds. Lang, a man of strong principles and prejudices who was later to become an ardent republican, never forgave him for this, and he and the Reverend Samuel Marsden eventually became his most relentless denigrators and enemies.

Brisbane's attitude was equally liberal in the matter of free expression. In 1824 he allowed William Charles Wentworth, who had recently returned to the colony as a barrister, to found *The Australian,* in partnership with another barrister, Robert Wardell, and he accepted without rancour its criticisms of himself and his policy. When the editor of the *Sydney Gazette* complained that this put his own government-censored newspaper at a disadvantage Brisbane at once lifted the censorship and the *Gazette* became in effect independent.

By far the most vital change during Brisbane's regime resulted from the passing in England in July 1823 of what became known as the N.S.W. Judicature Act. This not only greatly widened the power of the Supreme Court but directed the setting up of a Legislative Council of from five to seven members

with power to make laws 'for the peace, welfare and good government' of the colony. Although this was in fact little more than an advisory body it did provide certain safeguards against unduly autocratic rule and was an important first step towards self-government. Francis Forbes, a jurist of experience and integrity, arrived in May 1824 to replace Barron Field as judge of the reconstituted Supreme Court, and one of his first acts was to introduce trial by jury, though for a start only in civil cases in which the parties desired it. Brisbane and Forbes soon became close friends and both the Supreme Court and the Legislative Council, of which Forbes was virtually president, functioned smoothly from their inauguration.

Brisbane's liberalism was shown yet again in his attitude towards convicts. He strongly opposed excessive corporal punishment and reprieved many men sentenced to death; and he encouraged the rehabilitation of well-behaved, educated convicts by sending them to Bathurst where their surroundings were comparatively congenial and their duties light. On the other hand, when convicts at Liverpool attempted to organize for better rations and conditions their leader was solitarily confined for a month on bread and water, then given 500 lashes and sent

to hard labour at an out-station. During his term two new penal stations were formed – one at Moreton Bay and one, for secondary offenders, at Macquarie Harbour on the bleak west coast of Van Diemen's Land – and Norfolk Island was reoccupied after having lain abandoned for fifteen years.

It was John Oxley, his exploring days now over, who was responsible for the Moreton Bay settlement. In 1823, on the Governor's orders, he sailed north to inspect Port Curtis and Moreton Bay as possible sites for a penal station. At Moreton Bay he found the river which Cook had guessed must exist, explored its lower reaches and quickly realized its advantages over Port Curtis. In September 1824 he returned with soldiers and convicts and established a temporary settlement at what is now Redcliffe; but almost at once he found a more suitable site where the city of Brisbane now stands and on 2 December the settlement was transferred. In the same month Forbes inspected and approved Oxley's choice and called it Edinglaslie, which was perhaps fortunately abandoned in favour of its present name.

About the same time, 200 miles away, another outlying settlement was being created. During 1818 Captain Phillip Parker King – a son of Governor King – had made a marine survey of northern Australia, and on his return to England he had urged the establishment of a port in the area, mainly as a base for trade with the East Indies. Accordingly in 1824 Captain J. Bremer, of HMS *Tamar,* was sent there with a party of troops and volunteer convicts. King's own choice, Port Essington, was rejected in favour of a site on Melville Island; and here, after taking formal possession of the whole coast, Bremer built a fortified post which he named Fort Dundas.

On land there was much minor exploration during Brisbane's term. In 1823 his aide-de-camp, Major John Ovens, discovered the rich Monaro districts to the south of what is now Canberra; and in the same year Allan Cunningham, a noted botanist, pene-

Left The first house in Brisbane. It was still standing in 1892 when this drawing was published.

Right Allan Cunningham, explorer and naturalist, who discovered the rich Darling Downs, west of Brisbane.

Below A French artist's impression of a roadside store in southern Queensland.

Left Bushmen making camp. Coloured etching by George Hamilton.

Bottom left Queensland bushmen playing cards around a camp fire.

Right Another Hamilton etching, of bushmen handwatering their horses from a mudhole.

trated the rugged mountains north of Bathurst and opened a practical route to the Liverpool Plains. In both cases squatters followed close behind with their flocks. A more spectacular achievement was that in 1824 of two free settlers, a former ship's captain, William Hovell, and Hamilton Hume. Forcing their way south-west from the settled area through a tangle of hills and mountains they discovered the Hume River (now the upper Murray) which divides the present states of New South Wales and Victoria, and beyond it other rivers including the Mitta Mitta, Ovens and Goulburn. Continuing on they reached what they thought to be Western Port but was in fact Corio Bay, on the western shore of Port Phillip. They found much good land and the general westerly flow of the rivers they encountered set intriguing problems which other explorers were soon to solve.

Brisbane's relations with Sorell, his Lieutenant-Governor in Van Diemen's Land, were always cordial, and during his term the island's continuing prosperity was further increased by the influx of a large number of free settlers, most of whom were of an excellent type with capital and the will to succeed. In 1824, to the dismay of the whole colony, Sorell was recalled on the specious ground that the woman with whom he was living was not and could not be his legal wife – a fact which the British government had known at the time of his appointment and had tactfully ignored for seven years – and was replaced by Colonel George Arthur, a former Governor of British Honduras.

This shoddy treatment of so outstanding an administrator may well have contributed to Brisbane's growing dissatisfaction with his own lot. There were other reasons, of course. His feud with Goulburn had now become open and irreconcilable; the exclusives, led by Marsden, Lang, Macarthur and the Blaxlands, continued to undermine him in England; a long and grossly unfair criticism of him published in the London *Morning Chronicle* further damaged his reputation; and his policy restricting land-grants was virtually nullified when in June 1824 the British parliament approved by a special law the formation of the Australian Agricultural Company. This was headed by John Macarthur Junior and its stated objects were to improve the fine wool industry in the colony and to cultivate grapes, flax, olives and other products. Its capital was to be £1,000,000, it was to receive a grant of 1,000,000 acres, it was to employ 1,400 convicts and no rival company was to be permitted in New South Wales for twenty years. Reaction in the colony was strong. *The Australian* said the authorities had obviously been 'hoodwinked and duped by artful men', and the *Gazette* said its founders clearly 'meant to enrich themselves at the expense of the colonists'. Brisbane's own opinion was never officially expressed but the government's action must have warned him that his recall was near. In May 1825 he received advice from Earl Bathurst that he was to be replaced by Lieutenant-General Ralph Darling. He accepted the decision 'without regret'; and when he sailed for home near the end of the year he left as a gift to the colony his astronomical instruments and a library of 350 scientific books.

On his way to Sydney Governor Darling called at Hobart Town to meet Governor Arthur, to proclaim Van Diemen's Land a separate colony, and to wangle a job as surveyor-general for his wife's brother, Edward Dumaresq. Another brother-in-law, Colonel Henry Dumaresq, was already his secretary; and a third, William, he appointed civil engineer soon after his arrival in Sydney. This early example of nepotism did not endear Darling to the colonists, nor did his stiff and formal military manner, his passionate zeal for efficiency, his strict enforcement of regulations, his lack of magnanimity and his complete inability to accept criticism. As his record was to show, Darling had many sterling qualities to offset these faults; but he was certainly not the man to have been sent to govern a colony growingly aware of its own identity and groping towards self-rule.

Brisbane had created a free press, and it was Darling's misfortune to be its first victim. Soon after the new Governor's arrival Edward Smith Hall, a man of passionate convictions, founded the *Monitor* as a rival to the *Gazette* and *Australian* and though all three papers treated Darling for a time with a certain wary respect his own overbearing attitude made an ultimate explosion inevitable. It was triggered off in November 1826 when Privates Joseph Sudds and Patrick Thompson, of the 57th Regiment, deciding that a convict's life was better than a soldier's, deliberately stole from a shop to get themselves convicted, and were duly sentenced to seven years' transportation. Determined to deter others from following their example, Darling commuted their sentences to seven years' hard labour in irons. They were paraded in felon's garb with iron collars round their necks linked by chains to leg-irons and then ignominiously drummed out of the regiment. Sudds, who was in poor health, died five days later in prison, and at once the storm broke. The blame for his death was laid firmly on Darling. His action in varying the sentences of the men was denounced as illegal – as, in fact, it was – and he was called

Below left Lady Darling, wife of the governor, with her son and daughter. Portrait by John Linnell.

Below The agony of Privates Sudds and Thompson after having been drummed out of their regiment.

Right Macquarie Harbour penal settlement, Van Diemen's Land, by the convict artist William Buelow Gould.

Centre right Boa Vista, a genteel establishment for young ladies in a suburb of Hobart Town.

Below right Malahide, a typical homestead of a successful pastoralist in Van Diemen's Land.

Studies of Australian life in the late 1820s by Augustus Earle. *Above* Debauched Aborigines in a Sydney street. *Left* Mrs Macquarie's Chair, a favourite spot in the Government domain. *Below left* A convict chain gang setting out from Hyde Park barracks. *Above right* Government House and gardens, Sydney. *Right* Bungaree, a native chief, one of Sydney's best-known identities.

everything but a murderer. As the intensity of the newspaper campaign against him mounted it developed into a general attack on his administration and on his rejection of the demands of Wentworth and his liberal followers for an elected house of assembly. In April 1827 Darling hit back by submitting to the Legislative Council a bill which required newspapers to be licensed annually and to pay a stamp-duty of fourpence a copy; but Chief Justice Forbes, already alienated by Darling's interference in judicial affairs, nullified the bill by refusing to certify that it was 'not repugnant to the laws of England'. One result was a duel between Henry Dumaresq and Wardell. Fortunately their marksmanship was poor. Three shots were fired on each side without effect and then Wardell apologized. Darling's next move was to instruct his officials to sue whenever they considered they had been libelled and as a result the Supreme Court became clogged with libel actions. Hall was tried no less than seven times, heavily fined and sentenced to an aggregate of three and a half years' imprisonment. Attwell Edwin Hayes, who in 1828 bought out Wardell's interest in *The Australian,* was fined and imprisoned; and the remarkable situation was created of two editors running their newspapers from jail at the same time. Eventually even the public tired of it, sympathy swung towards Darling, more than a hundred leading citizens signed an address expressing their confidence in him and the newspapers took the hint and modified the fury of their campaign.

At the same time a similar battle for the freedom of the press was being fought in Van Diemen's Land.

Arthur, even more stiff-necked and coldly efficient than Darling and certainly more ruthless, had quickly antagonized almost everyone on the island, and came under vigorous attack from Andrew Bent, editor of the *Hobart Town Gazette,* and Robert Lathrop Murray, a journalist who had been transported for bigamy. When Arthur withdrew government printing and launched a rival *Gazette* Bent changed the name of his newspaper to the *Colonial Times;* when Bent was fined £500 and sent to jail for libel his wife carried on as editor; when Arthur introduced newspaper licensing Bent refused to apply for one, put his paper into 'mourning' with thick black columns and published only advertisements. Bent won his fight eventually when Arthur's licensing act was disapproved in England but by then he was a tired and sick man.

Apart from Darling's prolonged battle against the Sydney press much occurred during his six years' regime. In 1826 a French ship, *L'Astrolabe,* appeared in Australian waters on a scientific voyage. To counter any possible territorial claims by her commander, Jules Dumont d'Urville, settlements were hurriedly formed at Western Port and at King George's Sound, which came to be known as Albany. The former survived less than two years and in 1831

More studies by Earle. *Above left* An Aboriginal family outside a settler's homestead. *Left* A native camp near Port Stephens, N.S.W. *Above* The governor meeting native tribes at their annual meeting at Parramatta. *Right* A night bivouac of travellers. *Below* A skirmish between bushrangers and police in the Illawarra district, south of Sydney.

Left Colonel George Arthur, fourth Lieutenant-Governor of Van Diemen's Land; and Captain James Stirling, founder and first Lieutenant-Governor of Western Australia.

Centre left Sealers and their hut at Westernport, Bass Strait.

Below King George's Sound, Western Australia, where a settlement was formed to thwart possible French ambitions. It is now the town of Albany.

Right Early map of the Swan River settlement.

Below right A French artist's impression, based on various sketches, of an Aboriginal family on walkabout.

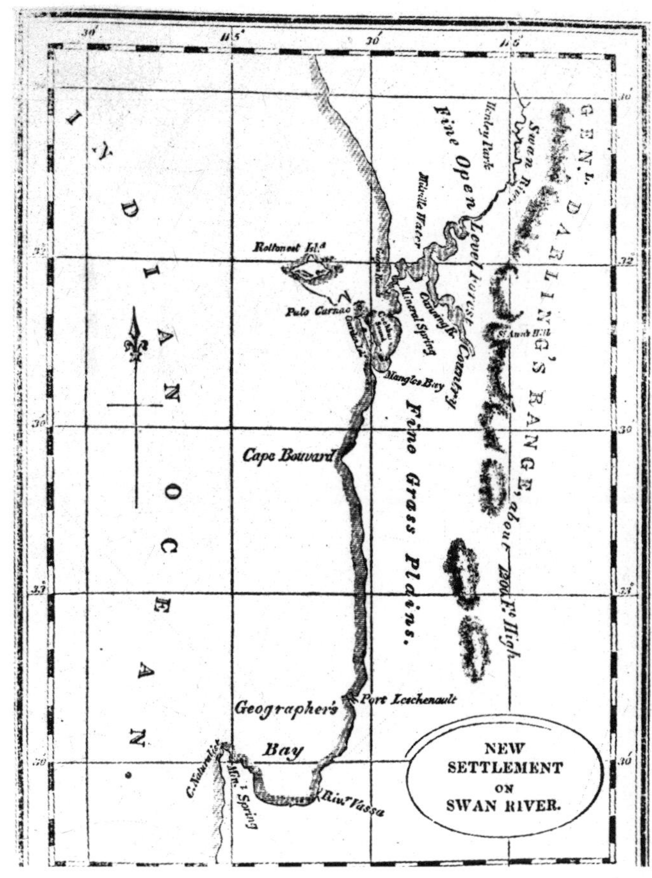

all convicts at Albany were withdrawn and it ceased to be a penal station. Meanwhile, things were going badly at Fort Dundas in the north. The Aborigines were hostile, many settlers died from tropical diseases and pirates captured the *Lady Nelson* off Timor and murdered her crew. In 1827, on orders from London, Darling sent Captain James Stirling, of HMS *Success,* with two transports to form an alternative settlement at Raffles Bay, on the nearby mainland. This proved no more successful than Fort Dundas, and in 1829 both were abandoned.

Soon after his return from Raffles Bay Stirling was sent to examine the Swan River, on the west coast of the continent and came back with a glowing report of its possibilities. His suggestion, supported by Darling, that a new colony should be founded there was at first not well received in London; but on his return home he won the support of investors and speculators, including Thomas Peel, a nephew of the statesman Robert Peel, who added their pressure to his. The government changed its mind and sent Captain Charles Fremantle in HMS *Challenger* to claim possession of the western part of the continent, which he did near the mouth of the Swan River on 2 May 1829. Within a month Stirling had arrived as first superintendent with his wife and family, some officials and an advance party of settlers. The new colony was proclaimed on 18 June, and on 12 August a site some miles upstream was chosen as its capital and named Perth.

In New South Wales in the meantime Darling was encouraging explorers to press even further inland. During 1827 Cunningham made his way north from the Liverpool Plains and discovered a vast area of good pastoral land, west of the dividing range, and Brisbane, which he called the Darling Downs. The following year Captain Charles Sturt, on the first of several historic expeditions, followed the Macquarie River north-west from Bathurst to where it joined a much larger river flowing south-west between high banks. Like Cunningham, he named it after the governor. Late in 1829 Sturt set out by boat to follow the Murrumbidgee, passed its junction with the Lachlan, and to his delight emerged into a 'broad and noble' stream which he named the Murray, unaware that it was the same river which Hume and Hovell had discovered further upstream and named the Hume. For a while the river flowed west and Sturt wondered whether Oxley's mythical inland sea might actually exist. Then it turned abruptly south and on 9 February 1830 the explorers reached its mouth, a lake separated by an isthmus from Encounter Bay, where Flinders and Baudin had met twenty-eight years before, and which Sturt named

Left 'Cousin Tom or the Swan River Job', an English satirist's commentary on Thomas Peel's land and emigration agreement with the government.

Below left 'The Foundation of Perth'. Oil-painting by G. Pitt Morison.

Right John Batman, one of the founders of Melbourne; and Captain Charles Sturt, one of the greatest of Australia's inland explorers.

Centre Right The bivouac of Captain Stirling during his exploration of the Swan River in 1827.

Below Early Fremantle, from the Canning Road. Swan River entrance is on right, and the tall building on Arthur's Head is the local jail.

Above Australia's first steamer, the *Sophia Jane* (256 tons).

Right Mrs John Piper, Sydney's leading hostess of the early 1820s, with some of her family. The portrait is possibly by Richard Read, a convict artist.

Below The Old Tank Stream, Sydney's first fresh water source. From a watercolour by John Skinner Prout.

Far right Captain Piper. Portrait by Augustus Earle.

Lake Alexandrina, after the future Queen Victoria. All efforts to get the whaleboat across the isthmus failed and with no other choice Sturt and his men began the long pull back upstream against the current. Rations were short and some of the party were ill and often men collapsed or fell asleep at the oars; yet for six agonizing weeks they rowed each day from dawn to dusk, with a single mid-day break of an hour. They returned to civilization gaunt, starving wrecks, but all miraculously still alive. Soon afterwards Sturt went blind and remained so for several months.

In Van Diemen's Land this was the year of the 'Black War'. Arthur had already had trouble enough coping with a resurgence of bushranging inspired by Matthew Brady, an escapee from Macquarie Harbour; but this had ended with Brady's capture by John Batman, a young free settler who was to be one of the founders of Melbourne, and his public execution in Hobart Town. Now the Governor had to face a more serious problem – the increasingly savage hostility of the island's Aborigines, now reduced to a roaming handful, denied access to their tribal areas and hunting grounds, brutalized by almost three decades of oppression and understandably accounting every white man their enemy. Stock and crops were destroyed, isolated settlers and their families murdered and it became unsafe to venture beyond settled areas. Arthur's attempt to cope constituted perhaps his most spectacular failure. He organized a massive campaign in which 2,000 men tried to drive the whole native population into a corner of the island. However the Aborigines slipped through the supposedly impregnable net at will, and the operation ended ludicruously with the capture of one old man and one boy. Soon enough, however, disease and sheer despair were to succeed where military strategy had failed and within Arthur's own lifetime they were to be reduced to a pitiful remnant of less than fifty.

In July 1831 Governor Darling learned, to his bitter disappointment, that as his six years' term had almost expired he was to be replaced by Major-General Richard Bourke. Without awaiting his successor he and his family sailed in October; and that night there were bonfires, fireworks and other celebrations at Vaucluse House, the home of William Charles Wentworth. But though Darling had never become widely popular there were many who regretted his departure and few who denied his considerable contribution to the colony's progress. During his regime a chamber of commerce was established, the first insurance company was formed and Macarthur and his friends opened a second bank, the Bank of Australia, which quickly and not inaccurately became known as 'the squatters' bank'. Country roads were vastly improved and extended and work began to provide Sydney with a more adequate water supply than the old Tank Stream offered. Sydney had its first subscription library, its first grammar school, its first museum (now the Australian Museum), and its first public concert. The first steamship – the *Sophia Jane,* a small but elegant paddle-wheeler – arrived from England; a second – the *Surprize* – was launched in Sydney; and the first hackney cab plied for hire. The first cricket clubs were formed and the first regular matches were played, often for substantial wagers, and Hobart Town held the colonies' first regatta. In 1827 there was a major scandal when Captain John Piper, collector of customs and Sydney's most popular and lavish host, defaulted for £12,000, had to sell his handsome harbourside villa and tried without success to drown himself. The first bank robbery occurred in the following year when thieves dug their way underground into Macarthur's new premises, decamped with about £20,000, and were never caught. In 1829 compositors on the *Australian* staged the country's first strike.

But more significant than the changing face of the colony was the changing composition of its population which, at the time Darling left, stood at about 75,000. Although convicts were still arriving at a formidable rate of about 4,000 a year an increasing flow of settlers and a thriving birth-rate were steadily reducing the ratio of prisoners to free people; and what had begun more than forty years earlier as a penal settlement was now beginning to take on the character of a free colony.

7 The Restless Years

Richard Bourke was Irish, a man of great warmth and charm, a qualified barrister, a distinguished soldier, and – as he had proved during a term as governor of the eastern district of South Africa – a liberal, just and humane administrator. His reputation had preceded him to Sydney and when he arrived with his wife and family on 3 December 1831 he was given a great welcome. However, his hopes of a trouble-free regime were soon to be dashed. By early 1832 he was in conflict with the colony's exclusives and in May his initial enthusiasm was further dampened by the death of his wife. Nevertheless, with backing from England he achieved a number of reforms which were to be of great benefit to the colony.

One of Bourke's first acts was to introduce trial by jury in criminal cases and this was followed by the abolition of the death penalty for sheep-stealing and forgery. He introduced a licensing system to control squatters who, hitherto, had helped themselves without permission to large grazing areas beyond the settled districts; he overhauled and tightened the system of convict assignment; and he abolished land grants and used the money from the sale of Crown lands to finance free immigration. His attitude towards emancipists was generous and he warmly supported a Supreme Court decision which fully restored their civil rights. He believed the colony was ready for at least partial self-rule and urged the formation of a Legislative Assembly of thirty-six, of whom two-thirds were to be elected by the people. His recommendation was eventually adopted and to this extent Bourke deserves to be regarded as the father of self-government in Australia.

Inevitably Bourke's severest critics included John Macarthur. But Macarthur was in his mid-sixties now, a choleric, incoherent old man, who had to be removed from the Legislative Council because he had been 'pronounced a lunatic' and seemed unlikely to recover. He died on 11 April 1834, a legend in his own lifetime and a legend still today. Macarthur was, of course, no mere political firebrand. He was the man who virtually founded Australia's greatest single industry; the man who as early as 1820 sold fine wool in England at 10/– lb and stud merino rams to his fellow-breeders at £300 a head; the man who lived to see realized his prediction that the colony could and would carry 'millions of sheep'. As such his place in history is assured.

The changes during Bourke's regime were not all political. When he arrived there were three colonies; when he left there were four with a fifth in process of creation.

Left Departure from Adelaide of Captain Charles Sturt and his expedition for the centre of Australia, 1844. From a drawing by S. T. Gill.

Right Hyde Park Barracks, Sydney, built by Macquarie to house convicts, it was used during the 1840s as a hostel for immigrants.

Above Boys on parade, Normal Institution, Hyde Park, Sydney, 1838.

Left The once-notorious penal station of Port Arthur, Van Diemen's Land, as it is today.

Bottom left Convicts building a new road over the Blue Mountains to Bathurst. Watercolour by the convict artist Charles Rodius.

Below Sir Richard Bourke, eighth governor of N.S.W.

Above right Convicts of Van Diemen's Land during a rest period.

Right Port Arthur in its heyday, from a drawing by John Skinner Prout.

Van Diemen's Land, despite the unpopularity of Governor Arthur, still flourished. Capital, free settlers and convicts continued to pour in; stock now grazed in their hundreds of thousands; wealthy merchants and pastoralists were building elegant mansions; Hobart Town and Launceston had become thriving small cities. Nevertheless it remained basically a penal colony and Arthur ruled it as such with justice of a kind but little humanity. He introduced a system of close and stringent control over convicts and for secondary offenders he built Port Arthur, a name many were to curse in the years ahead. When he was recalled in 1836 and replaced by the polar explorer Sir John Franklin the whole island celebrated. One newspaper brought out its largest type and proclaimed: 'Rejoice! For the Day of Retribution has Arrived.'

In Western Australia the reverse was true. Governor Stirling had the full confidence of his people; but Peel's ambitious land settlement scheme had already foundered and the whole colony was in danger of doing the same. Because holdings had to be so large most settlers lived miles from each other. There were no roads and no cheap convict labour to draw on, and the Aborigines were numerous and hostile. So many people moved east or went home

that by 1832 the population had fallen from 4,000 to 1,500 and only the energy, resource, patience and optimism of Stirling and his young wife averted a complete collapse.

The problems of these two colonies affected Bourke only indirectly. On the other hand New Zealand, still a dependency of New South Wales, was very much his responsibility. Since the 1790s it had been exploited by sealers, timber-getters and whalers. Marsden had sent two missionaries there in 1814 and gradually small settlements had sprung up – wild and lawless places under no effective control. The Maoris, already debased by liquor and venereal disease, had been given firearms and were killing each other off in a series of civil wars; and Captain Collet Barker, sent by Darling in 1831 to stop the senseless slaughter, had himself fallen a victim. In 1833, on orders from London, Bourke sent James Busby there as resident magistrate but without troops to back him he was, as a contemporary wrote, 'like a warship without guns'. The Maoris, who respected a show of force, were not impressed; but in fact his main trouble was with the whites, who ignored the authority he could not enforce. In 1835 he had to cope with the activities of the self-styled 'Charles, Baron de Thierry', a Frenchman who had served in the British army and who held a dubious claim to some land in New Zealand. De Thierry had big plans – to annex New Zealand and make himself king, to populate it with French settlers, to dig a canal across Panama isthmus, and to establish a fortnightly shipping service from there. Alarmed when some French settlers actually arrived, Busby persuaded the Maori chiefs to form a federation, the United Tribes of New Zealand, to be self-governing under British protection. Bourke was appalled and said so and London quickly repudiated the whole thing.

With the death of Oxley in 1828 Major Thomas Livingstone Mitchell had become Surveyor-General of New South Wales. Jealous of Sturt's success as an explorer, Mitchell set out in 1831 to investigate a report by a runaway convict that a great river, called by natives the Kundur, existed north-west of Bathurst. All he found were a few small streams which flowed into the upper Darling and when Aborigines stole his supplies he had to turn back. In 1835 he followed the Darling downstream for 300 miles, hoping to disprove Sturt's belief that it flowed into the Murray and again clashes with the natives, this time fatal, forced him to turn back. Undeterred, Mitchell set out once more in 1836. He followed the Murray down to its junction with the Darling, admitted grudgingly that Sturt had been right, after all; then having retraced his steps upstream for a

Left Sir John Franklin, Arctic explorer and governor of Van Diemen's Land; and his wife Lady Jane Franklin, who brought wit, charm and culture to the convict colony.

Right Boombana Bay, or Port Leschenault, an early settlement in the south-west of Western Australia.

Below Major Thomas Livingstone Mitchell, explorer and surveyor-general of N.S.W.

Below right Mitchell's impression of Turandurey and her daughter Ballandella, who accompanied him on his exploration of western Victoria.

while he plunged south into what is now the western district of Victoria and passed through an area so rich and well-watered that he called it Australia Felix. Following a river which he named the Glenelg down to its mouth in Bass Strait he was astounded to find, in nearby Portland Bay in what he had thought to be unknown territory, a well-established pastoral run and whaling station occupied by Edward and Francis Henty, who, with their father Thomas and other brothers, had been among the early settlers in Western Australia. On his way home Mitchell climbed Mount Macedon, looked across to Port Phillip, and saw 'a mass of white objects which might have been tents'. In fact they were and he had been forestalled yet again.

For years settlers in Van Diemen's Land had known of good grazing land in the Port Phillip area and had sought and been refused permission to settle there. In 1835, disregarding the ban, John Batman crossed with a party, noted a site at the mouth of the Yarra River as suitable for a village, 'bought' 600,000 acres of land from the local Aborigines for a few axes and other trade goods, returned to Launceston and there formed the Port Phillip Association to exploit his purchase. In his absence his party rescued William Buckley, an absconder from Collins's expedition of 1803, who had lived with the natives for more than thirty years – a huge, long-bearded, awesome figure in kangaroo skins, who had so completely forgotten his English that it took him months to relearn it. While Batman was still in Launceston John Pascoe Fawkner, an inn-keeper and former convict, organized his own party for the mainland and it was his tents, pitched on the village site Batman had chosen, that Mitchell saw on his way home. The trickle across Bass Strait soon became a flood. In 1836 Bourke vetoed Batman's purchase and sent Captain William Lonsdale to the rapidly-growing settlement as resident magistrate; and the following year during a personal visit, he named the place Melbourne and had a plan of streets drawn up, with building lots measured and offered for sale.

Meanwhile in England the failure of Peel's scheme in the west had inspired a spate of theories of systematic colonization, including one from Edward Gibbon Wakefield, propounded while he was in Newgate jail for having abducted a young heiress. Wakefield's theory was that all land in a new colony should be sold in a concentrated area at 'a sufficient price' to finance the immigration of free labourers and their families, who would eventually save enough to buy their own land a little further out, thus providing more money to bring out more

Above Mitchell meets Bogan River natives.

Above right William Buckley, the wild white man, who lived for thirty-two years with the natives of Port Phillip.

Top right Batman's Hill and the village of Melbourne, 1837.

Right Two studies by Charles Rodius – Morirang, a girl of the Shoalhaven tribe; and Nunberri, chief of the Nunnerahs.

Above Fawkner's hotel and the lockup, Melbourne.

Left Founders of two cities – John Pascoe Fawkner of Melbourne, and Colonel William Light of Adelaide.

Below left Site for the proposed town of Adelaide. Aquatint from a drawing by Colonel Light.

Right An early view of Port Adelaide, S.A.

Below right 'Emigrants about to leave England for Adelaide'. Watercolour by Robert Alexander Hillingford.

labour and so on. On this general basis the government decided in 1834 to establish a colony in South Australia, with authority vaguely divided between the Crown and a board representing investors, of whom the largest was the South Australian Company, formed by George Fife Angas, a London banker and shipowner. When the official party, which included Captain John Hindmarsh as Governor, reached the area on 28 December 1836 about 300 settlers were already there. The colony was proclaimed; and early in 1837, against Hindmarsh's stubborn opposition, the government surveyor, Colonel William Light, chose a site on the Torrens River as a capital, to be named Adelaide after King William IV's queen.

In these years much was happening in Sydney. Encouraged by Bourke the Congregationalists opened a chapel in 1833 and the Baptists followed suit in 1835. In the same year Bishop J. B. Polding arrived as the first Roman Catholic vicar-apostolic of New South Wales and on 5 June 1836 William Grant Broughton, formerly the colony's archdeacon, was enthroned as its first Anglican bishop. A month later Bourke passed a Church Act which put all denominations on an equal footing and provided state subsidies for the salaries of clergy and for

building churches, chapels and parsonages. The Governor's efforts to create a state schools system were defeated by sectarian differences but during his regime three grammar schools were opened – The King's School at Parramatta and Sydney College and the Australian College (founded by the Reverend J. D. Lang) in Sydney. He created the first savings bank in 1832 and sponsored the first school of arts in 1833. In the same year Sydney had its first philharmonic society and in 1836 William Vincent Wallace, composer of *Maritana* and other operas, and his wife opened its first music school. Sydney cabinet-makers formed the colony's first trade union in 1833, quickly followed by tailors, bakers and upholsterers; and it is ironical that convict arrivals in the following year should include the 'Tolpuddle Martyrs', six Dorset farm-labourers whose only crime had been to combine together to ask for a weekly wage of 10/–.

Charles Darwin, soon to win fame as a naturalist, was in Sydney for a while in 1835 aboard HMS *Beagle,* a naval survey ship; and Conrad Martens, a former shipmate and an artist of great skill, arrived about the same time. Martens liked the place and stayed and in the next fifty years his influence was to have a profound effect on art in Australia. In 1836 Van Diemen's Land also acquired an artist of some

Mrs Eliza Anne Fraser (*left*) and incidents illustrating her ordeal as a captive of the natives of Queensland. *Below left* Survivors of the shipwrecked *Stirling Castle* captured and stripped as they venture ashore. *Above* The murder of Captain Fraser. *Below* John Graham, convict, and a friendly native help Mrs Fraser to escape her captors.

note – Thomas Griffiths Wainewright, transported for forgery and thought by some to have poisoned his sister-in-law for her insurance. Wainewright's flair was for portraiture and many surviving likenesses of Tasmanian worthies and their families testify to his sensitive talent.

One incident during Bourke's regime which became a favourite subject of authors was the ordeal of Eliza Anne Fraser, wife of the captain of the brig *Stirling Castle*. In May 1836 the ship foundered on a reef off Queensland and after four days in an open boat Mrs Fraser gave birth to a child which died almost at once. Soon afterwards she, her husband and four others were captured by natives. Fraser and another man were killed and Mrs Fraser was stripped and subjected to many indignities by the women of the tribe, who looked on her as a freak. Eventually she was located by John Graham, who as a convict absconder from Moreton Bay had lived six years with the Aborigines. To win the confidence of her captors Graham shed his own clothes and at great risk to himself helped her and the other survivors to escape. His bravery earned a reward of £10, a ticket-of-leave, and presumably the lifelong gratitude of young Mrs Fraser, who later married another sea-captain and returned to England.

In 1837 Bourke resigned when the government failed to support him in a quarrel with a colonial official and was succeeded by Major Sir George Gipps. Gipps was an able and fearless administrator, whose misfortune was to get off to an appallingly bad start. For years there had been virtually open war between the Aborigines and the squatters who encroached on their land and to many it was no more a crime to kill a native than a kangaroo. Early in 1838 some overlanders and several shepherds were killed by Aborigines; and in June 1838 some station-hands at Myall Creek, near the present town of Inverell, retaliated by callously murdering a whole tribe of twenty-eight men, women and

Above left Convicts boarding the prison hulk at Portsmouth in which the Tolpuddle Martyrs were confined while awaiting transportation.

Below left Aborigines about to attack a dray carrying stores to an outlying sheep station. From a drawing by S. T. Gill.

Below 'Ways and means', a rare cartoon commenting on Governor Gipps's enforced economies during the depression of the 1840s. His companion is the immigration agent in Sydney, Francis Mereweather.

children. Gipps ordered the arrest and trial of these men for murder and seven were found guilty and hanged. It took great courage for Gipps to impose such stern justice in the face of outraged public opinion. Inevitably his action created bitter feeling against him, particularly among the increasingly-powerful squatters and this was to continue throughout his regime.

For some years there had been doubts in England regarding the effectiveness of the transportation system and in 1840, adopting recommendations made by a committee of the House of Commons, the government decided that in future convicts would be sent only to Van Diemen's Land and Norfolk Island. As a result 20,000 prisoners poured into Van Diemen's Land in five years, creating a hopeless labour glut; whereas in New South Wales Gipps's abolition of the assignment system, on orders from London, deprived the squatters of cheap, semi-slave labour; and this and his efforts to bring unauthorized squatting under control by restricting sheep-runs to twenty square miles increased his unpopularity to a point where there were even threats of rebellion. To add to the Governor's problems a series of droughts between 1837 and 1842 contributed to a disastrous fall in land sales and widespread economic depression. As free immigration was financed from Crown land sales Gipps now found himself without money to continue the system yet unable to check the flow of immigrants which had now reached 20,000 a year and unable to provide work for those who arrived. This crisis produced its champion in the person of Mrs Caroline Chisholm, a dedicated social worker, who had reached the colony in 1838 and who against formidable odds managed to look after and find employment for literally thousands of female immigrants.

Even London's approval in 1842 of Bourke's recommendation to add twenty-four elected members to the Legislative Council, though hailed as a vital step towards self-rule, brought little relief to the harassed Governor, for the franchise excluded two-thirds of the adult male population and when the reconstituted council first met in August 1843 most of its elected members were squatters or their friends, who opposed on principle almost every measure Gipps introduced. One result of the depression was the failure of the Bank of Australia in 1842; yet when Gipps opposed granting charters to two other banks on the ground that thrift, rather than more capital, was needed to get the economy under way again, he came under fierce attack once more.

The depression was felt particularly in Van Diemen's Land where, from 1841 on, as wool and grain prices fell, there was a spate of bankruptcies

Left An English satirist's view of emigration to Sydney. The porter asks why the woman is going, and she replies: 'Vy, they says as how there's lots of good husbands to be had cheap there, whereas the brutes in England can't see no charm in a woman unless she's got plenty of money to keep 'em in idleness'.

Below left Sir George Gipps.

Right Mill at North Adelaide in the 1840s. Watercolour by S. T. Gill.

Below Lyons Terrace, a fashionable quarter of Sydney facing Hyde Park, 1844. Oil-painting by George Edward Peacock.

Left Adelaide racecourse, 1 January 1840. Watercolour by J. M. Skipper.

Centre left West front of Adelaide barracks. On far left is the Methodist chapel. Watercolour by Samuel Thomas Gill.

Below left Village of Klemsig, near Adelaide, founded by German settlers.

Below An Aboriginal pupil at Poomindie mission, South Australia, playing cricket, 1835.

Below right Penny's Stopes, Burra Burra copper mine, S.A. Watercolour by S. T. Gill.

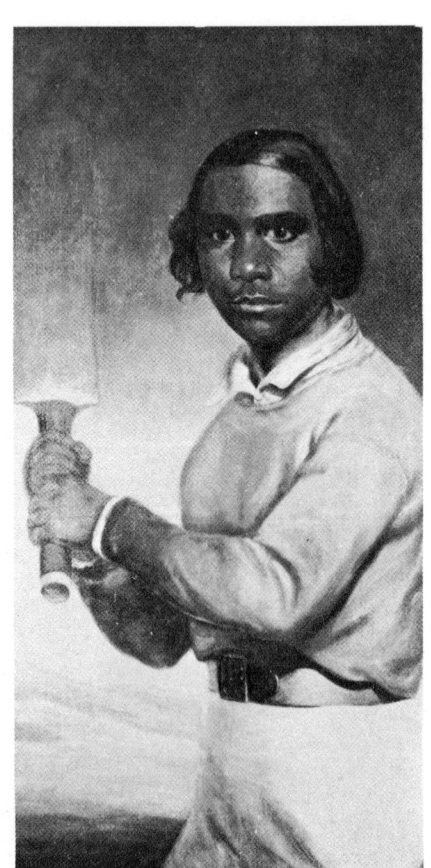

and forced sales. Franklin tried to help the settlers, but with the colony now 'the jail of the Empire' and with no money from England to pay for the supervision of the convicts who poured in his situation soon became impossible. In 1843 he was recalled and the unenviable task of restoring the colony's economy fell to his successor, Sir John Eardley-Wilmot.

In South Australia the folly of divided control had become apparent by 1838. The Wakefield plan was abandoned as impracticable, Governor Hindmarsh was recalled and his successor, Colonel George Gawler, combined the position of Governor and Commissioner. By 1841 the population had risen to 14,000, and the new settlers included many Lutheran refugees from Germany who built their own villages of Klemsig and Bethany. However, most newcomers preferred to stay in Adelaide, which in 1840 had been proclaimed Australia's first municipality, and as a result land speculation sent prices soaring until town sections were fetching £10,000 each. The boom collapsed with the onset of depression; the Colonization Commission in London went bankrupt; and South Australia lost its semi-independent status and became just another Crown colony. In 1841 Gawler was replaced by Captain George Grey who achieved a balanced budget after three years of drastic economy; and the depression finally ended with the discovery of rich copper deposits at Kapunda in 1842 and Burra Burra in 1845.

Although too isolated to feel the full effects of the depression in the east, Western Australia continued to have troubles of its own. There had been some exploration on and around the north-west coast by George Grey, who was soon to become Governor of South Australia but settlement remained confined to a small pocket in the south and the population was still under 5,000. Little capital was coming in, settlers were still hopelessly short of labour to clear their large holdings and they lacked markets for their products. Stirling, still a young man and anxious to resume his naval career, resigned in 1838 and early in the following year handed over to John Hutt, a firm supporter of the Wakefield system.

Depression notwithstanding, Port Phillip continued to expand rapidly as settlers poured in from Van Diemen's Land and north of the Murray. In 1839 Charles Joseph La Trobe, a man of culture and considerable character, arrived from England as first superintendent. By the following year 600,000 sheep were grazing over almost the whole western district, including Mitchell's Australia Felix, and Melbourne's population had soared to 4,000, with

thirty hotels and three newspapers. Attempts to land convicts at Port Phillip were frustrated by the angry residents; there were frequent protests against the proportion of local revenue which went to Sydney; and when the district was allotted six seats on the reformed Legislative Council its spokesmen persistently and vociferously demanded separation from New South Wales.

The problem of dealing with wholesale land-grabbing in New Zealand by London and Sydney syndicates was dropped into Gipps's lap in 1839 when both islands were formally incorporated within the boundaries of New South Wales. One of the first acts of Captain William Hobson, sent there as Lieutenant-Governor, was to proclaim that no land sales would be recognized unless ratified in London. Hobson went further when he gathered the Maori chiefs at Waitangi and concluded a treaty under which, in return for yielding sovereignty to Queen Victoria, they were promised 'full and undisputed possession' of their lands. The land speculators including Wakefield, who had formed a New Zealand Company, blamed Gipps personally for this set-back and lobbied so effectively against him in London that in 1841 they succeeded in having New Zealand proclaimed a separate colony and thus re-

Left G. A. Robinson with Aborigines of Van Diemen's Land. As official protector he won their friendship where other means had failed. Drawing by Benjamin Duterreau, 1835.

Below left Early Melbourne from the south bank of the Yarra. John Batman's cottage is on extreme left.

Right Collins Street, Melbourne, 1839. Watercolour by W. Knight.

Below 'Beautifully Linked', a rare political cartoon of the 1840s advocating the separation of the Port Phillip district from N.S.W. The mother colony is shown as a convict woman and Port Phillip as her free-born daughter. On the left are the Reverend J. D. Lang and other representatives of Port Phillip in the N.S.W. Legislative Council.

Left Arrival of Eyre and his native companion, Wylie, at Albany after their hazardous trek across the continent.

Below left Victoria Square, Port Essington, goal of the German explorer, Ludwig Leichhardt, on his epic journey through northern Australia.

Right Residents of Adelaide farewell Edward John Eyre on his departure for central Australia. Defeated in his attempt to reach the north coast, Eyre changed his plans and crossed the continent east-west to Albany.

Below right Leichhardt after his return to Sydney, 1846, by W. Romaine Govett.

moved from his control.

Explorers were active during Gipps's regime. In 1840 Count Paul Strzelecki, a Pole, penetrated the rugged Snowy Mountains in south-eastern New South Wales and discovered and named Mount Kosciusko, Australia's highest peak. Continuing south he and his party passed through the thickly-timbered area of Gippsland and reached Western Port exhausted and starving.

The following year Edward John Eyre, who had already probed the barren country north and west of Adelaide, set out from Fowler's Bay with John Baxter and three Aborigines on a cross-continental journey of almost 1,000 miles to Albany. Two of the Aborigines treacherously killed Baxter and escaped with most of the provisions, and only a chance meeting with a French whaler at Rossiter Bay saved Eyre and the third Aborigine, Wylie, from starvation. Eventually they reached Albany after a heroic journey of four and a half months which did no more than confirm that the area they covered was mostly uninhabitable desert.

On the other hand many important discoveries were made by an expedition led by Ludwig Leichhardt, a German, which left Brisbane in August 1844 to reach Port Essington, recently established to re-

place the abandoned settlement at Raffles Bay, a distance of about 2,000 miles through completely unknown country. Near the Gulf of Carpentaria Leichhardt's second-in-command, John Gilbert, was killed and two others were wounded by Aborigines; and it was only after fourteen months of appalling hardships that the party reached its destination in December 1845.

While Leichhardt was still on his long trek Charles Sturt and a well-equipped party left Adelaide in August 1844 hoping to solve the riddle of the inland. After following the Darling upstream they turned north-west into barren and almost waterless country and survived six months of blazing heat at a depot near what is now Milparinka. In 1845 from a more forward depot which Sturt called Fort Grey they managed to press on about 450 miles but failed in several attempts to penetrate the surrounding desert; and when they reached Adelaide in January 1846 Sturt was broken in health, too ill even to mount a horse.

About the same time but 500 miles further east in much more hospitable country, Major Mitchell was seeking a practical route north to Carpentaria. He too failed but discovered in what is now central Queensland several rivers and the fertile Maranoa plains.

When Mitchell returned to Sydney Governor Gipps, relieved at his own request, had already sailed for England, a tired, ill and disillusioned man, reviled by the press and those he had done his best to help. He was succeeded by Sir Charles Augustus FitzRoy.

8 The Golden Revolution

When FitzRoy reached Sydney in August 1846 Australia was on the verge of political, economic and social developments which, in a few years, were to change completely its whole character and aspect, and it was his task to steer the country through this period of radical and exciting change. Although no great statesman he was very much a man of the world, shrewd in assessing people and situations, flexible in his ideas and with an easy uncondescending manner which earned him instant popularity among all classes. No Governor in the colony's history had got away to such a good start but it was not to last. In December 1847 a carriage which FitzRoy was driving into Government House, Parramatta, overturned and his wife and aide-de-camp, Lieutenant C. C. Master, were killed. For a while sympathy for the bereaved Governor was overwhelming but within a year much of this was alienated by his own indiscretion. Scandalous reports regarding his private life were circulated, including an allegation by the Reverend J. D. Lang that he had seduced the daughter of a Berrima innkeeper; and although ignored by some these persistent attacks did much to undermine his reputation both in the colony and in England.

There were four vital changes during FitzRoy's term of office. Three of these were political. The principle of self-government was conceded, Port Phillip became the colony of Victoria and transportation to the eastern colonies was finally abolished. The fourth was the discovery of gold.

For years in England there had been a growing realization among liberal statesmen that the best way to retain an empire was to let its constituent colonies govern themselves. The Act of 1842, which gave New South Wales a partly-elective Legislative Council, had been a step in this direction. But more was needed and it was achieved in August 1850 with the passage of what was to be known as the Australian Colonies Government Act. This recon-

Far left A party of prospectors strike it lucky at the gold diggings.

Left Sir Charles FitzRoy, tenth Governor of N.S.W.

Left Official opening of Prince's Bridge, Melbourne, by Lieutenant-Governor La Trobe, 1850.

Below Immigrants disembarking in Sydney Cove. From a painting by Oswald Brierly.

Right Prince's Bridge, Melbourne, from the south side of the Yarra, 1853.

Below right Melbourne post office, 1853, at the height of the gold rush.

stituted Port Phillip district as a separate colony, with La Trobe as its first Lieutenant-Governor and brought Victoria, South Australia, Western Australia and Van Diemen's Land (soon to change its name to Tasmania) into line with New South Wales by giving them two-thirds elective Councils. It went far beyond this, however. It empowered all five colonies to alter their own constitutions, decide their own terms of franchise and modify their form of government without reference to London. In short, it removed the last vestige of autocractic power from their various governors and gave them the right to rule themselves as they chose.

In Melbourne joy was unrestrained and the people, free at last to shape their own destiny, celebrated for a fortnight. Elsewhere the reaction was more cautious. In Sydney, faced with the reality he had fought a lifetime to achieve Wentworth, grown conservative with the years, wrote apprehensively that he had no wish 'to sow the seeds of a future democracy'. He proposed what his critics derisively called 'a bunyip aristocracy' – in other words a hereditary Australian peerage – to form an upper house which would have power to veto any law passed by the elected lower house but the idea was received with such scorn that he dropped it.

Although willing to let the colonies govern themselves, England was reluctant to stop using them as a dumping ground for her surplus criminals. By 1847 it had become apparent that the policy of flooding Van Diemen's Land with convicts to the exclusion of the other colonies had failed; and it was decided to resume transportation to the mainland. The reaction was immediate and strong. In 1849 when two transports reached Port Phillip with a total of about 500 convicts the citizens refused to accept them and threatened to repel their landing by physical force. Eventually, though not without more angry protests, the convicts were landed in Sydney. Most were assigned at once to work in the country and about sixty were sent on to Moreton Bay, to the disgust of the free settlers there. In 1850 the four eastern colonies combined to form an Anti-Transportation League and England was flooded with protests, petitions, deputations and threats of secession. In ironical contrast Western Australia, hitherto proud of its free status, now decided that only cheap and plentiful convict labour could save it from foundering. England accepted the inevitable. Transportation to the east tapered off, to cease finally in 1853 and the convict flow was diverted to the west. During eighteen years almost 10,000 were landed; then even the west had had enough and said so, and the *Hougoumont*, which reached Fremantle on 9 January 1868, was the last convict ship ever to sail for Australia.

In the east much happened during FitzRoy's first five years in office. During April 1848 Ludwig Leichhardt set out from Brisbane with four white companions and two Aborigines to reach Perth and was never heard of again; in December of the same year Edmund Kennedy was killed by natives while exploring Cape York. In Sydney the late 1840s saw the completion of Circular Quay, on which work had begun in 1839, and the introduction of regular ferry services to suburbs on the north side of the harbour. In 1850 the Governor's daughter, Mrs Keith Stewart, turned the first sod of a railway line to run to Goulburn; and in the same year the University of Sydney was founded. The first overland mail between Sydney and Adelaide was inaugurated in 1846; and Sydney held its first swimming championships in the same year. In 1847 Melbourne laid down its first golf-course in the present Flagstaff Gardens and Sydney had its first art exhibition, two years after Hobart. Melbourne, Adelaide and Hobart were thriving; Sydney was booming. By 1848 its population had reached 50,000 and it had 223 flour mills, 62 tanneries, 30 soap and candle works, 27 foundries and 51 breweries.

With active encouragement from Caroline

Chisholm and her husband, who had returned to England in 1846, immigration figures continued to soar. Between 1841 and 1850 no less than 108,000 free immigrants reached Australia, compared with 32,000 convicts. Despite this considerable influx the squatters were still short of labour and determined to get it where and as cheaply as they could. In 1847 two shiploads of natives from the New Hebrides were landed at Twofold Bay, on the south coast of New South Wales, for pastoral work and in the following year 270 Chinese coolies reached Sydney. Inevitably there were protests but FitzRoy was reluctant to antagonize the squatters and failed to take a firm line. The New Hebrideans proved useless as shepherds and most were sent home. The Chinese stayed.

The islanders had been imported by Benjamin Boyd, one of the colony's most spectacular characters of the 1840s. Boyd, who had genius of a sort, had arrived in Sydney in 1842 in his yacht, the *Wanderer,* with a handsome sum of £200,000 to invest on behalf of British clients. By 1846 he had built Boydtown and a whaling station at Twofold Bay, he operated nine whalers and several other ships, his pastoral leases in the Riverina and Monaro areas alone exceeded 2,500,000 acres, and he

Left Benjamin Boyd, Australia's most spectacular commercial entrepreneur of the 1840s.

Below The University of Melbourne, founded in 1853.

Right The death of explorer Edmund Kennedy near Cape York. His faithful native companion, Jacky Jacky, is fighting off other attackers.

Above Sydney about 1850 looking towards Darling Harbour and Goat Island.

Left Ben Boyd's yacht *Wanderer* in Sydney Harbour, 1849. Watercolour by Oswald Brierly, who accompanied Boyd from England.

Top right The old wharf, Hobart Town.

Right The man who started the Australian gold rush, Edward Hammond Hargraves.

grazed 160,000 sheep and several thousand cattle. By 1848 he had so utterly overreached himself that his 'empire' collapsed in financial chaos. A year later he sailed for the Californian gold-diggings in the *Wanderer,* which his creditors had allowed him to keep. Unsuccessful there he was on his way back to Australia in 1851 when he was murdered by natives on Guadalcanal, in the Solomon Islands. A month later his yacht was wrecked off Port Macquarie.

Of the thousands lured across the Pacific to the Californian diggings many who returned felt sure there must be equally rich gold in Australia. In fact, during the 1840s there had been several finds, notably by Count Strzelecki and the Reverend W. B. Clarke, a keen geologist. But Governor Gipps feared the social upheaval that a gold-rush might create particularly among the convicts and in 1846 when Clarke showed him a specimen he said nervously, 'Put it away, Mr Clarke, or we shall all have our throats cut', and the discovery was hushed up. By 1850, with a rapidly diminishing convict element, the situation had changed and FitzRoy, realizing how gold could benefit the economy, actively encouraged the search for it.

In California in 1849-50 a prospector named Edward Hammond Hargraves observed that the richest finds were made in country which closely

resembled the Bathurst district, where he had had a sheep run. On his return early in 1851 he went to Summer Hill Creek, a spot he knew well about twenty-five miles north-west of Bathurst, and on 12 February the first pan he washed yielded gold. Hargraves, who eventually received a government reward of £10,000, made no secret of his find and there was an immediate rush to the area. Within six weeks a canvas town called Ophir had risen on the site of his discovery and people were pouring across the Blue Mountains in hundreds; in carriages and coaches, drays and carts, on horseback but mainly on foot humping their belongings or trundling them in wheelbarrows. Soon even richer gold was found at Sofala on the Turon River and the flow became a flood. The lure of gold drew men from all classes – doctors, lawyers, merchants, clerks, farmers, shepherds, labourers. Seamen deserted their ships, shopkeepers put up their shutters and in Sydney's once-bustling streets were to be seen only women, children and old men. Melbourne, Adelaide and Hobart became equally denuded as the great trek to the diggings continued. Alarmed by the rapid decline of population in Victoria wealthy citizens offered a large reward to anyone finding payable gold within 200 miles of Melbourne. It was soon

Left Thompson's Point on the Turon River near Bathurst, N.S.W. Rich gold finds were made here during the winter of 1851.

Below left Bay whaling off Boydtown lighthouse, Twofold Bay, N.S.W.

Above Commissioner Hardy collecting licence fees from diggers at the Turon, while others hide to evade payment. Watercolour by George Lacey.

Below Men, women and children on their way to the diggings from Sydney, 1851.

claimed. Within weeks there were rich-yielding fields at Clunes and Mount Alexander (now Castlemaine) and fabulous discoveries followed at Ballarat in August and Bendigo in November. By the end of 1851 Victoria had yielded gold worth almost £1,000,000.

There were some dramatic individual finds. In the Bathurst district an Aboriginal shepherd uncovered a block of quartz which contained 106 lb of pure gold. His employer sold it for £4,000 and rewarded him with a flock of sheep. At Ballarat one lead was so rich that it was called 'The Jeweller's Shop', and the digger who tapped it earned £1,800 in his first day. A single claim worked by several successive parties yielded more than £50,000 in two months. However, these were the exceptions and for every digger who made his fortune there were fifty who earned little more than wages and some not even that.

The work was hard and conditions on the diggings, particularly in winter, were primitive. There were no hospitals and few doctors. Supplies had to be hauled long distances over rough tracks by bullock dray, and all goods, including food, were expensive. During the first year or so there were no public houses and sly-grog sellers did a thriving trade. Most diggers went armed but there was surprisingly little crime. During the week men worked from dawn to dusk; on Sundays, by mutual consent, there was no work at all.

From the beginning FitzRoy kept the situation well under control. He proclaimed that all gold was Crown property and that only those licensed by the government were entitled to dig for it. The fee was fixed at 30/– a month and commissioners were sent to the fields to issue licences and maintain law and order. This lead was followed in Victoria by La Trobe.

By the beginning of 1852 the Turon fields, though still yielding well enough, had been completely overshadowed by those in Victoria and as gold-seekers began to arrive from overseas ships originally bound for Sydney got no further than Melbourne. Many were deserted by their officers and crews and Hobson's Bay became a forest of masts. In a year Victoria's population of 77,000 more than doubled; in three years it increased fourfold. Canvas towns which sprang up on the banks of the Yarra could not cope with the increase. Rent and food prices soared at such a rate that thousands of newcomers found themselves on the breadline. Administratively there was chaos. Schools had to close, law-courts could not function, government departments were reduced to skeleton staffs and at one time only five

Below left King Billy and the Ballarat tribe at the time of the first gold discoveries there in 1851.

Right Successful diggers, armed and alert for bushrangers, on their way to Melbourne to deposit their gold. Drawing by S. T. Gill.

Below Gold prospectors panning and cradling.

Left A meeting of diggers at Mount Alexander on 15 December 1851 to protest against the imposition of a licence fee.

Below 'Prospectors at work'. Oil-painting by an unknown artist.

Right Bushranger in flight pursued by mounted troopers.

Below right Gold escort from Bathurst on arrival at the Treasury, Sydney. Drawing by Marshall Claxton.

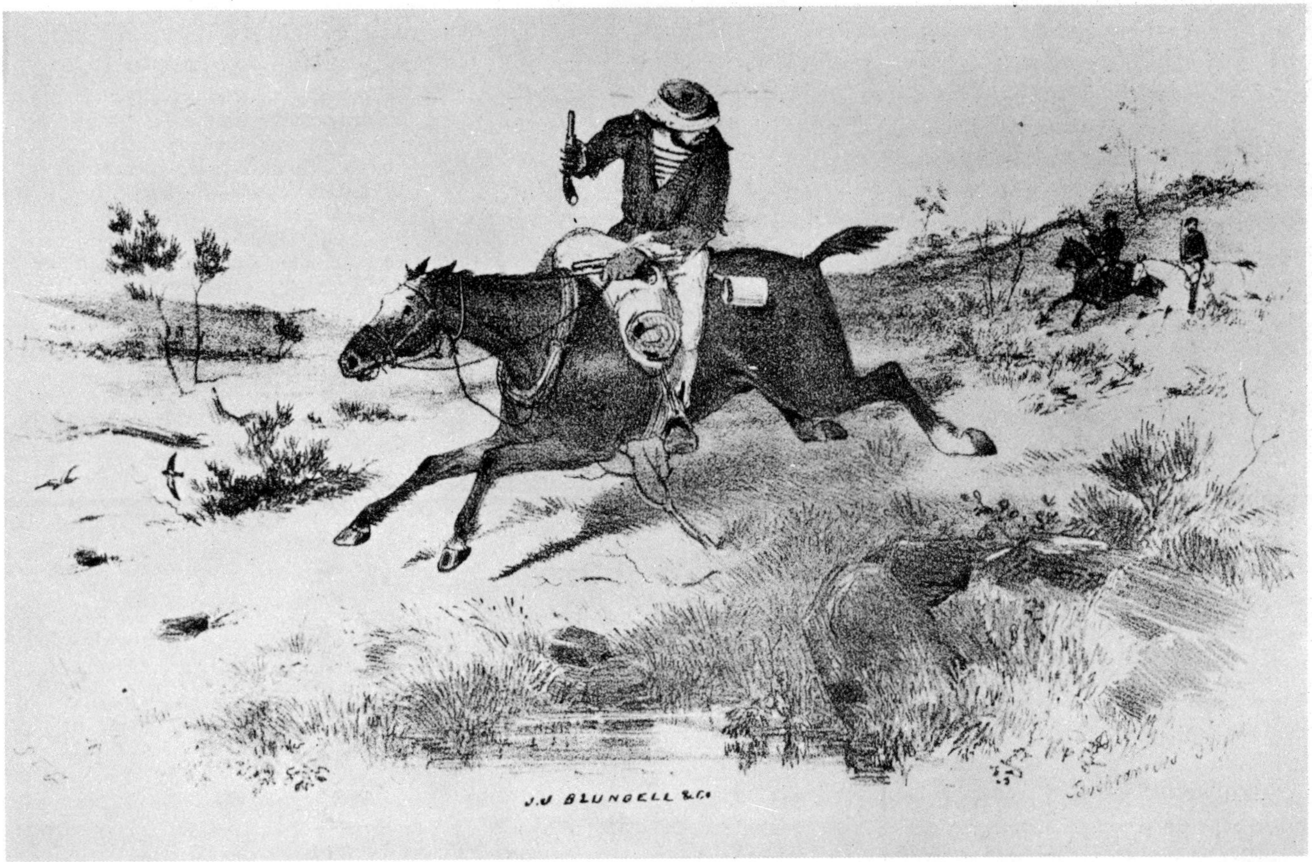
J.J BLUNDELL & Co

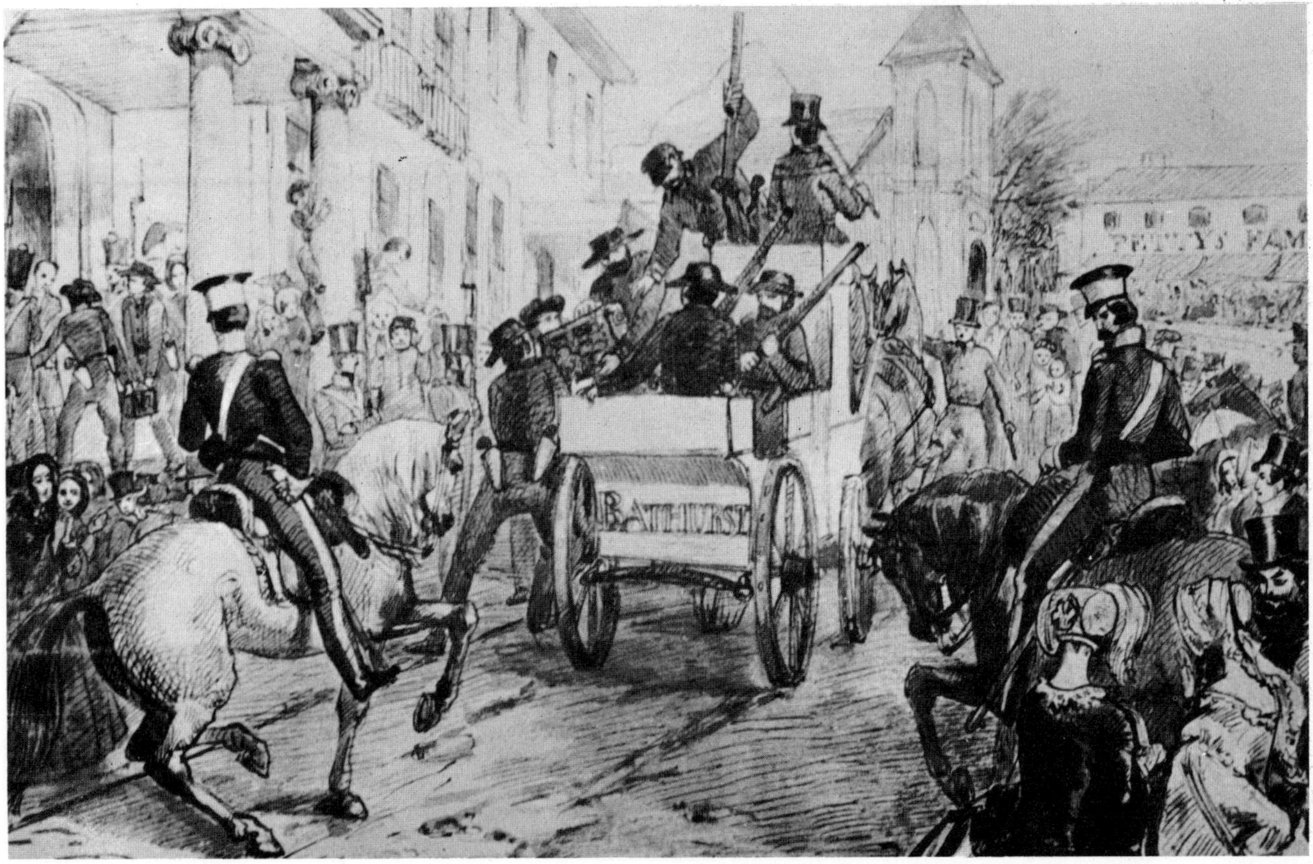
BATHURST
PETTY'S FAM

Left Gold escort attacked by bushrangers.

Below Arrival of the first gold escort, William Street, Melbourne, 1852. The clerks and draughtsmen of the Surveyor-General's office, seen watching from their office windows, resigned in a body next day to try their luck on the fields.

Below right Gold escort leaving the chief commissioner's camp at Castlemaine for Melbourne.

constables remained in Melbourne. To meet the acute need for more police and troopers inflated salaries were offered but even these attracted only young, inexperienced and often corrupt recruits.

Ticket-of-leave convicts who swarmed over from Tasmania, universally known as 'Vandemonians', introduced an ugly element which was lacking in New South Wales. In Melbourne robbery and crimes of violence became prevalent and bushranging gangs preyed on those on their way to and from the diggings. Mostly they operated in the Black Forest, where pursuit was difficult, but even on St Kilda Road, within sight of Melbourne, travellers were held up and robbed. A masked gang of twelve attacked a gold escort on its way from the McIvor diggings, shot three of the troopers and made off with gold worth £7,000. In Hobson's Bay robbers boarded the ship *Nelson,* overpowered the crew and stole 8,183 oz of gold, worth about £25,000. In Ballarat four men with unloaded pistols walked casually into a bank and got away with £14,000. The most notorious bushranger of this period was a former Tasmanian convict, Frank McCallum, who called himself Captain Melville. Caught and sentenced to thirty-two years' imprisonment, he escaped while working in a quarry after having killed a guard, was retaken, sentenced to death, reprieved and eventually committed suicide in his cell.

On the goldfields agitation steadily grew for the repeal of the licence fee. La Trobe suggested replacing it by an export duty on gold but was overruled by his council and compromised by reducing the fee to £1 a month. However, it was not the fee itself so much as the mode of its collection that antagonized the diggers. According to law those unable to produce their licences on demand were liable to arrest and fine, half of which went to the arresting officer. The police took full advantage of this chance to augment their wages. 'Digger hunts', as they were known, became increasingly frequent and men who resisted arrest were roughly handled.

La Trobe was not the man to deal with a social upheaval of such magnitude. By the end of 1853, harassed and hounded on all sides, he had had enough; and in June 1854 he was glad to hand over to Sir Charles Hotham, a former naval officer. Hotham received a rousing welcome, and a triumphant tour of the goldfields with his wife satisfied him that La Trobe's fears of trouble were groundless. He ruled his Council like a martinet; and, faced with a prospective deficit of £1,000,000, he ordered that in future licences should be checked at least twice a week, thus forfeiting the goodwill of the diggers.

Early in October in Ballarat a digger named James Scobie was killed in a drunken brawl near the Eureka Hotel. The publican, James Bentley, a man of dubious reputation, and three others were charged with his murder but despite strong evidence against them they were discharged by the stipendiary magistrate, John D'Ewes. D'Ewes was known to be corrupt and a friend of Bentley's and on 17 October about 5,000 diggers held a protest meeting. This started quietly but eventually got out of hand. There were clashes with the police, the enraged mob stormed the hotel and burned it down and Bentley narrowly escaped lynching. Three men who had played only minor parts were arrested as the alleged ringleaders and sent to jail. Another protest meeting followed, at which a Ballarat Reform League was formed, with Peter Lalor, the son of an Irish M.P., Frederick Vern, a German, and Raffaello Carboni, an Italian, prominent among its members. A deputation sent to Melbourne to demand the release of the prisoners was reproved by Hotham for using the word 'demand' and he refused to intervene. He promised there would be reforms on the goldfields; then nullified the good impression he had created by sending extra troops to Ballarat.

At another meeting several hundred diggers, now

Right McLaren's boxing saloon, Ballarat, Victoria, in 1854. Watercolour by S. T. Gill.

Below 'Topsy-Turvy', an ironic comment on life at the diggings by the English cartoonist John Leech.

Far right A concert at the diggings.

Below far right Troops from Melbourne arriving at the government camp, Ballarat, 1854.

openly defiant, burned their licences. Next day when police conducted their usual check-up they were violently resisted. The Riot Act was read, the military were called in and many arrests were made. The same evening the flag of 'the Victorian Republic' – a Southern Cross on a blue background – was raised and with Lalor as their leader about 500 diggers swore to stand truly by each other and to fight to defend their rights and liberties. Arms were requisitioned, companies were formed and drilled and an area of about an acre at Eureka was enclosed by a stockade of slabs. There was no real discipline. Men came and went at will and many who had taken the oath lost heart and deserted. On the evening of 2 December spies reported that only about 150 remained inside the stockade. Vigilance was relaxed and it seemed the right moment to strike. Before dawn next day, a Sunday, a mixed force of 276 troops and police stormed the stockade. The diggers, disorganized and many still half-asleep, were routed and within fifteen minutes it was all over. Six attackers and an estimated twenty-four diggers, most of them Irish, were killed. Lalor, badly wounded in the right arm, was helped by friends to escape. The same evening a doctor amputated the arm and in the next weeks while he remained in hid-

V. R.

Colonial Secretary's Office,
Melbourne, [illegible] December, 1854.

£400 REWARD

Whereas Two Persons of the Names of

Lawlor & Black,

LATE OF BALLAARAT,

Did on or about the 13th day of November last, at that place, use certain

TREASONABLE AND SEDITIOUS LANGUAGE,

And incite Men to take up Arms, with a view to make war against Our Sovereign Lady the QUEEN:

NOTICE IS HEREBY GIVEN

That a Reward of £200 will be paid to any person or persons giving such information as may lead to the Apprehension of either of the abovenamed parties.

DESCRIPTIONS.

LAWLOR.—Height 5 ft. 1[illegible] in., age 35, hair dark brown, whiskers dark brown and shaved under the [illegible], no moustache, long face, rather good looking, and is a well made man.

BLACK.—Height over 6 feet, straight figure, slight build, bright red hair worn in general rather long and brushed backwards, red and large whiskers, meeting under the chin, blue eyes, large thin nose, ruddy complexion, and rather small mouth.

By His Excellency's Command,

WILLIAM C. HAINES.

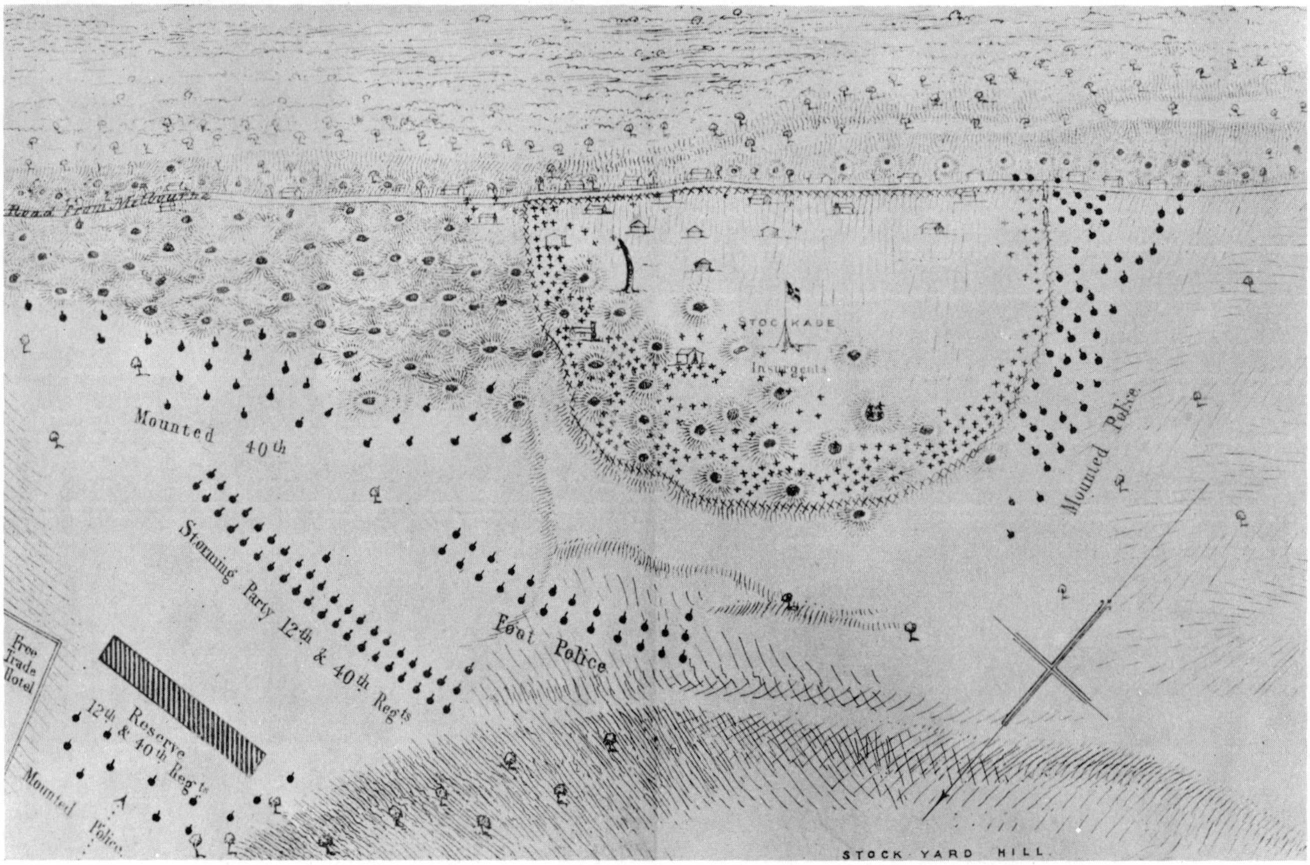

Road from Melbourne
Stockade
Insurgents
Mounted 40th
Storming Party 12th & 40th Regts
Foot Police
Mounted Police
Free Trade Hotel
12th Reserve & 40th Regts
Mounted Police
STOCK YARD HILL

ing with a price on his head, he was nursed back to health by Alicia Dunn, a schoolmistress, who later became his wife. Vern and George Black, another leader, also escaped; but Carboni, although not present at the time of the attack, was among about 120 arrested. Eventually he and twelve others were tried for treason and acquitted.

The tragedy of Eureka need never have happened. Hotham had already initiated steps for a comprehensive inquiry into affairs at the diggings and on 7 December he appointed a commission for this purpose. Its recommendations, issued in March 1855 and adopted soon afterwards, included replacement of the licence fee by a miner's right to cost £1 a year, an export duty of 2/6d. an ounce on gold, the establishment of courts on all fields to deal with local problems and disputes, the subdivision and sale of Crown lands to those who wished to settle in the colony and the franchise of all registered miners when responsible government was introduced later in the same year. The rewards offered for Lalor and others were withdrawn. Lalor emerged from hiding to bid at the first public auction of Crown land and in November he and J. B. Humffray, the Reform League secretary, were elected to represent Ballarat on the reformed Legislative Council. On 31 December Eureka claimed its last victim with the sudden

Far left Sir Charles Hotham, governor of Victoria.

Above left Government poster offering rewards for the arrest of the diggers' leaders Peter Lalor and George Black.

Below left Plan of the attack on Eureka Stockade, showing positions of police and troops.

Above Peter Lalor, the hero of Eureka.

Below The storming of Eureka Stockade, 3 December 1854. Watercolour by J. B. Henderson.

Top left Eureka shortly after the attack.

Left Australia's first mail steamer, the *Chusan*.

Below Melbourne and Hobson's Bay railway station at St Kilda.

Above The gold rush attracted thousands of Chinese. Here a long line of them pass through Flemington on their way from Melbourne to the diggings.

Above right Passengers cling on as a coach bumps over a corduroy log culvert.

collapse and death of Governor Hotham, worn out by his turbulent eighteen months in office.

Among the many colourful characters attracted to Australia at this period were G. V. Brooke, described as 'the greatest English actor since Edmund Kean', who was paid £10,000 for a hundred performances, and the dancer Lola Montez, former mistress of Louis of Bavaria, whose performances on the goldfields won showers of nuggets and who publicly horsewhipped the editor of the *Ballarat Times* for giving her a bad notice.

One result of the gold-rushes was a considerable development in various forms of transport. Despite a shortage of labour many railway lines were under construction in New South Wales and Victoria. The first to open – in September 1854 – was a single track of two and a half miles linking Melbourne and Port Melbourne; and a year later a line of fourteen miles from Sydney to Parramatta was opened. The first mail steamer, SS *Chusan*, owned by the Peninsular and Orient Company, reached Sydney in August 1852 eleven weeks out from England and in the same year three other steamers arrived. In 1853 Freeman Cobb imported the first stagecoaches from America and opened regular services to the various goldfields. Cobb soon sold out and returned home but the company retained his name and within a few years it was operating over a wide network in New South Wales and Victoria. In the same year Francis Cadell, a former naval officer, took a flat-bottomed steamer with a barge in tow 950 miles up the Murray from its mouth to Swan Hill in about three weeks and so pioneered the transport of wool by river from the interior to Adelaide.

Another result of the gold-rushes was the rapid growth of the trade union movement, stimulated by the arrival of politically-minded artisans from England. Seamen, tailors, coalminers, engineers, printers and others formed unions between 1852 and 1855; and in the latter year stonemasons in New South Wales won general recognition of the principle of an eight-hour working day.

Not all the tragedies of the period occurred on the goldfields. On 6 February 1851, ever since remembered as 'Black Thursday', the worst bushfires in colonial history devastated thousands of square miles of Victoria and caused many deaths; and in June 1852 a flood on the Murrumbidgee River totally destroyed the town of Gundagai and drowned eighty-nine of its population of 250.

9 Mid-Victorian

By the end of 1856 the changes brought about by or coincidental with the gold discoveries had transformed Australia almost beyond recognition. The four eastern colonies were now virtually masters of their own fate, with governments elected by the people and empowered to legislate on most matters without approval from England. In six years the population had doubled to about 1,000,000 and there had been a dramatic change in its distribution. About 450,000 – almost half the total – were now concentrated in Victoria. New South Wales, no longer the premier colony, claimed 350,000, South Australia more than 100,000, with Tasmania well behind and Western Australia a poor last. Now that transportation had ceased except to the west the proportion of convicts to free people was reducing rapidly and the once-familiar sight of chain-gangs at work had become rare.

The economy was now based overwhelmingly on gold and wool. Gold worth £12,000,000 a year was being exported, mostly from Victoria. The country had 20,000,000 sheep producing an annual greasy wool clip of about 55,000,000 lb and cattle totalled about 3,500,000. Lack of shepherds had forced many squatters to fence their runs with the result that stock, left to graze in peace, were improving considerably in condition and quality. The invention by John Ridley of a stripping machine which reduced harvesting costs by about 7d a bushel had greatly encouraged wheat-growers, particularly in South Australia and land under crop was now at a record level of about 800,000 acres. Manufactured goods were pouring in from England and elsewhere and imports to Victoria alone were at a rate of £18,000,000 a year.

With most of the surface gold now won alluvial diggings were giving way to deep-shaft mining which needed expensive equipment and considerable capital. There were occasional new finds and rushes but in general the day of the prospectors was over and most either worked in the mines for wages or left the fields for the cities and went back to their old occupations. Local secondary industries were thriving, wages were high and living standards had improved. Ornate and opulent mansions were beginning to appear, particularly in Melbourne and successful squatters were building new and imposing homesteads. Although most leading financial and commercial entrepreneurs were now headquartered in Melbourne, Sydney still had its men of enterprise of the calibre of Thomas Sutcliffe Mort, whose interests included wool-broking and auctioneering, shipping, mining and dairying and who in 1856 opened Australia's first dry dock at Balmain.

Left This graphic painting by John Longstaff of the arrival of Burke, Wills and King at Cooper's Creek after their overland journey to Carpentaria symbolizes the hardship and tragedy of much inland exploration.

Right A picnic on Sydney Harbour. The more genteel aspects of social life in Victorian Australia inspired many artists and popular composers.

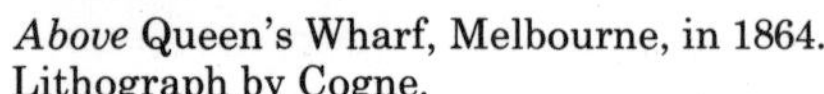

Above Queen's Wharf, Melbourne, in 1864. Lithograph by Cogne.

Below Two panoramic views of Melbourne in the 1860s. The first features the Exhibition Building; the second is from the Observatory, looking towards Sandridge.

Centre Anything from a Timor pony to a racing thoroughbred could be bought at Tattersall's Horse Bazaar, Melbourne.

Above right Gaiety is unconfined at this fete organized by the Ancient Order of Foresters in the Melbourne zoological gardens, 1866.

Below right Dry-dock under construction at Waterview Bay, Sydney. One of the many enterprises of Thomas Sutcliffe Mort.

The various Governors had now only a shadow of their former power. After eight years of intensely personal administration in Tasmania Sir William Denison had succeeded FitzRoy in New South Wales in 1855 and had soon found that his real task was no longer to rule but to accustom the people to rule themselves. He accepted his new and reduced role gracefully, became an enthusiastic patron of the arts and sciences and wrote several learned papers on scientific and engineering subjects. In all the eastern colonies there was a new and exhilarating sense of freedom and constitutional changes continued at a bewildering rate. In 1856 Victoria and South Australia introduced voting by ballot to replace the old 'show of hands' system. A year later Victoria gave the vote to all adult males and New South Wales followed suit in 1858. Queensland was proclaimed a separate colony in 1859 with Sir George Bourne as its first Governor; boundaries between New South Wales, South Australia and Queensland were considerably readjusted in 1861; and in 1863 South Australia was given jurisdiction over the Northern Territory. The determination of each colony to control its own destiny led to many serious problems. For instance, Victoria, New South Wales and Queensland all had different rail-

POST OFFICE
POST OFFICE

ARGUS OFFICE

BULL & MOUTH HOTEL
VICTORIA BOOKING OFFICE

AUCTION MART
FOOTSCRAY
FOR SALE
POSITIVE SALE BANKRUPTS STOCK JEWELLERY
AT 12 o Clock Sharp
OILMENS STORES SLOPS

1 o'Clock at Harry Jenkins CORPORATION DINING ROOMS SOUPS, HOT JOINTS &c. &c.

SANDERS & CO 68 TAILORS 68
MUFFINS
ALBION HOTEL
BILLIARDS
EDINBURGH
SAWELL, WILSON & CO WHOLESALE GROCERS
COLLINGWOOD

HOTEL

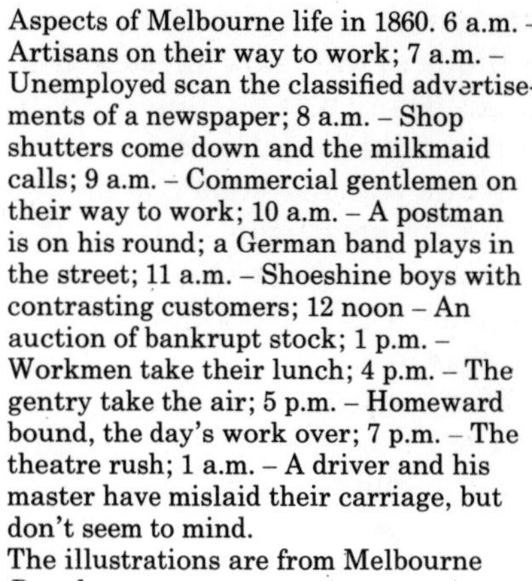

Aspects of Melbourne life in 1860. 6 a.m. – Artisans on their way to work; 7 a.m. – Unemployed scan the classified advertisements of a newspaper; 8 a.m. – Shop shutters come down and the milkmaid calls; 9 a.m. – Commercial gentlemen on their way to work; 10 a.m. – A postman is on his round; a German band plays in the street; 11 a.m. – Shoeshine boys with contrasting customers; 12 noon – An auction of bankrupt stock; 1 p.m. – Workmen take their lunch; 4 p.m. – The gentry take the air; 5 p.m. – Homeward bound, the day's work over; 7 p.m. – The theatre rush; 1 a.m. – A driver and his master have mislaid their carriage, but don't seem to mind.
The illustrations are from Melbourne *Punch*.

way gauges, a folly which was to cost untold millions in the years ahead and which persists until today. There was no uniformity in tariff rates, taxation or land laws. Each colony had its own education and postal system and its own immigration policy. In an attempt to straighten out some of these problems the first of several intercolonial conferences was held in 1863 but it was not notably successful.

One particular problem concerned the massive influx of Chinese to the gold diggings. Even when surface gold had petered out on a particular field the Chinese stayed on to work over the tailings discarded by earlier prospectors, and their ever-increasing numbers caused great resentment. In an effort to keep them out Victoria imposed a landing tax of £10 a head but as entry to South Australia remained unrestricted they simply went ashore there and trekked overland to the fields. By 1858 there were an estimated 42,000 of them in Victoria. A riot at Buckland River in which angry diggers destroyed Chinese camps and drove their occupants into the bush was followed in 1860 by a much more serious one at Lambing Flat, New South Wales. Although extra police and troops were called in to protect the threatened Chinese many were brutally treated and some were killed or died. Restrictive laws on the Victorian pattern were passed in South Australia and New South Wales but the remedy, although effective for a while, was only temporary and the same problem was to arise again in later years. Because of their inept handling of the situation at Lambing Flat the prestige of the N.S.W. police suffered greatly and one result was the emergence of a new school of bushrangers who were to plague the colony throughout the 1860s. These were not convict escapees driven to crime by circumstances but 'wild colonial boys' – bush-bred youths and young men, the sons in most cases of poor free settlers, who combined contempt for authority with a spirit of reckless adventure; and it is significant that three who were to become the most notorious of them – Frank Gardiner, Ben Hall and Johnny Gilbert – had all been present during the Lambing Flat riots.

Gardiner began his bushranging career in 1861 with John Piesley and they soon became familiar and feared figures on the roads around Lambing Flat, Yass and Gundagai. When Piesley was caught and hanged early in 1862 Gardiner was joined by Gilbert and others. In June of the same year the gang stuck up a gold escort at Eugowra Rocks and got away with gold and notes valued at £12,000. Gardiner vanished after this exploit but several men were arrested, among them – to the surprise of his

Below left The ex-mining camp of Ballarat, now a sober Victorian city, welcomes the governor on a visit from Melbourne.

Left Sheep-shearing in the 1860s.

Below The rise of the 'squattocracy' is symbolized in this sentimental engraving, from a drawing by Nicholas Chevalier, of the old and new homesteads of a sheep station.

friends – Ben Hall. Hall was married with a small son, his record was clean and he was known to be honest and hard-working. The police evidence against him was flimsy and he was eventually released without being brought to trial. On his return home he found his wife had deserted him, taking their child, and all his cattle, which were his only capital, had strayed or died of neglect. Soon afterwards, harassed by the police, Hall turned bush-ranger and became the leader of a gang which included Gilbert. Many of his exploits in the next three years have become legendary. In September 1863 he and his gang occupied the town of Canowindra for three days, and a month later he captured a police magistrate and held him to ransom for £500. In November 1864 near Jugiong on the road to Melbourne Hall, Gilbert and a new recruit named John Dunn rounded up sixty travellers and while Dunn held them captive Hall and Gilbert stuck up and robbed a mail coach after a gun duel with its police guard. All three were declared outlaws. In May 1865 Hall was trapped and shot dead and a week later Gilbert – betrayed by his friends, it is said – met the same fate. Dunn remained free for a while but was caught early in 1866 and hanged for the murder of a police constable. In the meantime

Far left Bushrangers robbing the mail, a favourite subject of artists of the time. Pen drawing by George Lacy.

Left 'Brave' Ben Hall, a legend in his own brief lifetime and the hero of many bush ballads.

Below left Ben Hall, said to have been betrayed for the reward on his head, is ambushed and killed by police.

Below centre The death of Gilbert. His mate John Dunn (left) escaped the police trap, but was later caught and hanged.

Right The shooting of Sergeant Parry by Gilbert.

Below right 'Black' Dan Morgan, the most feared of the bushrangers, callously shoots a Chinese gold prospector.

police had traced Gardiner to a small town in Queensland where he was running a store under an assumed name. He was sentenced to thirty-two years but after eight years in prison he was released on condition that he left the colony. He became the proprietor of a saloon in San Francisco and is believed to have died there in 1895.

Other notable bushrangers of this era included Daniel Morgan, known as 'Black Dan' and Frederick Ward, who called himself 'Captain Thunderbolt'. Both were lone workers but whereas Morgan was a brutal and ruthless killer with a price of £1,000 on his head Ward was known for his gentleness and courtesy, particularly to women. Eventually both were shot dead – Morgan by a stockman at Wangaratta, Victoria and Ward by a policeman at Uralla, N.S.W.

While the gold fever had been at its height there had been little serious exploration but as it died down explorers became active again. Between 1856 and 1861 the Gregory brothers made several sorties into the unknown north-west of Western Australia and their discoveries disproved the general belief that it was all barren and useless desert. In 1860 John McDouall Stuart, who had been with Sturt on his last expedition, set out from Adelaide to cross the

Left The death of Morgan at Peechelba station, near Wangaratta, Victoria.

Below Explorers digging for water. Engraved from a drawing by Thomas Baines, who was with the Gregory expedition in northern Australia in 1855.

Right Members of the Gregory expedition tending their horses at the Victoria River. An oil-painting by Baines.

Below right Start of the ill-fated Burke and Wills expedition from Royal Park, Melbourne. Burke is on the white horse and Wills (also mounted) is on the far left. From a drawing by William Strutt.

continent from south to north. After reaching the geographical centre he pushed on doggedly through harsh spinifex country; but lack of water, an outbreak of scurvy among his men and the hostility of the natives combined to defeat him and at Newcastle Waters, within 400 miles of his objective, he was forced back.

Meanwhile the Victoria Government and the public of Melbourne had contributed £12,000 to outfit another expedition which aimed to reach the Gulf of Carpentaria by way of the Darling River and Cooper's Creek. Robert O'Hara Burke, a police officer with no previous exploring experience, was appointed leader of a party of eighteen, and twenty-five camels were imported from India to carry supplies and equipment. The expedition was rousingly farewelled when it left Melbourne on 20 August 1860; but public confidence was soon shaken when it was learned that G. J. Landells, the second-in-command, had quarrelled with Burke and resigned. His place was taken by William J. Wills, the expedition's astronomical and meteorological observer. A base was established at Menindee on the Darling; then Burke, Wills and six others pressed on to form a forward depot at Cooper's Creek, where the others were to join them. As time

I hope we shall be done justice. We fulfilled our task but we were ~~aband~~ not followed up as I expected and the Depot party abandoned their post – R O'H Burke

passed with no sign of them Burke became impatient and rather than wait any longer he decided, as he wrote, 'to dash into the interior and cross the continent at all hazards', a journey of about 600 miles each way through almost completely unknown country. It was an incredibly foolhardy decision. On 16 December he set out with Wills, John King, Charles Gray, six camels, a packhorse and provisions for twelve weeks. The going was hard and when, two months later, they reached the tidal estuary of the Flinders River which flows into the Gulf of Carpentaria they were too weak to force a way through the mangrove swamps to the open sea.

The journey back was a nightmare. Gray was flogged by Burke for stealing some flour and died a few days later. Food supplies gave out, some of the camels died and their emaciated packhorse was killed for its meat. On 21 April 1861 when the three survivors staggered, exhausted and starving, into the depot at Cooper's Creek it was deserted and they found a note advising that the rest of the party had left for Menindee a mere seven hours before. Too weak to go after them they lingered around the depot for a while then set off with the vague and hopeless intention of reaching Adelaide. Occasional gifts of edible roots and fish from local Aborigines

Above left Burke's last written words, addressed to his sister.

Above Burke, Wills and King on the long trek back from the Gulf of Carpentaria. Engraved from a drawing by Nicholas Chevalier.

Left The death of Wills. King (supporting Wills) received occasional food from Aborigines, and was the only survivor.

Right The hazards of exploring are pictured light-heartedly by John Davis, who was a member of the McKinlay expedition. The 'alligators' which threatened their crossing of a river in northern Australia were, in fact, crocodiles.

kept them precariously alive for two months but by the time a rescue party from Melbourne under W. A. Howitt eventually arrived both leaders were dead and only King survived, 'wasted to a shadow and barely to be distinguished as a civilized being'. In the meantime three other relief parties had set out from different points and though they failed to find the missing men two of them, led respectively by John McKinlay and William Landsborough, did some notable exploratory work on their own account in central and north-western Queensland.

In October 1861, while the search for Burke and Wills went on, McDouall Stuart, undeterred by earlier failures, left Adelaide in his second attempt within a year to reach the north coast. This time knowing the various hazards ahead he and his party were better able to cope with them. Newcastle Waters was reached after six months of hard but unspectacular slogging; and a final dash brought them on 24 July 1862 to the coast not very far from the present town of Darwin. On the return journey they were harassed by Aborigines and Stuart became paralysed and lost his sight for a while but he had partly recovered by the time Adelaide was reached.

Between 1856 and 1866 there was much progress in the sphere of communications. The idea of linking the various colonies by electric telegraph had been brought to the country by S. McGowan, who had worked in the United States with Samuel Morse, and under his supervision the first telegraph line, from Melbourne to Williamstown, had been established as early as 1854. Thereafter progress was rapid. Hobart and Launceston were linked in 1857, Melbourne and Adelaide in July 1858, Sydney and Melbourne in October 1858 and Sydney and Brisbane in 1861. An attempt in 1859 to span Bass Strait by submarine cable was unsuccessful and another ten years were to pass before communication was established between Tasmania and the mainland.

By now there were extensive networks of roads particularly in Victoria and New South Wales but until the late 1850s most were in deplorable condition and many were impassable in wet weather. In Victoria, where a Central Roads Board was financed by government grants and where the distances between towns were relatively short, there was considerable improvement in the 1860s. In New South Wales, however, road upkeep continued to be financed mainly from tolls. By 1865 there were no less than thirty-four toll-bars on the three main roads alone but even so the revenue they yielded was inadequate and travelling, even in Cobb and Co.'s well-sprung coaches, remained an uncomfortable and often hazardous business.

Railway construction, which had practically ceased in the gold-rush period through lack of labour, was now going ahead again at a great rate, particularly in Victoria. Melbourne and Geelong were linked by rail in 1860; Melbourne and Ballarat in 1862; and a line of 156 miles from Melbourne through Bendigo to Echuca, on the N.S.W. border, was opened in 1864. In New South Wales the Parramatta line was extended west to Penrith in 1862; the main southern line had got as far as Picton (fifty miles) by 1863; and a branch from Blacktown to Richmond was opened in 1864. In Queensland a line from Ipswich west towards the Darling Downs had been completed as far as Helidon; and in South Australia there were lines from Adelaide to Port Adelaide and to the copper centre of Kapunda (fifty miles). By 1866 the eastern colonies had a total mileage of about 460.

The first fatal railway accident occurred at what is now Lidcombe, N.S.W. on 10 July 1858, when several carriages of a train from Campbelltown were derailed on a curve. Four people were killed and thirteen injured.

However, the dangers of rail travel were as yet not to be compared with those faced at sea. Even with the coming of steam about fifty ships were wrecked or simply disappeared on and around the Australian coast in the ten years to 1866. The most

Left Another oil-painting by Thomas Baines, which shows Aborigines watching him at work.

Right A train arriving at the Sydney terminal at Redfern. By the 1860s rail transport was beginning to open up much of the interior.

Below When transportation to the eastern colonies ceased many English criminals were sent out as 'exiles' in the hope that they would reform. This graphic picture, subtitled 'A Hint For Downing Street', was inspired by an opponent of the scheme, which in fact was a failure.

Above South Australia's first train crossing a bridge in Adelaide. From a drawing by H. Glover.

Left Emu-hunting was for long a favourite sport in Australia. Watercolour by an unknown artist.

Right In at the kill. A fox-hunting scene in the English tradition by an unknown Australian artist.

notable of these disasters was the wreck of the *Dunbar* (1,321 tons) off Sydney on 20 August 1857. It was a dark night with a south-easterly gale and high seas and it is possible that the captain mistook the Gap, near South Head lighthouse, for the harbour entrance. Before he could get the ship clear she was dashed broadside on to the rocks at the foot of the high cliffs and within minutes was pounded to pieces. Of the 122 persons on board the only survivor was James Johnson, a young seaman, who scrambled on to a ledge of rock and was seen and rescued about thirty-six hours later. Afterwards Johnson was employed at Newcastle lighthouse and on 12 July 1866 he helped to rescue the only survivor of the steamer *Cawarra* which was wrecked with the loss of sixty lives while trying to enter Newcastle harbour. Only two months after the *Dunbar* disaster there were twenty-one deaths when the *Catherine Adamson*, an Aberdeen clipper, went ashore on Inner North Head at the entrance to Sydney harbour; and on 4 August 1859 the steamer *Admella*, bound from Adelaide to Melbourne, was lost off Cape Northumberland, South Australia, with only twenty-one survivors of a total complement of 104.

A disaster of a different kind, in which fortunately no lives were lost, was the destruction by fire of St Mary's Roman Catholic cathedral, Sydney, on the night of 29 June 1865. A temporary building was erected on the site and plans were at once ordered for a new cathedral. The old one, consecrated in 1836, had been in the Gothic revival style, as the new one and most other cathedrals and churches built in the latter half of the century were also to be. Indeed, the old colonial eighteenth-century architectural tradition was now virtually dead. Australia's first public art gallery (actually a wing of the public library), opened in Melbourne in 1861, was in the Italian Renaissance style, as were the Adelaide and Brisbane town halls, both opened in 1865 and many other public buildings, banks and commercial houses.

One effect of the general prosperity was the growing popularity of many sports and their more efficient organization. In New South Wales horse-racing was now largely controlled by the Australian Jockey Club and in Victoria by the Victoria Racing Club. The first big intercolonial race was the Australian Champion Sweepstakes, run over three miles at Flemington, Melbourne, on 1 October 1859 and won by Flying Buck, owned by W. C. Yuille, a Victorian squatter. The Melbourne Cup, eventually to become one of the world's great handicap races, was first run in 1861 and won by Archer, a Sydney

Above An English cricket XI, captained by George Parr, playing against a Victoria XXII. Melbourne cricket ground, 1 January 1864. Because of the ability of the English visitors, colonial teams of up to twenty-two players were chosen to make a match of it.

Left Tom Curran, Victorian middleweight champion, wearing the gold belt he won with the title in 1860.

Above right Lineup for the start of Australia's first big intercolonial horse-race, the Australian Champion Sweepstakes, run on 1 October 1859. The winner was Flying Buck, a three-year-old. Drawn by Herbert Palmer.

Right A hunt club meeting at Melton Mowbray, Tasmania. Hunting on the English pattern was a feature of Australian social life of the 1860s.

horse owned by Etienne de Mestre. Heavily weighted at 10 st. 2 lb. Archer won again in 1862; but his entry for the following year was rejected because of the late delivery of the telegram. The first Adelaide Cup was run in 1865 and the first Sydney and Brisbane Cups in 1866. In cricket the first of what became an annual series of matches between Victoria and New South Wales was played in Melbourne in March 1856. The New South Wales side turned down Victoria's suggestion of a side-wager of £500 but nevertheless won by three wickets. The pitches at this time strongly favoured the bowlers, and it was not until 1867 that R. W. Wardill, of Victoria, scored the first century of the series. The first English team, captained by H. H. Stephenson, was brought to Australia at the end of 1861 by a Melbourne catering firm. The visitors were far too good for their colonial rivals and although opposed by teams of as many as twenty-two they lost only two of their fifteen matches. The late 1850s – the actual year is still in some doubt – saw the evolution in Melbourne of what was to become known as Australian Rules football. Its founders, T. W. Wills, who had played Rugby at school in England, and H. C. A. Harrison, worked out a set of rules which combined some of the more spectacular features of Rugby and Association football (soccer) and the game quickly became popular. In time it spread to Tasmania, South Australia and Western Australia but it was never widely accepted in New South Wales and Queensland, where Rugby was preferred. Among other sports which enjoyed a considerable vogue at this time were sculling, prize-fighting and professional footrunning.

10 Towards Federation

Because the Australian colonies had no common policy regarding such vital matters as foreign affairs, defence, immigration, tariffs and financial and industrial affairs it seemed to many that eventually there would have to be some form of federation. This had been suggested as early as 1847 by the Secretary of State for the Colonies, Earl Grey. But inter-colonial rivalries were strong; there was a basic conflict between the free-trade advocates of New South Wales and the protectionists of Victoria; the smaller colonies, Tasmania and Western Australia, feared that federation would destroy their independence; and the larger colonies felt that the smaller ones would become a financial burden on them. Most politicians were spokesmen for the vested interests of their colonies and although they claimed to favour federation they argued that the time was not yet ripe for it. One man who disagreed was Henry Parkes, who had come to Sydney as an assisted immigrant in 1839 and was now Australia's rising political star and her most brilliant orator. In a memorable speech at an intercolonial conference in Melbourne in 1867 Parkes came out strongly in favour of federation as the only way to resolve common problems. In 1870 a royal commission was appointed to consider the subject but it got no further than submitting a preliminary report. However, Parkes was a patient man and bided his time.

Meanwhile the eastern mainland colonies continued to enjoy unprecedented prosperity, though the pattern of it differed widely among them. In Queensland sugar production, centred at first near Brisbane, was emerging as a major industry. In 1867 six mills produced 168 tons of cane-sugar; three years later there were twenty-eight mills producing 2,854 tons. When the climate and soil further north were found to be more suitable Mackay and Cairns became the new centres of production and by 1888 the annual output had risen to 60,000 tons. To work the plantations cheap coloured labour was recruited from the islands of the south-west Pacific but recruiting soon degenerated into straight-out, brutal kidnapping – euphemistically called 'blackbirding' – and from 1868 on laws were introduced, with varying success, to regulate the importation, working conditions and repatriation of the islanders. The discovery of gold at Gympie, though greatly beneficial to Queensland's economy, created yet another problem. As other rich finds were made notably at Charters Towers and at Palmer, inland from Cook's Endeavour River, Chinese began to

Left Climax of a famous man-hunt. Police shoot it out with the Kelly gang at Glenrowan Hotel.

Right Town transport of the 1880s. The scene is outside the Town Hall and Public Library, Ballarat East.

An international incident was narrowly averted in 1883 when Queensland, fearing German aggression, annexed part of New Guinea and raised the British flag.

Above In pre-Federation days each colony was responsible for its own defence. Picture shows the Victorian navy in 1886.

Below The burning of the Garden Palace, Sydney, on 22 September 1822. In the foreground is Macquarie Street, and the isolated colonial house is on the site of the Public Library of N.S.W.

Above right The fighting was almost over when Australian volunteers reached the Sudan in 1885. This satirical cartoon of their return is from the *Bulletin*.

Below right Sturt Street, Ballarat. By 1880 the old tent-town of the gold-diggers had become a solid and dignified city.

pour in as they had to the south years earlier and by 1877 there were 17,000 on the various fields. Restricting legislation was introduced in the same year and eventually similar laws were passed in the other colonies, though Tasmania, for instance, did not fall into line until 1887.

Profitable gold was still emerging from the deep-shaft mines of Victoria and in 1869 a record-sized nugget of 2,284 oz., called the Welcome Stranger, was found at Moliagul. However, gross production was now well below its peak and steadily declining; and in one memorable year Queensland's total production actually exceeded Victoria's, due largely to a record yield from the mine at Mount Morgan.

In New South Wales in 1870 rich gold was found at Hill End, in the Bathurst area, and at Gulgong about fifty miles further north. In its first five years Gulgong produced thirteen tons of gold. By 1872 Hill End had a population of 30,000 with fifty-two hotels. In the same year Bernard Holtermann, a German, found the largest single mass of gold ever known. It was 4 ft 9 ins high, it weighed 630 lb and it was valued at £12,000. Later Holtermann built a mansion at North Sydney and engaged photographers to make an extensive – and now historically invaluable – camera record of the main

Above left Rich gold finds in Queensland in the 1870s brought thousands of Chinese to Australia. Their alien customs and frugal ways created much ill-feeling.

Left Not only whites resented the mass intrusion of the Chinese. Here gold-diggers on the Gilbert River, northern Australia, are being attacked by hostile Aborigines.

Above A gold prospector at Gulgong, N.S.W., in 1871 shows the nuggets he has won.

Right A typical shop in the boom town of Hill End, N.S.W., during the gold rush of the 1870s.

gold-mining areas and towns of New South Wales and Victoria. In 1875 silver ore deposits were found near Broken Hill in the far west of New South Wales but their richness was not confirmed until 1883, when there was a rush to the area. Charles Rasp, a boundary rider, and a syndicate of six friends who contributed £70 each, found rich silver in a claim they had staked at Broken Hill itself and in 1885 they floated the Broken Hill Proprietary Company, which has since played a dominant part in Australia's industrial development.

Despite these rich mineral finds, however, prosperity in New South Wales, as in Victoria, continued to depend mainly on wool. By now most of the colonies had introduced free selection laws which aimed to break up the huge leasehold lands of the squatters and enable small farmers to buy limited areas on deferred terms at £1 an acre. The scheme worked fairly well in Victoria but in New South Wales loopholes in the law led to many abuses and much bitterness between squatters and 'cockies', as the small farmers came to be known. Many unscrupulous squatters acquired sites which denied the selectors access to water – a practice known as 'peacocking' – and bought large areas through dummies. A commission appointed to investigate the situation found itself involved in

Left Bernhard Otto Holtermann, a German prospector, with the mass of almost solid gold which he unearthed at Hill End in 1872. It weighed 630 lb, and was valued at £12,000.

Below left In contrast to the opulence of the 'squattocracy' is this humble selector's homestead in Victoria.

Right The imposing masion built by a successful squatter, Sir William J. Clarke, at Sunbury, Victoria.

Below Miners' wives outside a bark-roofed wattle-and-daub cottage at Hill End.

PUTTING THE HOPS INTO THE BOILER
THE REFRIGERATOR
CARLTON BREWERY
THE FERMENTING VATS
ONE OF THE CELLARS
TOPPING UP
THE BREWERY FROM VICTORIA STREET

Left From her earliest days Melbourne has prided herself on the quality of her beer. These pictures of Carlton Brewery were published in 1886.

Above The character of the Australian bush is caught superbly in this painting by Edward Roper of a kangaroo hunt at Mount Zero, in the Victorian Grampians, in 1880.

Below 'Christmas Day down south'. It took British immigrants many years to get used to celebrating Christmas in midsummer.

unintelligible chaos' and the scheme eventually collapsed in almost total victory for the squatters. Other factors were combining to increase the wealth and power of the big pastoralists and graziers. In 1879 the presence of vast underground water supplies was proved by the successful sinking of an artesian bore in north-western New South Wales. By 1888 several hundred bores were flowing in the eastern mainland colonies and the stock-carrying capacity of much hitherto arid land was greatly increased. In 1880 the successful shipping of refrigerated meat to England, an enterprise pioneered by T. S. Mort, encouraged the cross-breeding of English sheep with merinos to produce mutton for export and greatly stimulated the cattle industry. By 1888 Australia's cattle exceeded 10,000,000, of which more than half were in Queensland; there were 80,000,000 sheep and the annual wool clip was 450,000,000 lb.

In South Australia the emphasis was still on agriculture. The invention in 1876 of the stump-jump plough had brought much otherwise difficult land into production and by 1888 the colony had 2,000,000 acres under wheat, more than half the Australian total. Tasmania, depopulated by the gold rushes, remained a pastoral backwater and Western Australia was still the Cinderella of the colonies.

AUSTRALIA
SHIP HOPE

Left and below left A famous pair of colour-prints by George Baxter, titled *'News from Home'* and *'News from Australia'*. It is doubtful whether the artist ever visited the colonies.

Below The late Victorian era was not a happy one for the Aborigines of Australia who, although no longer hunted down were shamefully neglected. This lithograph, by an unknown artist, shows a typical encampment in South Australia.

Right The last four Tasmanian Aborigines. With the death of Truganini (seated, right) the race became extinct.

However, the discovery of tin at Mount Bischoff in 1871 and of silver-lead at Mount Zeehaen in 1885 gave hope for the future in Tasmania; and Western Australia was similarly heartened by gold finds in the Kimberleys in 1885 and at Pilbara and Yilgarn two years later.

This rapid economic growth led inevitably to conflicts between employers and workers on such questions as wages, working hours and general conditions. Stonemasons had long since won an eight-hours working day but only after long agitation was the principle extended to other trades. The trades union movement was growing rapidly and from 1879 on there were regular intercolonial congresses to discuss common problems. Strikes, although frequent, were mostly local and brief. The first with intercolonial ramifications occurred in 1878. In protest against the employment by the Australasian Steam Navigation Co. of cheap Chinese labour on their ships trading with the islands the Seamen's Union called out its members as the ships reached port. The strikers received financial support from other unions and the public; coal-miners refused to load the company's ships; the Queensland government, still coping with its own Chinese problem, withdrew its mail subsidy; and after much bitterness a compromise settlement was reached. The first industrial dispute involving women occurred in Melbourne in 1882 when female employees in the tailoring industry struck for better wages and conditions. One result was the appointment of a commission whose revelations regarding 'sweating' led to many reforms. In 1886 a strike of Melbourne wharf-labourers, unimportant in itself, became notable as the first to be settled by arbitrators representing both sides with an independent chairman.

At this time unionists felt strongly that if too many people were let into the country there would not be enough jobs to go round and that hard-won concessions would be threatened. Despite their opposition, however, the various colonies continued to encourage immigration, and in the fifteen years to 1880 there were about 270,000 new arrivals, mainly from Britain. A year later the country's first simultaneous census revealed a total population of 2,250,194. By 1888, Australia's centenary year, the figure was not far short of 3,000,000 and Governor Phillip's belief that he was founding an empire was being proved true.

Through the 1870s and 1880s railway construction was at its peak and vast areas were being brought within easy reach of the seaboard cities. In New South Wales the Sydney-Albury line (386 miles) was completed in 1881, the Sydney-Bourke line (503 miles) in 1885, and the line from Sydney to Wallangarra, on the Queensland border, in 1889. In Victoria a line from Melbourne to Wodonga, on the Murray, had operated since 1873; and among many important lines opened in the early 1880s was one to the South Australian border to link with a wide-gauge line from Adelaide. In Queensland the Brisbane-Wallangarra line was opened in 1887 and the Brisbane-Charleville line (483 miles) a year later. A line from Rockhampton to Longreach (427 miles) was nearly complete and others radiating from Maryborough, Mackay and Townsville were under construction. In Tasmania Hobart and Launceston were linked in 1876 and Launceston and Devonport in 1885. Through traffic between Melbourne and Sydney began in 1885, though passengers had to change at Albury because of the differing gauges. In 1887 trains ran direct from Melbourne to Adelaide and two years later Sydney and Brisbane were conconnected, again with a change at the border. Throughout the country there were now more than 8,000 miles of railways, almost all government-owned. Sydney had its first steam trams in 1879 and Melbourne its first cable trams six years later.

An epic achievement was the construction during 1871-72 of an overland telegraph line from Port Augusta, South Australia, to Darwin, following the route which McDouall Stuart had pioneered a mere

Above Colonial railways bought most of their rolling stock from England. This Baldwin engine, imported from the United States about 1877, was one of the few exceptions.

Left A double-decker steam tram in Elizabeth Street, Sydney, in 1879.

ten years earlier. At Darwin it linked with a submarine cable from Java, and on 21 October 1872 England and Australia exchanged their first direct cable messages. The event was celebrated by public banquets in Sydney, Adelaide and London, and Charles Todd, Postmaster-General of South Australia, who had planned it all, was knighted. A telegraph line between Adelaide and Perth was opened in 1877 and another between Perth and Derby (1,700 miles) in 1888. The first long-distance telephone conversation in Australia took place in February 1878 between Port Augusta and Semaphore (240 miles). In the same year Melbourne opened the first telephone exchange and by 1887 all the other capitals had followed suit.

The opening of the overland telegraph line virtually brought an end to the heroic age of exploring. On the other hand it made a convenient starting or finishing point for explorers and in the 1870s there were several expeditions from the line to the Western Australian coast or *vice versa*. The most notable were led by Major Peter Warburton (1873), Ernest Giles (1873, 1875 and 1876), John Forrest (1874), and his brother Alexander Forrest (1879). All contributed greatly to geographical knowledge but most were across arid desert country and only Alexander Forrest, who crossed well to the north of

Above left 'The Emigrant', a coloured lithograph which tells its own story. For many years it graced the walls of thousands of English parlours.
Below left A popular pastime of small boys was to 'scale' a free ride on Sydney trams of the 1880s. Fifty years later they were still doing it.

Above Victoria was the first colony to install a telephone service in 1878, thus opening a new avenue of employment for genteel young ladies, here seen at work at the multiple switchboard at Melbourne exchange.

Below The men who built the overland telegraph line in 1871-2. The Postmaster-General of South Australia, Charles Todd (second from right) was knighted for his achievement.

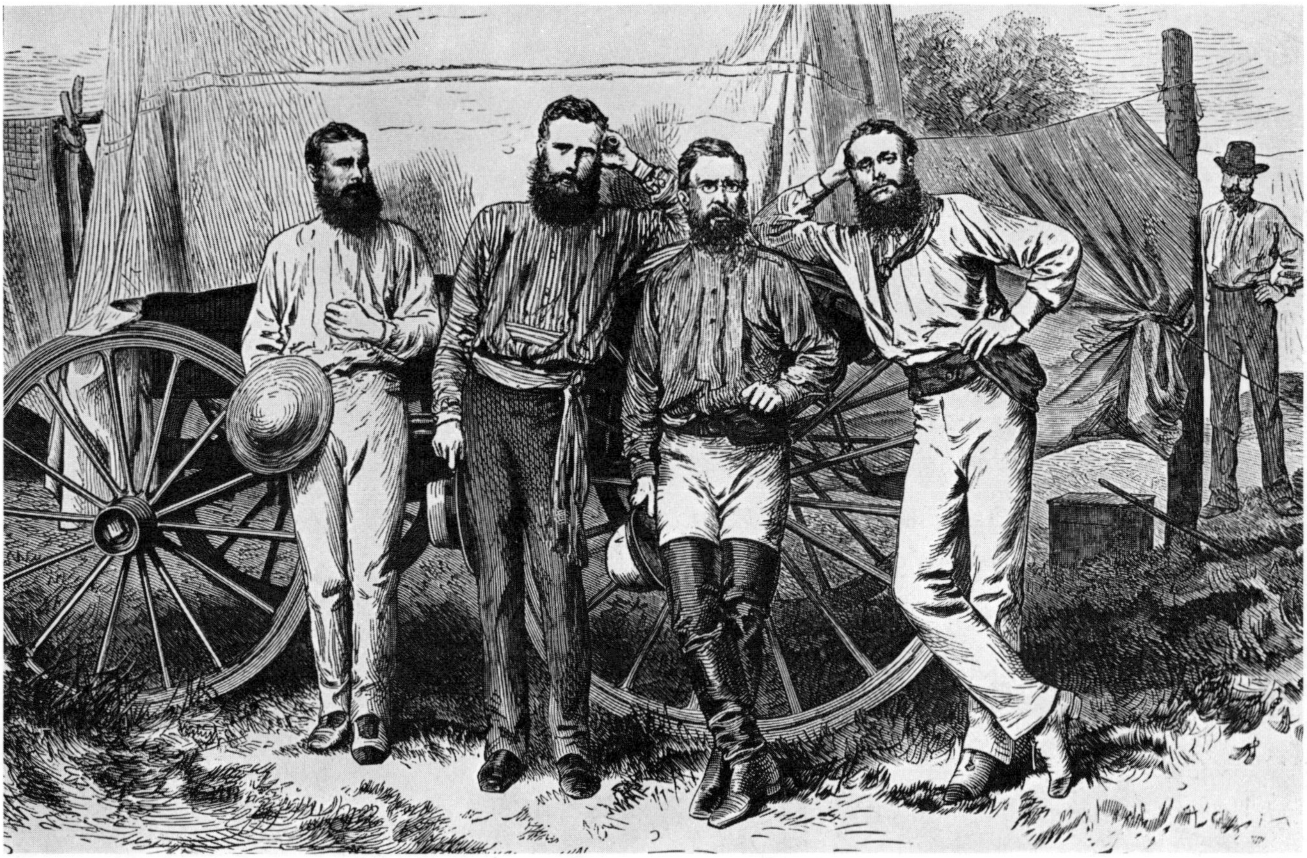

the others, found good grazing land on the Nicholson Plains.

The 'heroic' age of bushranging was not, however, quite at an end yet. One night in May 1869 a masked man who called himself 'Captain Moonlite' broke into a bank at Mount Egerton, Victoria, held up the manager and got away with £1,000 in gold and notes. The manager's claim that the robber was a local lay preacher named Andrew George Scott, ridiculed at first, was proved true when an ingot of gold which Scott sold in Sydney was identified as part of the loot. Scott was returned to Victoria and sentenced to eleven years. He proved a model prisoner and on his release in 1879 he lectured for a time on prison reform and became an open-air preacher. Then unaccountably he turned bushranger, enlisted five recruits of whom the youngest was only fifteen, and crossed into New South Wales. In November after several minor robberies the gang took Wantabadgery, a station homestead near Wagga, detained a total of fifty-two residents and visitors and held the place for two days. An escapee gave the alarm and a strong police force set out from Wagga. Eventually the gang was cornered in a selector's hut and in a pitched battle two bushrangers and a policeman were shot dead. At the trial in Sydney Scott took all the blame. His plea

Above left Aborigines attack explorer John Forrest and his party at Weld Springs, W.A., in 1874. This depiction of the incident is by a present-day Aboriginal child.

Left Andrew George Scott, alias 'Captain Moonlite'.

Above The last stand of the Moonlite gang in a shepherd's hut at Wantabadgery, near Wagga Wagga, N.S.W., in November 1879.

Right When the notorious Kelly gang raided Jerilderie, N.S.W., they locked the police in their own cells and plundered the town's only bank at leisure.

for the lives of his three surviving companions saved two of them, and on 20 January 1880 he and the third were hanged.

Scott was a comparatively minor bushranging figure; his contemporary, Ned Kelly, was to become the most famous of them all. Kelly, the son of a poor widow who lived near Benalla, Victoria, was in trouble with authority from early adolescence and in 1871, at the age of sixteen, he was jailed for three years for receiving a stolen mare. Two years after his release he began a profitable business of stealing horses in Victoria and selling them in New South Wales. In 1878 his brother Dan, then aged seventeen, was arrested for a similar crime but escaped after slightly wounding a constable and took to the bush. Next day his mother, who had been present, was arrested for aiding and abetting an attempted murder and despite the flimsiness of the charge was sent to jail for three years. The Kelly brothers went into hiding in wild mountain country with two friends, Steve Hart and Joe Byrne; and soon afterwards in a gun duel with pursuing police Ned Kelly shot and killed a sergeant and two constables. All four were proclaimed outlaws with rewards of £500 each on their heads. They lay low for a year, then in December 1878 they emerged to rob a bank at Euroa of £2,000 in notes and gold. Two months later they crossed the Murray to Jerilderie in New South Wales; locked the two local policemen in their own cells; took over the town and escaped with £2,140 from its only bank. With rewards for their capture now increased to £2,000 a head they stayed under cover for another sixteen months. Then in June 1880 Byrne shot and killed an informer named

Above and centre left Native police, superbly skilled in the art of tracking, were the opponents feared most by the Kelly gang.

Below left Ned Kelly at bay.

Above Ned Kelly and his mates were declared outlaws after they had ambushed and killed three pursuing policemen at Stringybark Creek, Victoria.

Below A bird's-eye view of Glenrowan, where the Kelly gang made their last stand. The railway-station is in foreground, and beyond is the Glenrowan Hotel with yards and outhouse. The tree marked (11) is where Ned Kelly was wounded and captured.

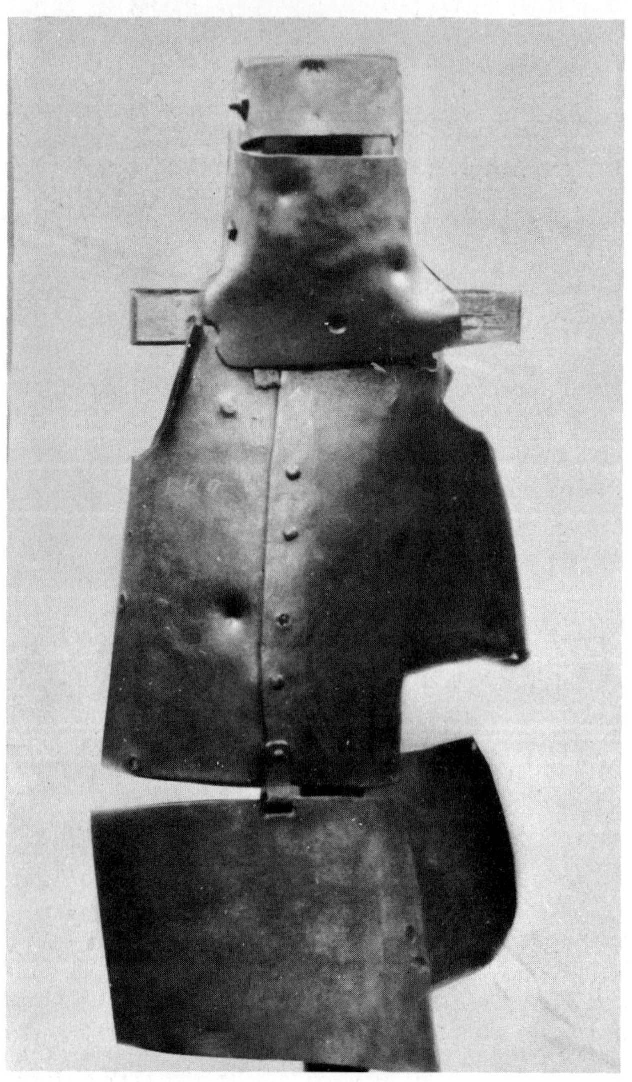

Aaron Sherritt, and next day the gang took possession of the township of Glenrowan and detained about thirty people in its only hotel. Their plan to wreck a special train bringing police by tearing up a length of railway line was frustrated by the local schoolmaster who escaped and warned the driver. Police poured out of the train and surrounded the hotel, the gang donned some crude armour they had made from ploughshares and a running battle continued throughout the night. Byrne was killed by a stray bullet; and soon after dawn Kelly emerged – armour-clad and grotesque in the swirling morning mist – to fight it out alone. The police fired at his

Left The dead body of Joe Byrne propped up for the benefit of photographers and the curiosity of spectators.

Far left Ned Kelly's armour, fashioned from ploughshares.

Below left The hanging of Ned Kelly at Pentridge jail, Melbourne, on 11 November 1880.

Right Alfred, Duke of Edinburgh, who was wounded slightly by a would-be assassin, during his visit to Sydney in 1868.

Below The Duke of Edinburgh's escort, HMSs *Galatea, Challenger* and *Charybdis,* at anchor in Farm Cove, Sydney. The picture also shows Government House, Fort Macquarie and part of Sydney Cove.

Left 'The Duke of Edinburgh's welcome by the natives'. A satirical cartoon.

Right Australia's social event of 1881 was the visit of Princes Albert and George (later King George V), as midshipmen aboard HMS *Bacchante*. Pictures show incidents during their tour of Brisbane and south Queensland.

unprotected legs and he was brought down and captured. Later that day police set alight to the hotel and the charred bodies of Hart and Dan Kelly were found in its smouldering ruins. They had apparently taken poison rather than be caught. Ned Kelly was hanged four months later but his name lives on and today Australians say that a recklessly brave man is 'as game as Ned Kelly'. Some see him as a martyr driven to crime by the persecution of corrupt police; others as a reckless hoodlum, a compulsive criminal and a cold-blooded killer. Perhaps the truth lies somewhere in between.

Not all life was on the same violent level but English newspaper readers may justifiably have thought so when they learned that on 12 March 1868 at Clontarf, Sydney, Australia's first royal visitor, Alfred, Duke of Edinburgh, the second son of Queen Victoria, had been shot in the back by an Irishman named O'Farrell. Luckily the wound was superficial (though O'Farrell was hanged for it) and the Duke's tour, which lasted seven months, was a huge success. So was the visit in 1881 as midshipmen aboard HMS *Bacchante* of Prince Albert and Prince George, the teen-age sons of England's future monarch Edward, Prince of Wales. Prince George was to return in 1901 as the Duke of York, and nine years later was to become King George V. Other visitors of note in this period included the novelists Anthony Trollope, in 1872 and again three years later, and Joseph Conrad, who made four visits between 1879 and 1893. Trollope was delighted by the country but shocked by the degree of intercolonial jealousy. Later he wrote *Australia and New Zealand* and a novel with an Australian setting called *Harry Heathcoate of Gangoil*; and Conrad recorded his impressions of Australia in *The Mirror of the Sea*.

Until the 1870s education continued to be a generally haphazard business. Most schools were run by churches, fees were charged and there was no compulsion to attend. Inevitably the rate of illiteracy was high. In 1872 Victoria brought education under state control and introduced free and compulsory primary education and the other colonies followed this lead. However, secondary schools remained under church control and only a small and privileged minority attended universities. From its opening in 1876 Adelaide University admitted women; and Melbourne and Sydney were shamed into following suit in 1879 and 1881 respectively.

By this time an indigenous literature was beginning to emerge. Henry Kendall, a lyric poet with a romantic feeling for the Australian bush, published *Poems and Songs* in 1862, and followed it with

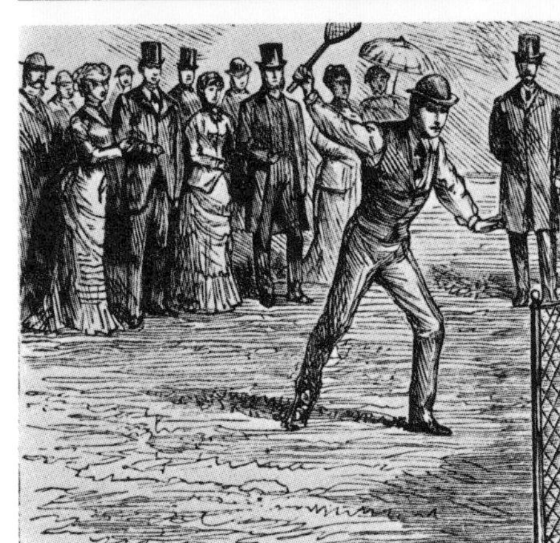

Above left Adam Lindsay Gordon, whose poems of the outback won him fame but so little financial reward that he committed suicide.

Above centre Charles Bannerman, one of the great figures of nineteenth-century Australian cricket.

Above right Fred Spofforth, Australia's 'Demon Bowler'.

Centre left The new sport of lawn tennis caught on quickly in Australia, and in the 1880s no garden party was complete without a few sets of mixed doubles.

Centre right Interior of the Prince of Wales Opera House, built in 1872 and in its time the pride of Melbourne.

Left By the 1880s cricket Tests between England and Australia were attracting great crowds. The picture shows a Test at Lord's ground, London, in July 1886. England won by an innings and 103 runs.

Leaves From Australian Forests (1869) and *Songs From the Mountains* (1880). Adam Lindsay Gordon, a migrant from England in 1853, worked for a while as a mounted trooper and then as a horse-breaker until a legacy made him independent for a time and these experiences were vividly reflected in his verse. He published *Sea Spray and Smoke Drift* (1867) and *Bush Ballads and Galloping Rhymes* (1870) but neither was financially successful and he shot himself soon afterwards at the age of thirty-six. Marcus Clarke, who also died in his thirties, is best remembered today for his powerful novel of convict days, *For the Term of His Natural Life*, which first appeared as a magazine serial and was published in book form in 1874. Thomas Alexander Browne, who wrote under the name of Rolf Boldrewood, was far more prolific. From his experience as a police magistrate on the Gulgong goldfield emerged his most famous novel, *Robbery Under Arms*, a story of bushranging based largely on fact. A weekly magazine, the *Bulletin*, founded in Sydney in 1880, gave writers a wider market than they had had before and encouraged them to develop an aggressive pro-Australian attitude.

Australian artists were also beginning to think in positive Australian terms. The influence of Conrad Martens, whose romantic landscapes had dominated Australian painting for almost fifty years, had waned before his death in 1878; and a new school had risen, inspired by Louis Buvelot, a Swiss painter, who had settled in Victoria in 1865. Tom Roberts, a brilliant young painter, became converted to impressionism during a visit to Europe, and on his return in 1884 he greatly influenced the work of such men as Arthur Streeton, Louis Abrahams, Fred McCubbin and Charles Conder. From the association of this group in various camps around Melbourne emerged what is now regarded as the first truly Australian school of painting.

In the theatre the 1880s were notable for the rise of James Cassius Williamson, an American actor, who became the country's leading impresario; and October 1887 marked the triumphant debut at Brussels of a young Australian opera singer named Helen Mitchell, who was to win fame as Nellie Melba.

Apart from horse-racing cricket was now firmly established as Australia's favourite sport. The first Australians to visit England were, oddly enough, a team of Aborigines in 1868, who combined cricket with exhibitions of boomerang-throwing. Although hardly in international class they held their own in a long programme of matches, mainly against club sides. What is now regarded as the first Test match was played at Melbourne in 1877 between John Lillywhite's English XI and a combined team from New South Wales and Victoria. To their own surprise the locals won by forty-five runs, due mainly to a superb innings by Charles Bannerman, who scored 165 and then retired hurt. Five years later at the Oval, London, an English side led by W. G. Grace was routed by Fred Spofforth, known as 'the Demon Bowler'; and a London newspaper, recording the 'death' of English cricket, added: 'The body will be cremated and the ashes taken to Australia'. In June 1876 sculling had its greatest boost when Edward Trickett, of Sydney, won the world championship from J. H. Sadler on the Thames. Sydney had its first Rugby club in 1870 but it was 1888 before a British team visited Australia; and in the early 1880s the public fancy was caught by a sport newly imported from England called lawn tennis.

11 Birth of a Nation

In a famous speech at Tenterfield, N.S.W. on 24 October 1889 Henry Parkes – who had been knighted the previous year – launched an all-out campaign for federation. Under his leadership the movement grew rapidly. General principles were discussed at a meeting of colonial leaders early in 1890 and this was followed in March 1891 by a massive convention in Sydney. After days of debate and argument committees were appointed, and by the end of the month a draft constitution had been completed which crystallized the ideal of federation into a practical and detailed scheme. Had the colonies been willing to sink their differences this could have been a decisive advance. But instead some demanded sweeping revisions and others found excuses to avoid committing themselves or to shelve the whole idea. All looked to New South Wales for a positive lead. But Parkes, on whom all seemed to depend, was now old and exhausted. His political influence was waning, he was harassed by debts and his health was failing. When he died on 27 April 1896 at the age of eighty it seemed for a while that the cause of federation had died with him. However a new champion arose in his place in the person of Edmund Barton, barrister and statesman. In a blaze of enthusiastic campaigning Barton won over many waverers and organized a second convention – this time of delegates elected by the people – which met at Adelaide on 22 March 1897. There had been so many objections to the original draft constitution that it was scrapped and a new one drawn up; and with many amendments this was eventually accepted at a third conference in January 1898. The approval of the people had yet to be obtained, so the next step was to hold referendums in the various colonies. The first, in the same year, was defeated; in a second, held in 1899, the five eastern colonies all voted in favour of federation and Western Australia abstained. Barton headed a delegation to London; various objections raised by the Colonial Office were over-

Left Australian troops riding through a Sydney street on their way to the Boer War, 1900.

Right Sir Henry Parkes, 'Father of Federation'. Portrait by Julian Ashton.

Left A bird's-eye view of Sydney in 1888, a hundred years after its foundation.

Below left Hyde Park, Sydney, in the 1890s.

Right Sir Edmund Barton, first Prime Minister of Australia.

ruled; Western Australia agreed to come in after some hard bargaining, which included a promise that a transcontinental railway would be built to link Perth with the east; and on 9 July 1900 Queen Victoria gave her assent to an Act which would, from 1 January 1901, unite the six colonies into the Commonwealth of Australia.

Although most Australians were aware of the importance of federation and the part it was bound to play in their lives they accepted its achievement quietly and with no great show of enthusiasm. Their apparent indifference was not surprising for in the previous ten years or so they had had problems enough of their own, more immediate and, as it seemed to them, more important. Until 1891 there had been barely a shadow on the economic horizon. In that year the country's sheep population exceeded 100,000,000 for the first time and seemed likely to go on rising indefinitely. There were more than 10,000,000 cattle, nearly 5,000,000 acres were under wheat, annual sugar production was approaching 100,000 tons, and gold production although declining, still exceeded 1,000,000 oz a year. These were impressive figures for a country of 3,200,000 people. Wool and other primary products were fetching satisfactory prices abroad, immigrants continued to arrive in great numbers, railway construction and other public works provided full employment and British capital flowed in freely.

But there were ominous signs. Huge areas were being denuded by reckless over-grazing and formerly fertile lands were turning into eroded wastes. Wheat-growers took all from the soil and put back little or nothing and average yields had halved in thirty years to about seven bushels an acre. Rabbits, which had crossed the Murray from Victoria in 1880, were moving north and west in multiplying swarms, unchecked by so-called 'rabbit-proof' fences, and millions of acres in the far west of New South Wales and southern Queensland were becoming barren and useless. To make matters worse there had been a country-wide drought in 1888 and since then rainfall in most colonies had continued well below normal.

Governments had borrowed large sums in London to finance public works; many pastoralists had run heavily into debt to buy their properties; city speculators, particularly in Melbourne, had sent property values soaring; merchants, manufacturers and builders were operating largely on credit; and bank and building society loans had reached record levels.

The crash came in 1893. Wool dropped to 7d lb, and there were corresponding falls in the prices of

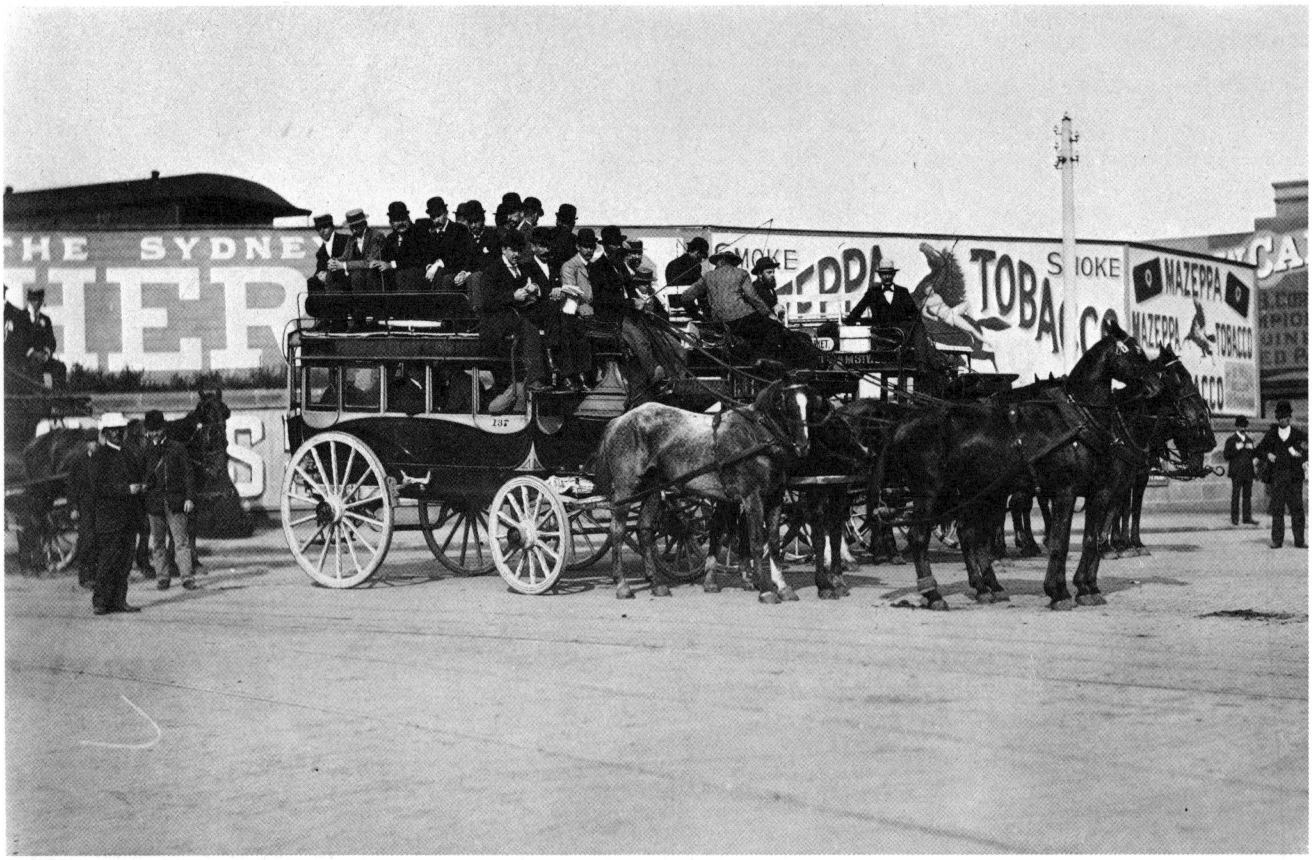
THE SYDNEY
SMOKE
SMOKE
MAZEPPA
MAZEPPA TOBACCO
137

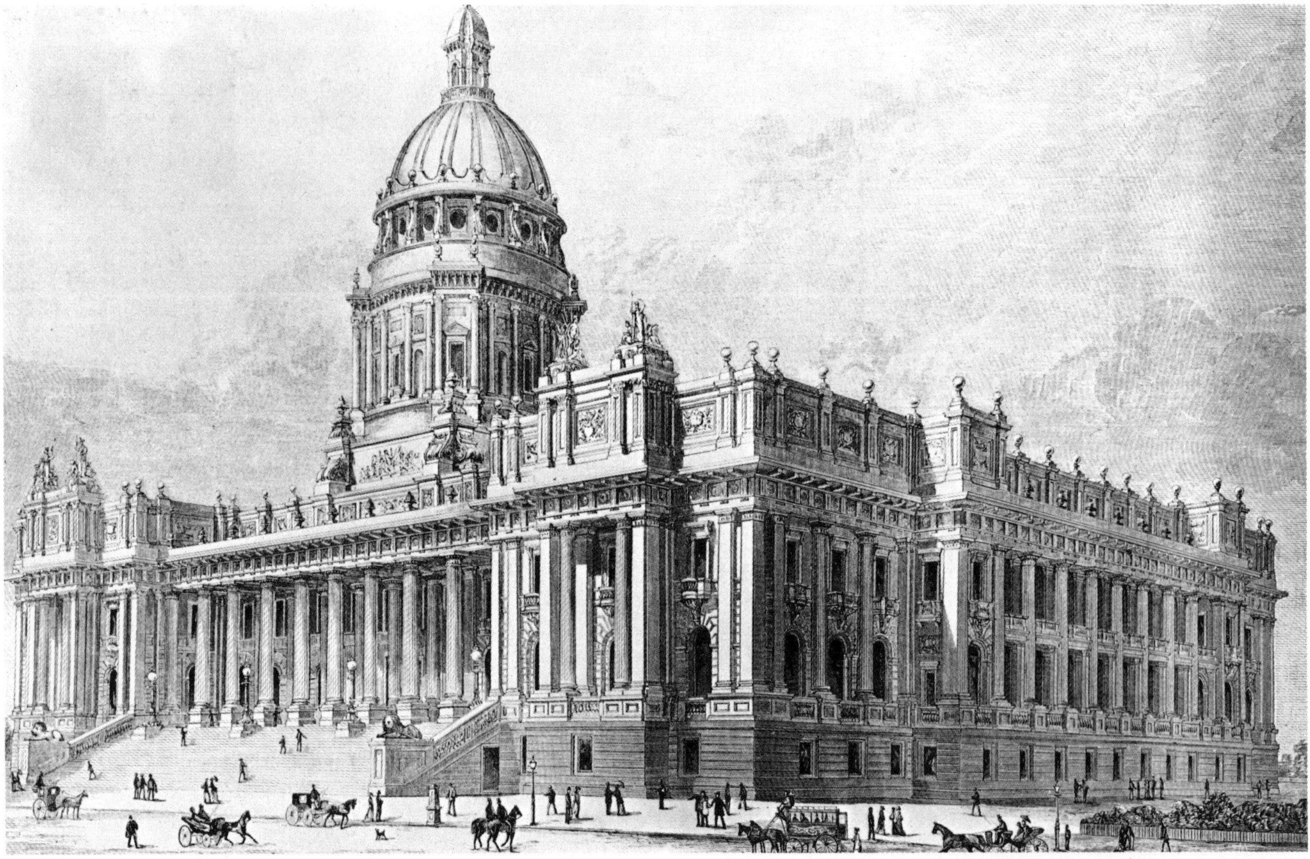

Left Horse buses outside Sydney railway station in 1892.

Below left The Houses of Parliament, Melbourne. From Federation until 1927 these were the headquarters of the Commonwealth House of Representatives and Senate.

Right The Federal Coffee Palace, Collins Street West, Melbourne, a spectacular example of late-Victorian architecture.

mutton, beef, wheat and minerals. As British investors lost confidence governments found it increasingly difficult to raise money in London. Public works had to be curtailed or abandoned and there was a sharp rise in unemployment. Many pastoralists and city speculators were unable to meet their overdrafts and went bankrupt. A run on the trading banks followed and within months twenty-three had been forced to suspend payment or had failed. Unemployment and general distress were particularly severe in Victoria and many thousands migrated to other colonies.

One colony which barely felt the effects of the depression was Western Australia. Here the struggles and hardships of the first fifty years were now all but over. Local railway lines and sensible land laws had opened up large areas to small farmers; cattlemen were moving in to the newly-found pastures of the north-west; by 1890 the population had reached 46,000; and in the same year the colony at long last won self-government with the explorer John Forrest as first Premier. The gold finds of the 1880s, although limited, had promised more exciting things to come; and in 1892 that promise was dramatically realized. In September two prospectors found rich gold in dry, barren

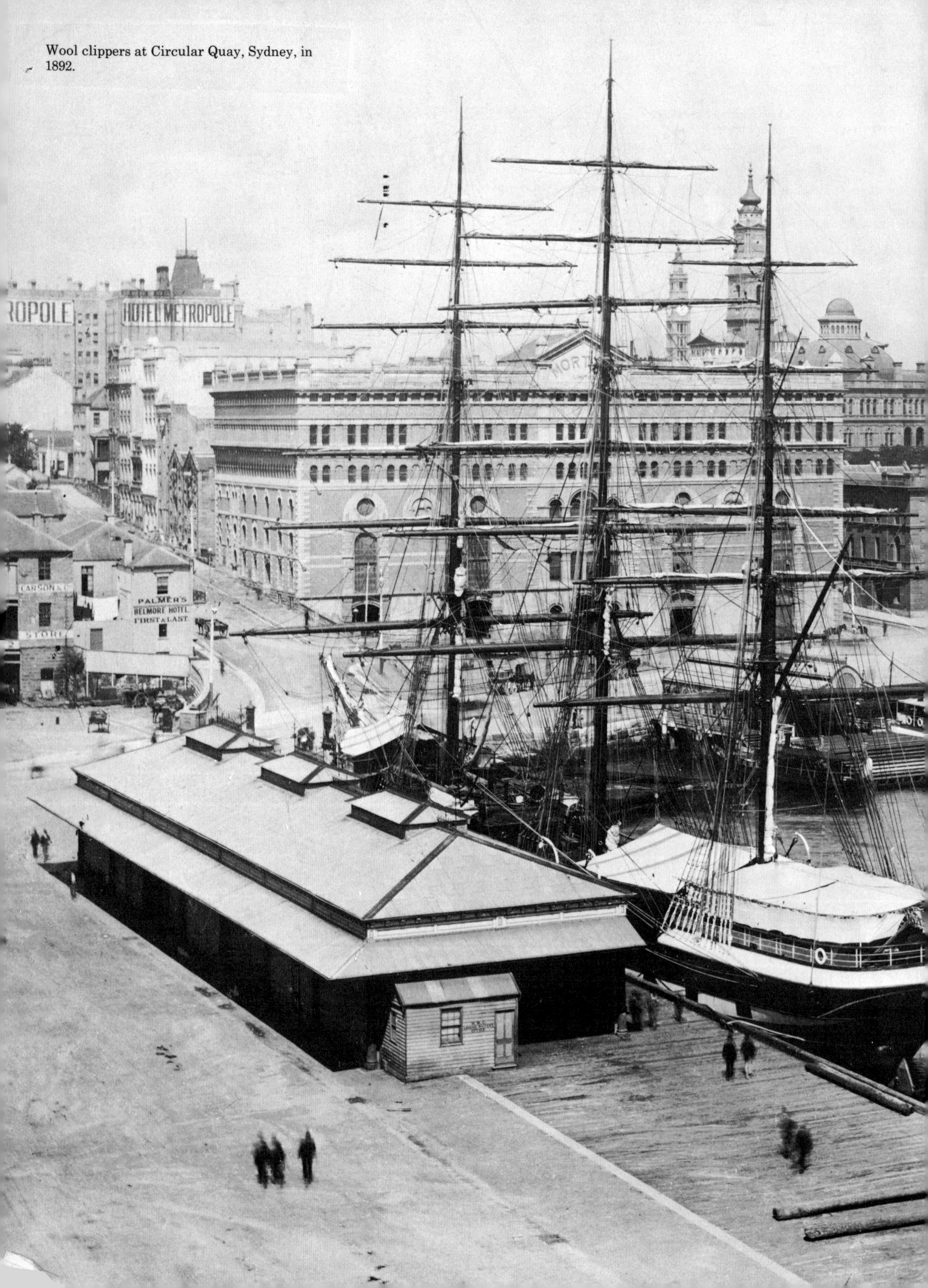

Wool clippers at Circular Quay, Sydney, in 1892.

country about 350 miles east of Perth at what is now Coolgardie. By the following June there were 2,000 miners on the field and new finds were being made almost every week. One reef yielded 5,000 oz in a few days; another was so rich that it was sold for £147,000. Then the most sensational find of all was made a few miles to the east at a place first called Hannan's, after its discoverer Paddy Hannan, and now famous as Kalgoorlie. In this Golden Mile, as it became known, were to be sunk some of the largest and most productive gold-mines in the world. Despite the handicaps of remoteness, a harsh and hot climate and lack of water prospectors swarmed in from the eastern colonies and gold production soon topped 1,000,000 oz a year. There was no lack of English money to finance the deep-sinking that was necessary; a single-track railway from Perth was hurriedly built to carry water to the parched fields; and when this proved inadequate the government borrowed £2,500,000 to build a pipeline from near

Left A striking portrait of a gold-miner on the Western Australian fields. Both subject and artist are unknown.

Centre left 'Bringing down the wool from a station on the Murray River, Victoria'. Oil-painting by Edward Roper.

Below left By the 1890s steamers had completely superseded sail as passenger ships. This is the *Ophir,* 6,814 tons, pride of the Orient Line, now amalgamated with P & O.

Right A miner's hut, Lithgow Valley, N.S.W.

Centre below The atmosphere of a shearing shed is brilliantly conveyed in this picture, *'Shearing the Rams',* by Tom Roberts.

Below 'Across the black soil plains, N.S.W.' By George W. Lambert.

Above Bayley Street, Coolgardie, W.A., in 1895 when the gold rush was at its height.

Below Printing and publishing offices of the *Western Argus* at Hannan's, now Kalgoorlie, W.A.

Above right Coach outside a hotel. A typical country-town scene by an unknown artist.

Below right Sir John Forrest, explorer and Premier of W.A., who was responsible for the water pipeline to the goldfields.

Perth, designed to provide 10,000,000 gallons a day. By 1900 Western Australia's population had trebled to 138,000. The Cinderella had become a golden princess.

Meanwhile economic conditions in the east were creating another problem. Industrial unrest, which had simmered through the 1880s, reached boiling point in August 1890 when maritime workers went on strike on the basic issue of whether or not employers were entitled to engage non-union labour. Transport workers, miners and shearers were soon involved, large sectors of industry were brought to a standstill and there were bitter and sometimes bloody struggles when the various governments called in troops and special police to protect strike-breakers, who became known contemptuously as 'scabs'. In the end victory went to the employers but the fight was by no means over. A shearers' strike in Queensland in 1891, in which the issue was essentially the same, was even more bitterly fought. Striking shearers established camps near the various sheds where free labour was being used; again troops and police were called in; sheep were killed and sheds were fired; there were mass riots that stopped just short of civil war; and many strike leaders were arrested and jailed. In 1892 there was trouble and some violence at Broken Hill when

Above Departure of a mail-coach from the gold-mining town of Cue, W.A., on the first leg of its 528 miles' journey to Perth.

Below Bush travellers take time off for a glass of beer.

Above right Settlers outside a timber and bark hut.

Below right A cattle abattoir in the Australian bush. Artist unknown.

miners were locked out for rejecting a variation of a wages agreement; and in 1894 there was a second shearers' strike in Queensland. From all of these the unions emerged on the losing side. Many were now practically bankrupt and on the verge of disintegration and for the time being at least there could be no further thought of direct action.

However, the cause was by no means lost, for in the meantime Labour had emerged as an organized political party. Labour candidates made their first appearance in New South Wales at the general election of 1891, and to the surprise of everyone, including themselves, they won no less than thirty-six seats and actually held the balance of power. Union-sponsored candidates won ten seats in Victoria in 1892, eight in South Australia in 1893 and sixteen in Queensland in the same year.

By the late 1890s the worst of the depression was over. Australian wheat was selling well abroad and rust-free varieties evolved by a brilliant scientist, William James Farrer, had greatly improved quality and yield. Pastoralists were introducing more economic methods to offset the low price of wool. At Mildura and Renmark on the Murray River two American brothers, George and William Chaffey, were demonstrating how intensive farming could be developed in low rainfall areas by modern methods of irrigation. In Queensland the introduction of centralized, steam-operated mills had reduced sugar production costs and output was still rising. The days of the famous wool and wheat clippers were now virtually over and fast cargo steamers and keen competition had substantially reduced freight charges to the benefit of producers.

As confidence returned English capital began to flow in again and governments were able to resume their public works programmes. In New South Wales, Victoria and Queensland alone 1,700 miles of new railways were built during the last few years of the century. In the main cities tramway systems

Left and above Two aspects of sporting life in Queensland in the 1890s by S. A. Lindsey. Kangaroo-sticking, a local adaptation of the popular Indian Army sport; and the finish of a race at a bush meeting.

Right The illustrator of an English book has managed to cram into one drawing many of Australia's best-known fauna – dingos, kangaroos, a lyre bird, an emu, a black swan and a platypus.

Above A steam-launch in Queen Street, Brisbane, during the floods of 1893.

Left The rescue of the Vernor family at Ferndale, in the Brisbane valley. An incident of the disastrous floods in south Queensland in 1893.

Below Lawrence Hargrave.

Right Over the long, dry coach-routes of the outback camels were sometimes used in place of horses. Their stamina compensated for their slowness.

Below right Henry Lawson. Portrait by John Longstaff.

were greatly extended and work began on electrifying steam and cable lines. Australia's first motor vehicle, a three-wheeler with a Daimler petrol engine, was built by Charles Highland, of Sydney, in 1894 but it tended to burst into flames after going a few yards. In the next few years, however, more successful models were built or imported and by 1900 it was apparent that a new form of transport had come to stay. As yet only a few visionaries – generally regarded as 'cranks' – had begun to think in terms of powered air transport. Foremost among them was Lawrence Hargrave, of Sydney, whose discovery in 1889 of the principle of the rotary engine was followed through the 1890s by extensive experiments with box-kites, which were greatly to affect early aircraft design.

The depression and industrial disturbances of the nineties emphasized to Australians that for good or ill they were citizens of one country rather than a number of separate and independent colonies and

Above *'Bailed Up'*, by Tom Roberts, perhaps the most famous of all Australian genre paintings.

Below An unusual volunteer is given a drink on his way to the Boer War.

Right Bushmen of the Australian outback receive a rousing welcome in Sydney on their way to the Boer War.

that what affected one affected all. Politically this did much to help the cause of federation. On another level it greatly heightened national awareness and pride, so that people began to think of themselves as Australians rather than transplanted colonials whose first allegiance was to Britain. Inevitably this attitude found its most lucid expression among writers of the period, of whom the most notable were Henry Lawson, A. B. ('Banjo') Paterson and Victor Daley. Lawson was a convinced socialist, a champion of the under-dog and a passionate believer in the ideal of 'mateship'. He wrote simply with pathos and humour in terms that appealed to the man in the street and his *In the Days when the World was Wide* (a book of verse) and *While the Billy Boils* (short stories), both published in 1896, did much to mould public opinion. Paterson and Daley shared Lawson's love of Australia and her people but lacked his acute social awareness. Paterson's most successful early poems, published in 1895 as *The Man from Snowy River and Other Verses*, were brisk, swinging ballads, vibrant with the life and atmosphere of the outback. In the same year he wrote what has been called Australia's unofficial national anthem, 'Waltzing Matilda'. Daley, who had migrated from Ireland as a young man, saw the Australian bush through a lyrical glow of Celtic

GOD SPEED to OUR BUSHMEN
FRED LEIST.
SYDNEY.

Above left Volunteers for the Boer War leaving Sydney in the troopship *Warrigal*.

Left Australian 15-pounders in action at the battle of Hartebeestfontein.

Above Australian troops watching a Boer outpost.

Right An Australian outpost on duty near Klerksdorp.

romance and mystery and this was reflected in the collection of his poems, *Dawn and Dusk*, which was published in 1898. Next to Lawson the best-known short-story writer of this time was Arthur Hoey Davis, who wrote as 'Steele Rudd'; and his humorous sketches of the tribulations of a small-farming family, first published in book form in 1899 as *On Our Selection*, were immensely popular.

Sections of the press, notably the *Bulletin*, so encouraged this new spirit of Australian patriotism that some writers began to advocate not only federation but complete secession from the Empire. Except among extremists they received little support. On a practical level Australia depended on Britain almost entirely for her markets, and more important, for her defence. In addition, of course, the population was overwhelmingly British in origin and sentimental attachment to the mother country was strong.

The strength of this attachment was positively demonstrated during 1899, when it became clear that war was imminent between Britain and the Boer Republics of South Africa. As far back as 1885 New South Wales had, in fact, sent a contingent of 750 volunteers to the Sudan but by the time they had arrived most of the fighting was over. On this occasion the situation was more serious and the response much wider. In July 1899 Queensland led the way with an offer to send a force of 250 mounted infantry to Britain's aid; and in September the military commandants of the various colonies agreed to despatch a joint contingent of 2,500. When hostilities actually began in October there was enthusiastic volunteering all over the country and in the first eighteen months more than 6,500 Australians sailed for South Africa. In the field they operated mainly as small, independent units scattered over a wide front and soon earned a reputation as outstanding fighting men. Perhaps their most notable single exploit was at Brakfontein, on the Elands River, western Transvaal, in August 1900 when 500 Australians held out against an overwhelmingly superior force of 3,000 Boers for eleven days before they were relieved. Conan Doyle, then a war correspondent, described this action as 'one of the finest deeds of arms of the war'. As the conflict dragged on additional contingents left Australia, including a unit of mounted Imperial Bushmen, who proved themselves superb horsemen and crack assault troops. When peace came at the end of May 1902 the country had sent a total of 16,175 and casualties amounted to 1,400, of whom 518 were killed or died of illness. Six Australians had been awarded the Victoria Cross and a great fighting tradition had been born.

Above Australian artillery crossing the Vaal Rover near Hoopstad, Orange Free State.

Left Centrepiece of Sydney's celebration of the relief of Mafeking in May 1900 was the illumination of the General Post Office.

Above right With sails for extra speed the Orient liner *Orient* was one of the fastest ships on the England-Australia run at the turn of the century. During the Boer War she served as a transport.

Right Clem Hill, the boy prodigy of Australian cricket in the 1890s.

As Australian soldiers were gaining a reputation abroad so were Australian sportsmen and athletes. Reciprocal visits between English and Australian cricket teams had now become regular and Test match rivalry was keen. Between 1890 and 1900 Australia won ten Tests to England's eight and many Australian cricketers achieved international fame, among them Clem Hill, who had been a schoolboy prodigy, Joe Darling, Victor Trumper and M. A. Noble, still regarded by some as the best all-rounder ever. Australian Rules football had taken a firm hold in the southern colonies and in the west; and although a British Rugby team visited Australia in 1899, winning three of four Tests, it was not until nine years later that the first Australian side visited Britain. At the first revived Olympic Games, held in Athens in 1896, E. H. Flack boosted Australian athletics when he won the 800 and 1500 metres events. In the following year Percy Cavill became Australia's first world champion swimmer by winning several races in England; and at the second Olympics in Paris in 1900 another swimmer, F. C. V. Lane, won the 200 metres. Australia's best-known boxer of this period was 'Young Griffo' (Albert Griffiths), a product of the famous Larry Foley school, who went to the United States in 1893, where after a series of victories among the world's leading lightweights he narrowly missed winning the world title.

As a sign of their increasing emancipation perhaps, women were now taking an active part in some sports. The first women's cricket match between New South Wales and Victoria was played in 1891. In 1894 – the year in which women gained the vote in South Australia – Mrs C. B. Mackenzie, of Victoria, won the first women's Australian golf championship; and in 1899 a Mrs MacDonald became almost a national heroine when she cycled from Sydney to Melbourne in a few hours over a week, no mean feat even for a man on the roads of that time.

12 Infancy

The Commonwealth of Australia was proclaimed and the first Governor-General, the Earl of Hopetoun, was sworn in at a ceremony in Centennial Park, Sydney, on 1 January 1901. About 60,000 people were present, including a mass choir of 15,000. On 9 May before a huge gathering in the Exhibition Hall, Melbourne, the Duke of York (later King George V) officially opened the first parliament. The future Queen Mary was with him on the platform and, dispensing with a choir, Nellie Stewart, Australia's leading musical comedy star, sang solo a specially-composed memorial ode.

The first Prime Minister was Edmund Barton but only after a bitter contest with Sir William John Lyne. Lyne had to be content with the Ministry of Home Affairs. Alfred Deakin, of Victoria, was Attorney-General and Sir John Forrest, of Western Australia, was Minister for Defence. It had been decided that a Federal capital would ultimately be built somewhere in New South Wales but argument was still going on as to its actual site. In the meantime parliament met and the first Commonwealth offices were established in Melbourne, which became the *de facto* capital of Australia.

Common tariffs were introduced, a common foreign policy was enunciated and a High Court was established. Defence and postal and telegraph services were united under federal control and immigration laws were unified. The main effect of these was to exclude coloured immigrants and they were the basis of what became known, and is still often criticized, as the White Australia policy. The various states were reluctant to give up more rights than they had to and each continued to administer, among other things, its own public health, education, transport, police and judicial systems.

Although most Australians thought federation a good idea it did not greatly affect their daily lives; and they were much more concerned, for instance, with the effects of a nation-wide drought which by 1902 had halved the country's sheep population to 53,000,000 and had reduced its cattle to 8,000,000. Even so, the economy was thriving. Wheat sold profitably abroad and the annual harvest had now risen to about 48,000,000 bushels, due largely to the perfection by Farrer of a strain called Federation which was prolific, drought-resistant and immune to most diseases. The gold yield was nearly 4,000,000 oz a year; coal production stood at about 5,000,000 tons; sugar at 110,000 tons; and wine – a growing industry – at well over 5,000,000 gallons, of which half came from South Australia. Refrigeration had greatly increased the export of butter, fruit and frozen meat; and overall exports exceeded imports

Left The birth of a national capital. The Minister for Home Affairs, King O'Malley, drives in the first peg at Canberra, 1913.

Right Lord Hopetoun coming ashore in Sydney on 1 January 1901 to proclaim the Commonwealth.

Far left Lord Hopetoun, Australia's first Governor-General.

Left Alfred Deakin, Australia's second Prime Minister, who succeeded Sir Edmund Barton in September 1903.

Below Drovers resting on the tracks. Wool was still Australia's biggest industry in the 1900s.

Right The Duke of York (later King George V) opening the first Federal Parliament. Painting by Tom Roberts.

Below right As Parliament House could not accommodate all the official visitors the Duke of York officially opened Australia's first Federal Parliament in the Exhibition Building, Melbourne, in May 1901.

by about £8,000,000 a year. There were 13,500 miles of railways, 45,000 miles of telegraphs, and the annual shipping turnabout was 27,000,000 tons, of which ninety per cent was British.

Having launched federation Barton felt he had done his bit and in 1903 he retired from politics to the peace and quiet of the High Court. He was succeeded by Deakin, a man of brilliant intellect and considerable political flair. For four months during 1904 there was a Labour government led by J. C. Watson but except for this and another small break Deakin remained in power until April 1910.

Watson's short term in office was notable for his vigorous fight to do away with cheap Kanaka labour on the Queensland sugar fields, even, he insisted, if it meant 'the absolute annihilation of the industry'. A Pacific Island Labourers' Bill was passed in 1904, sugar producers were compensated by a government bounty, and by 1907 the last islander had been sent home.

During these years most social legislation was enacted by the various states. Many laws were passed regulating working hours and conditions; employers became liable for accidents to their workmen; and compulsory arbitration was introduced to deal with industrial disputes. A Federal Arbitration Court was

formed to handle disputes which affected more than one state, and on the whole this functioned much more effectively than the state tribunals, although strikes and lockouts continued to be frequent. In 1907 Mr Justice Higgins, of this court, made an historic ruling that every man was entitled to a wage sufficient to satisfy his normal needs 'as a human being living in a civilized community'; and this principle of a basic wage, which is still almost unique to Australia, has been jealously guarded since. In 1908 the Federal Government assumed more social responsibility when it introduced old age and invalid pensions of 10/– a week.

By and large Edwardian Australia was a pleasant place to live in. Drought, low wool prices, high wages and heavy debts had forced some pastoralists to surrender their leases but most were able to hang on and with better seasons their flocks and wool cheques were soon increasing again. Life continued to be a struggle for the undercapitalized 'cockies' on their inadequate selections; but other primary producers were doing well and their prosperity affected the cities and towns. Wages were good, there was full employment and the people had more leisure than ever before. Paradoxically, now that Australia was officially a nation much of the aggressive

Above left Wool teams on the road in western N.S.W., 1909.

Below left Wool sorters and classers at work in a shed in western N.S.W., 1909.

Above The start of an early car reliability trial at Artillery Hill, National Park, N.S.W.

Below Silver mines at Broken Hill when production was near its peak in 1909.

Australianism of the 1890s had disappeared and England was regarded more affectionately than ever as 'the mother country' and 'home'. With new, fast passenger steamers of 12,000 tons and upwards the two countries were now within five or six weeks of each other; and the completion in 1902 of a Pacific cable, providing an extra link with Britain by way of Canada, helped further to reduce the old sense of isolation. Britain bought most of Australia's primary produce and supplied most of her manufactured goods. British investors looked increasingly to Australia and British capital continued to flow in. Although Australia was now creating her own little navy – the first ships were, in fact, put into commission in 1910 – it was a comfort to know that in time of trouble she still had Britain's naval might behind her. Australia's foreign policy almost automatically followed Britain's.

In Australia itself interstate rivalry was still strong but not nearly as bitter as it had been. The linking of the various capitals by rail had done a lot to break down this parochialism and now better roads and motorised traffic were breaking it down still further. Cars continued to be expensive and unreliable, and any journey over twenty miles was an adventure but public enthusiasm for this new form of transport – particularly in a country of such vast distances – was keen. Motoring associations were formed in Sydney, Melbourne and Adelaide in 1903; and two years later the first Sydney-Melbourne reliability trial was held.

The most popular Australian writers were still Lawson and Paterson but the fire had gone out of Lawson's work and Paterson, who had been a war correspondent in South Africa, was giving most of his time to journalism. In 1903 Joseph Furphy, writing as 'Tom Collins', produced a picaresque novel of the outback called *Such is Life* but it took a later generation to appreciate its qualities. Although Streeton and Roberts were still painting their influence among other artists was wider than among the general public. The theatre was booming. In 1902 *Sweet Nell of Old Drury*, starring Nellie Stewart, became the stage success of all time; and in the same year Nellie Melba, after years of operatic triumph in Europe, began a fabulously successful concert tour of Australia. In 1905 the Tait brothers produced what is claimed to have been the first feature-length film, *The Kelly Gang*. As a general rule, however, Australians were happy to import their culture from England.

Public interest in sport had now become almost obsessive. Every shop, office and factory – almost every household – had its Melbourne Cup sweep and

Left Surf-bathing on Sydney's numerous and now world-famed beaches had become all the rage by the mid-1900s.

Above A portent of things to come. Ships of the United States Navy at anchor in Sydney Harbour in 1907.

Right Australia's great batsman, Victor Trumper, in a typically aggressive attitude.

all work ceased while the race was being run. In the first decade of the century six cricket Test series were played between England and Australia, three in each country, with the tally fourteen matches to nine in Australia's favour and seven drawn. Clem Hill was still scoring centuries but Victor Trumper was the great Australian hero, and newcomers of promise included C. G. Macartney and Warren Bardsley. The first Australian tennis championships were held in 1905 and the men's singles winner was R. W. Heath of Victoria. In the same year Australia and New Zealand combined as Australasia to challenge for the Davis Cup. Their team, headed by Norman Brookes (Australia) and Anthony Wilding (New Zealand), was beaten in the second round; but the same pair won the cup from Britain in 1907, in which year Brookes also won the Wimbledon singles and successfully defended it in the next three years. It was a vintage decade for Australian swimmers. Richard Cavill introduced the 'crawl' stroke which he had learned from a young Hawaiian and broke many world records at home and in England. In 1904 he was overshadowed by Barney Kieran, who won all the Australian titles from 220 yards to a mile, set a new series of records and died a year later, aged nineteen. Kieran's successor was Frank Beaurepaire, who went to England in 1910 and was unbeaten in forty-eight races from 100 yards to three miles against the world's best swimmers. The most famous woman swimmer of the period was Annette Kellerman, a victim of infantile paralysis, who took up the sport to strengthen her legs. In 1904 she swam seventeen miles in the Thames but twice failed to swim the English Channel. Later she went to the United States, where she popularized the one-piece swim-suit and became a film star.

Australia's pre-eminence in swimming was no accident, for by now most Australians who lived within distance of a beach spent their summer week-ends on it and surfing had become the great popular pastime. This was partly due to the pioneering spirit of W. H. Gocher, a newspaper editor. Until 1902 surf-bathing in daylight hours was illegal. Gocher announced in his paper that he intended to defy the law by bathing at Manly beach at noon. He did so and as no prosecution followed he continued to do so. Scores of thousands followed his lead. For a while beaches were roped off to segregate the sexes but it was found impossible to keep them apart in the water and the ropes soon disappeared.

Alfred Deakin's long period as Prime Minister, during which he had virtually established a pattern for Australia's future development, came to an end in 1910 when a Labour government was returned with Andrew Fisher at its head and William Morris

Left One of Australia's greatest boxers, middleweight Les Darcy, who died tragically on an American tour.

Right Lord Kitchener, summoned to Australia in 1910 to advise on her defences, inspects a guard of honour of boy scouts.

Below The first of a long line of great Australian tennis-players. Pat O'Hara Wood and Norman Brookes (*right*) in a Davis Cup doubles match, in which they beat Tilden and Johnston, of the United States, in straight sets.

THIS STONE WAS LAID BY
THE RIGHT HONOURABLE ANDREW FISHER, P.C. M.P.
PRIME MINISTER OF THE COMMONWEALTH OF AUSTRALIA
ON THE 12TH MARCH 1913.

Hughes as Attorney-General. A site of 910 square miles, about 150 miles south-west of Sydney, had been chosen for a Federal capital. Competitive designs were invited and the winner was Walter Burley Griffin, an American who had been an associate of the famous Frank Lloyd Wright. Much controversy followed over a suitable name for the place. For reasons no longer clear somebody wanted to call it Shakespeare, and somebody else suggested Cookville. Eventually its native name of Canberra, which is interpreted as 'a meeting-place', was chosen. Many of Australia's most able politicians had been lured to the federal sphere and as a result state politics had sunk to a fairly low ebb, particularly in New South Wales. This was the era of the 'wild men of Sydney' such as John Norton, proprietor of the newspaper *Truth*, and 'Paddy' Crick, a noted criminal lawyer, who seemed to alternate their time between exposing unedifying political scandals and being involved in them.

A census of 1911 revealed that Australia's population had reached 4,455,005, an increase of more than a million and a quarter in ten years. Sydney and Melbourne had both passed the half-million mark and an estimated thirty-five per cent of the people lived in the six capitals. Primary productions levels were still rising and export prices were good. The number of factory workers in Victoria and New South Wales had almost doubled since federation. In 1911 the Commonwealth Bank was founded; Australia's first big hydro-electric project was established at Mount Lyell, Tasmania; and BHP (Broken Hill Proprietary) began to build extensive iron and steel works close to coal sources at Newcastle and Port Kembla. In the same year aviation progressed beyond the novelty stage when W. E. Hart, a Sydney dentist, made several successful flights in a Bristol biplane and became the country's first licensed pilot. A year later Harry Hawker, an Australian employed by the Sopwith Company in England, achieved world fame and a £500 prize with a flight duration record of almost eight and a half hours. Brisbane University was opened in 1911 and the University of Western Australia, the only free university in the country, in 1912. The popular heroine of 1912 was Fanny Durack, who won the 100 metres freestyle swimming event at the Stockholm Olympics in world record time.

Beneath this surface of well-being, however, lurked the growing threat of Germany's navy and her increasingly aggressive foreign policy. In 1910 Lord Kitchener had visited Australia to report on her hopelessly inadequate military defences and on his advice compulsory military training had been introduced the following year. In 1913 a naval college was established at Jervis Bay and the Federal government acquired Cockatoo Dock, Sydney, to build naval vessels. When Great Britain declared war on Germany on 4 August 1914 there was never any doubt which way Australia would go. As a dominion she was automatically and legally committed; but in any case Australian sentiment was overwhelmingly pro-British, and Andrew Fisher spoke for the whole country when he promised to support her 'to our last man and our last shilling'.

Australia's first acts of war were to destroy German wireless stations at Rabaul, Yap and New Guinea, and to occupy German New Guinea and

Above left Lady Denman, wife of the Governor-General, names Canberra. Others on the platform are Lord Denman, Andrew Fisher (Prime Minister) and King O'Malley. The place, Capital Hill; the date, 12 March 1913.

Left What Canberra may have looked like had the designs submitted by R.C.G. Coulter been accepted.

Right Volunteers for the First World War reach Sydney after a long journey in from the bush.

Right Artist George Lambert's impression of the landing at Anzac Cove, Gallipoli, on 25 April 1915.

Below Australia's first act of war. A naval brigade lands at Kabakaul, New Britain, to seize a German wireless station. Painting by C. Bryant.

Below right In Australia's first naval battle of the war HMAS *Sydney* beaches and destroys the German raider *Emden* after a running fight off Cocos Island. Painting by A. Burgess.

Left The front-line trench at Lone Pine soon after its capture. The enemy were only a few yards away, within grenade-range.

Above The Australian attack on Achi Baba, with Turkish prisoners being brought in. The artist was R. Caton Woodville.

nearby islands including New Britain, New Ireland and Bougainville. Resistance was weak and casualties were few. Meanwhile Brigadier-General W. T. Bridges had begun organizing a volunteer army for overseas service, to be known as the Australian Imperial Force and now famous in history simply as the AIF. The response exceeded all his hopes and in three months a complete first division of 20,000 men had been enlisted and partly trained and was ready to embark. It was joined by two brigades from New Zealand, and on 1 November the combined contingent sailed from Albany, W.A., in thirty-eight transports, escorted by the Australian light cruisers *Sydney* and *Melbourne* and a British and a Japanese cruiser. Its destination was England, via Suez. Nine days later a wireless station at Cocos Island, in the Indian Ocean, signalled that it was being attacked by a German cruiser, *Emden*. HMAS *Sydney* left the convoy and in a classic running battle disabled the enemy ship and ran her aground. Owing to a change of plan the troops were disembarked at Alexandria to complete their war-training in Egypt. Here they were joined by a second mixed contingent and united as the Australian and New Zealand Army Corps (ANZAC), with General W. R. Birdwood in overall command.

As a part of Allied strategy it was decided, early in 1915, to attack Turkey through the Dardanelles and so provide a safe sea-link with Russia. The First Lord of the Admiralty, Winston Churchill, was sure the British navy could force a way through the narrow passage but the attempt was defeated with heavy loss. The operation then became a military one against a forewarned and powerful enemy. On 25 April 1915 Anzac, British and French troops stormed ashore on the peninsula of Gallipoli against fierce opposition from five Turkish divisions. After a day of chaotic, heroic and bloody fighting the Anzacs had established a precarious foothold at what became known as Anzac Cove and during the

Above Sausage Valley, Gallipoli. During the eight months' campaign the Anzac troops were never out of range of the Turkish artillery. Painting by F. R. Crozier.

Below From Gallipoli to France. The morale of these Australians was high on their arrival in Flanders in 1916.

Above right A portrait by Augustus John of Australia's fiery wartime Prime Minister, W. M. ('Billy') Hughes.

Below right Australians resting before their attack on Mont St Quentin, described by one historian as 'one of the most brilliant feats of the war'.

next two days they held on grimly against continuous and savage counter-attacks. Then both sides paused to lick their wounds and the Anzacs dug in. During the next few months weeks of stalemate were interspersed with days of bitter fighting, with appalling casualties on both sides. From the start it was apparent that the campaign must fail – indeed, many thought it should never have been launched – and in December evacuation of the peninsula was ordered. This was carried out with such skill that the enemy was completely deceived and by 8 January the last Allied troops had left Turkish soil. In this futile holocaust of eight months Australian casualties had totalled 8,587 dead and 19,367 wounded; but from defeat the Anzacs had emerged as probably the best assault troops in history. One thing they never lost was their sardonic sense of humour and as they returned to Egypt, battle-shocked and weary they sang:

'We are the ragtime army,
  The A.N.Z.A.C.
We cannot shoot, we won't salute;
  What bloody use are we?'

Massive reinforcements arrived to fill their decimated ranks. By April four divisions were in France and two mounted divisions, including the

famous Camel Corps, remained to protect the Suez canal and challenge the Turks in Sinai and Palestine. An Australian Flying Corps had been formed and had already seen action in Mesopotamia.

In Australia W. M. Hughes had succeeded Fisher as Prime Minister. Primary production was soaring to new record levels to meet demands at home and abroad and the cessation of British and other imports was opening new fields for secondary industry. There were local war loans and savings campaigns and the first Federal income tax was imposed. Although more than 200,000 volunteers, drawn from a population of less than five million, were already overseas Hughes believed that only conscription would maintain the enlistment rate. His proposal was rejected in a referendum in October 1916 and the issue split the Labour Party asunder. In January 1917 Hughes and his followers formed a coalition Labour-Liberal government from which emerged the Nationalist Party, with Hughes still Prime Minister.

Meanwhile in France the Anzacs had been heavily involved in the first battle of the Somme. One of their great achievements was to take and hold the key village of Pozières after days of continuous assault in which casualties were astronomical. During the spring offensive of 1917 they were prominent in many battles around Bapaume, Bullecourt, Messines, Ypres and Passchendaele, again with heavy losses. In the east the Turks had been driven out of Sinai by early 1917 and late in the same year a full-scale invasion of Palestine was launched. A magnificent charge by Anzac light horsemen, under General Sir Harry Chauvel, broke the Turkish resistance at Beersheba. As a result Gaza was outflanked and taken, and in December the British commander, General Allenby, occupied Jerusalem without resistance.

At home the newspapers carried long daily lists of casualties and there was a growing sense of war-weariness and disillusionment. As taxes and prices

Left The 12th Battalion, A.I.F., on its way to the Somme.

Below left Artist Fred Leist's impression of the storming of Mont St Quentin.

Right A portrait by George Lambert of a sergeant of the Australian Light Horse in Palestine.

Below After the battle. Australian wounded on the Menin Road.

Above left Australian members of the Camel Corps at Magdhaba. Painting by H. S. Power.

Centre left Australian shock troops reducing a pillbox near Polygon Wood. Painting by Fred Leist.

Below left Australians, with tank support, breaching the Hindenburg Line. By Will Longstaff.

Above Impression by artist H. S. Power of Australians saving the guns at Robecq during the Palestine campaign.

Below A brilliant outflanking movement led to the capture of Damascus and the virtual end of the war in the eastern zone. Artist H. S. Power shows Australian Light Horsemen in the last dash on Damascus.

Right Surrounded and outfought, thousands of Turks surrendered in the last days of the war. Picture shows Australian Light Horse and long lines of prisoners near Negiddo on 22 September 1918.

Below Australian Light Horsemen receive aerial support during their advance in Palestine. Painting by H. S. Power.

rose the real value of wages declined. Industrial unrest became intense. There had already been a major strike in the coal industry, instigated by the Industrial Workers of the World (IWW, or 'Wobblies'). In New South Wales in 1917 a dispute among waterside workers spread to become a general strike of railwaymen. By the time the strike had been broken more than 4,500,000 working days had been lost and the effect on the economy had been disastrous. A second conscription referendum, held in December, was defeated even more decisively than the first.

In France during the great German spring offensive of 1918 Anzac troops figured prominently at Villers Bretonneux and elsewhere; and when the Allies launched their massive counter-offensive in August they distinguished themselves equally at Mont St Quentin. In Palestine in September a spectacular outflanking ride by Chauvel's Anzacs led to the capture of Nazareth, the near-encirclement of the hard-pressed Turkish and German forces and the fall of Damascus. By now the enemy resistance was crumbling on both fronts. The Turks surrendered unconditionally on 30 October and twelve days later an armistice was signed in France. The war was over, and all that remained now was to count its cost. Among 330,000 Australian troops sent overseas casualties totalled 226,000, of whom almost 60,000 were killed or missing. Australia's percentage of casualties was 68·5, New Zealand's 58, Britain's 52·5 and Canada's 51. The cost had been great indeed.

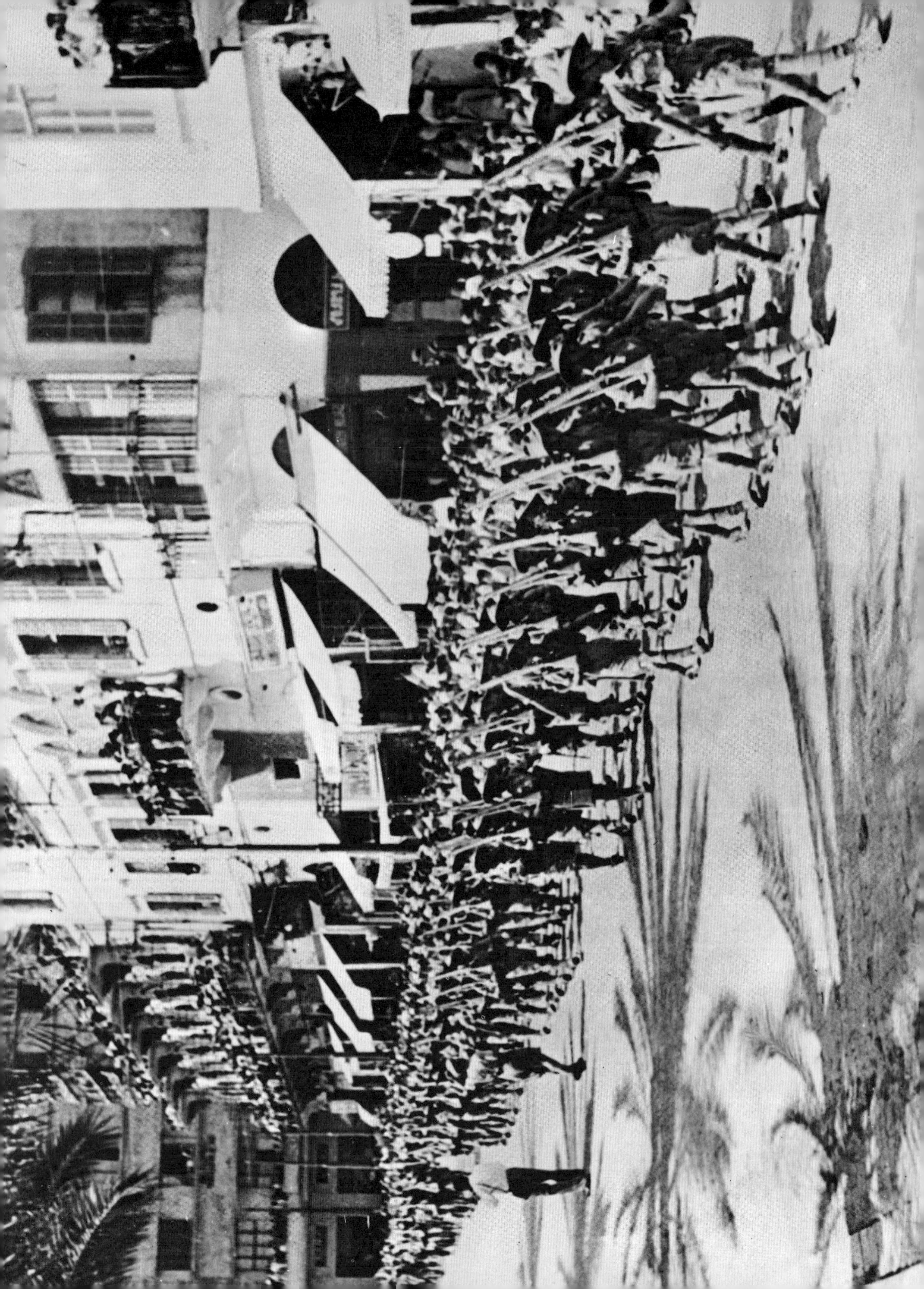

13 Adolescence

After the war came the boom. As soon as shipping was available large-scale immigration was resumed, with Britain's blessing and financial support. The Commonwealth and state governments borrowed freely at home and abroad to launch ambitious development programmes and various expansion incentives were offered to private industry. Many big estates were broken up and returning servicemen were encouraged to settle on the land. Extensive water-conservation and irrigation projects were introduced in Victoria and New South Wales. To counteract rising wages, increased freights and falling world prices primary producers were given subsidies in various forms, mainly at the expense of home consumers, so that prices for such commodities as meat, butter and sugar were higher in Australia than abroad. Tariffs were increased to protect industries which had been established during the war and to encourage the local manufacture of such things as electrical goods, motor vehicle bodies and textiles. The wartime expansion of BHP continued at an accelerating rate and under highly efficient management it became Australia's one industrial giant. The transcontinental railway linking Perth with the eastern capitals had been completed in 1917 and many new railway works were now put in hand. To cope with the rapid post-war rise in motor traffic existing main roads were greatly improved and new ones were built. In Sydney the suburban train system was electrified and work began on an underground railway system and a bridge to link the north and south shores of the harbour. As the pace of private building stepped up new suburbs began to appear in all the main cities. Wages were at new high levels, working conditions had never been better and unemployment barely existed.

In 1919 Australia had been a founder member of the League of Nations and in the following year she accepted the responsibility of a mandate over German New Guinea, New Britain and the Solomon Islands. At home the most significant political development of the immediate post-war years was the rise of the Country Party. Hughes failed to realize its potential power and rather arbitrarily rejected many of its demands. It was a fatal error. In the Federal elections of 1922 the party won enough seats to give it the balance of power and as a result Hughes was forced out of office and was succeeded by a coalition government led by Stanley Melbourne Bruce (Nationalist) and Dr Earle Page (Country Party). Although both Bruce and Page were able and sincere men, firmly committed to and believing in a policy of continued expansion their govern-

Left The final triumph of the Syria-Lebanon campaign in the Second World War. Australians marching through Beirut after its surrender by the Vichy French on 31 May 1941.

Right Beauty on the beach. Bondi, 1919.

Left Bathing girls on Bondi beach, Sydney, in 1919.

Below left Special constables and rioters clash in a Melbourne street during the police strike of December 1923.

Below The Duke and Duchess of York (later King George VI and Queen Elizabeth) at the opening of Federal Parliament House, Canberra, in 1927.

ment was never widely popular. On a superficial level Bruce irritated many Australians by his English accent and dress; on a deeper level it was felt by many that his concentration on economic and industrial development was at the expense of social experimentation, that in fact idealism was being swamped by materialism. Left-wing Labour and the Communist Party, formed in 1922, particularly stressed this point – perhaps not unjustifiably – and it was undoubtedly the basic cause of much industrial unrest during the 1920s. Strikes were frequent, bitterly fought and damaging to the economy. Among those involved were seamen, miners, transport workers and timber-workers and the average annual loss in working days was about a million. In Victoria in 1923 even the police went on strike and for a week there was considerable rioting and some looting in Melbourne. Emergency legislation was rushed through, special police were recruited, and eventually about a third of the regular force were dismissed and refused reinstatement.

However, strikes and lockouts did little to dispel the country's general sense of euphoria. A few people muttered darkly about living in a fools' paradise but most Australians were determined to take life as it came and enjoy it. The prevailing spirit

Far left Andrew ('Boy') Charlton, world record holder and winner of the 1500 metres freestyle at the Paris Olympics of 1924.

Left Gerald L. Patterson, winner of the Wimbledon singles in 1919 and 1922.

Below left The Prince of Wales (later King Edward VIII) arriving at Perth in August 1920 at the start of his triumphant tour of Australia.

Below: Ross and Keith Smith (centre) with the Vickers Vimy biplane in which they made the first flight from England to Australia in 1919.

was exemplified by the tumultuous welcomes accorded the Prince of Wales when he visited Australia in 1920, and the Duke and Duchess of York (later King George VI and Queen Elizabeth) when they came out in 1927 to open at Canberra the 'temporary' building which has ever since served as Federal Parliament House. A less welcome visitor was the English writer D. H. Lawrence who, after some months in Australia in 1923, wrote sourly that the more he saw of democracy the less he liked it and described Australians as 'healthy but almost imbecile, clattering around like so many mechanical animals'. However, despite the sensitivity of Australians to this sort of criticism, the bonds of Empire remained firm; though a few young intellectuals felt that England was becoming culturally effete and were beginning to look across the Pacific for their inspiration. Certainly on a popular level the American influence was becoming strong. Young people danced the Charleston and listened to American jazz. Such essentially American pastimes as pole-sitting, endurance piano-playing and miniature golf became the vogue in Australia. Rococo cinemas, described not unjustifiably as 'picture-palaces', proliferated in the cities and larger towns, there were Rudolph Valentino fan clubs everywhere and when talkies came huge placards appeared which announced simply in letters ten feet high: 'Garbo Speaks'. Radio, introduced in 1923, quickly caught on and soon the most popular programmes were American 'soap-operas'.

Sport had become almost a religion. In the first four Test series after the war Australia won twelve matches to England's two, and players like W. W. Armstrong, H. L. Collins, A. W. Kippax and W. H. Ponsford became national heroes. So did Gerald Patterson when he won the Wimbledon singles in 1922 and so did the swimmer Andrew ('Boy') Charlton when he won the 1500 metres freestyle at the Paris Olympics of 1924 in world record time.

Left 'Smithy's' famous aircraft, *Southern Cross*, in which he and Ulm made the first trans-Pacific crossing in 1928.

Below left Charles Ulm and Charles Kingsford Smith on their arrival in England in 1931 with the first airmail from Australia. With them, on right, is the British Minister for Air, Sir Sefton Brancker.

Right Bert Hinkler, Australia's most spectacular solo flying ace of the 1920s. He was killed when his plane crashed in January 1933 during an attempt to break the England-Australia record.

However, the country's popular idols were not all sportsmen. The great development of aviation during the war had emphasized the peacetime possibilities of commercial flying and many Australian pilots who returned home were eager to exploit this. The Commonwealth government, equally eager, offered £10,000 for the first successful flight from England to Australia within thirty days. It was won by Ross and Keith Smith, brothers who had served with the Australian Flying Corps in Palestine. Flying a Vickers-Vimy biplane, and accompanied by J. M. Bennett and W. H. Shiers as mechanics, they reached Darwin on 10 December 1919 with two days to spare. Exhibition flights and 'barnstorming' tours by other pilots did much to make the public air-minded. In 1921 the country's first commercial airline, Queensland and Northern Territory Aerial Services Ltd. (Qantas), founded by W. Hudson Fysh and P. J. McGinness, began operations with two small aircraft and by the following year it was conducting a regular service between Charleville and Cloncurry (577 miles). Other companies were formed and among other services inaugurated were Perth to Derby (1,442 miles), Adelaide to Cootamundra, N.S.W. (578 miles) and Melbourne to Hay, N.S.W. (233 miles). By 1926 commercial aircraft were flying 7,500 miles a week. In the meantime there had been some notable flights, including one round Australia by S. J. Goble and I. E. McIntyre in a Fairey 3D seaplane. In 1926 an Englishman, Alan Cobham, flew from England to Australia and back in easy stages in a DH50 seaplane. Two years later Bert Hinkler, an Australian test pilot employed in England, flew solo from London to Darwin in a single-seater Avro Avian in under sixteen days. He received a hero's welcome and cheques from the Queensland and Commonwealth governments totalling £2,500. But even Hinkler's achievement was overshadowed in the same year by those of Charles Kingsford Smith and

Charles Ulm. In June 1928, flying a Fokker monoplane called the *Southern Cross* and with an American navigator and radio operator, Smith and Ulm crossed the Pacific from California to Brisbane with stops at Honolulu and Fiji in thirty-three flying hours. In the same year and in the same aircraft they flew non-stop from Melbourne to Perth, crossed the Tasman Sea to New Zealand, and returned to Australia over the same route. In March 1929 while attempting to fly to England Smith and Ulm were forced down on a mud flat at the estuary of the Glenelg River, W.A. and were found only after a search of thirteen days in which two other airmen lost their lives. In June they made a fresh start and reached London in the record time of twelve days eighteen hours. Meanwhile in 1928 John Flynn, a Presbyterian clergyman, had introduced Australia's first Flying Doctor service, based at Cloncurry, Queensland.

Not only aircraft were vanquishing the vast distances of Australia. By 1929 the country had 650,000 motor vehicles. Interstate road travel had become commonplace and racing drivers such as Norman ('Wizard') Smith were constantly setting new intercity records. A railway of more than a thousand miles linked Brisbane and Cairns, the Oodnadatta, S.A. line had been extended north to Alice Springs and a standard gauge coastal line between Sydney and Brisbane was nearing completion.

In every way the country seemed to be going from strength to strength. Sheep again exceeded 100,000,000, the wool clip was proportionately up and ninety woollen mills were operating in the eastern States. Cattle totalled 12,000,000, and in western Queensland and the Northern Territory were huge station properties such as Alexandria, on the Barkley tableland, about equal in size to Belgium. Wheat production was at 140,000,000 bushels, coal at 12,000,000 tons and sugar at 500,000 tons. After only five years enough rice was being produced in irrigated areas to fill all the country's needs. The population had risen to 6,500,000, including 300,000 postwar immigrants, and of this total about forty-five per cent lived in cities. Sydney alone had more than a million and Melbourne was close behind with 900,000.

But there were cracks in this façade of prosperity. The national debt had become formidable and interest payments totalled many millions a year. At home there was a spiral of increasing wages and prices. On the other hand world prices were falling and freight rates had soared. Inexperience on the land had put many soldier-settlers heavily in debt. The spread of prickly pear in southern Queensland and northern N.S.W., which at one time had engulfed 65,000,000 acres of good land, had been checked by the introduction of *Cactoblastus cactorum*, an insect from the Argentine; but no equally effective means had yet been found to deal with rabbits and every year millions of acres of once good sheep-grazing land were becoming eaten out and useless.

In the political field the Bruce-Page government was losing its grip. A revolt within the party led by Hughes hastened its end and in the elections of October 1929 a Labour government was returned under the leadership of J. H. Scullin. It was Scullin's and the party's misfortune to take office just as the world was drifting into a state of economic depression.

When the depression hit Australia it hit hard. Export markets disappeared and loan sources dried up almost overnight. Primary producers and employees on public works were the first to feel the impact but soon almost everyone in Australia was affected. Soon one wage-earner in three was unemployed and many lived on the dole. Thousands of businesses failed and there were many bankruptcies. Every government economy worsened the general situation. In New South Wales the Labour Premier, J. T. Lang, repudiated interest payments on the public debt, started a run on the State Savings Bank which

Above left John T. Lang, Premier of N.S.W., who was dismissed from office during the depression.

Left The tragedy of the depression is poignantly expressed in this painting by Noel Counihan *'At the Start of the March 1932'*.

Above right Sir Isaac Isaacs, first Australian-born Governor-General of Australia.

Right Dole queues in Sydney during the depression. Australians bitterly resented being forced to beg, as it seemed to them, and many refused to accept dole money.

Above left Jean Batten, after breaking the Australia-England solo record in 1937.

Above right C. W. A. Scott and Campbell Black after the England-Australia air race of 1934.

Below Captain Cook's cottage. To celebrate the centenary of Melbourne in 1934 it was transferred stone by stone from Great Ayton, Yorkshire, and re-erected in Fitzroy Gardens, Melbourne.

Right Australia's first luxury train, the *Spirit of Progress,* which made its first run between Melbourne and Albury, on the N.S.W. border, in 1937.

forced it to suspend payments, and was dismissed from office by the governor, Sir Dudley de Chair. The currency was devalued by twenty-five per cent, with few of the dire results predicted by the experts and by 1932, as economic conditions improved elsewhere, the worst of the depression in Australia was over. However, its scars were to remain for many years.

By this time Scullin's government had fallen. One of his ministers, J. A. Lyons, had quit the party and linked up with the opposition under the new title of the United Australia Party and in January 1932 a coalition UAP-Country Party Government had swept overwhelmingly into power with Lyons himself as Prime Minister. While in office Scullin had been responsible for the appointment of Sir Isaac Isaacs, a distinguished jurist, as Australia's first native-born Governor-General, a precedent which had aroused considerable controversy at the time. During Lyon's first year a return to prosperity was further accelerated by an agreement signed at Ottawa which provided for preferential tariffs between the United Kingdom, the dominions and British colonies. Two years later the Commonwealth budget showed a surplus and Australians began to speak of the depression in the past tense.

A big event of 1932 was the opening of the Sydney harbour bridge, marred only slightly by an ardent right-wing militia officer, who anticipated the cutting of the ceremonial ribbon by riding up to it and slashing it with a sword. The bridge soon became known affectionately as 'the coat-hanger' and it soon superseded The Gap as a favourite spot for would-be suicides. In 1934 Melbourne celebrated its centenary by importing, stone by stone, a cottage which Captain Cook had built for his father at Great Ayton. The Hume reservoir, the largest in the country, was completed in 1936; and in the following year Victoria introduced luxury rail travel with its *Spirit of Progress,* which ran between Albury and Melbourne.

During and after the depression flying records continued to be broken with what became almost monotonous regularity. In 1930 Amy Johnson became the first woman to fly solo from England to Australia and in the next few years there were many memorable flights by, among others, C. W. A. Scott, James Mollison, Jean Batten and, of course, Kingsford Smith. In 1934 Scott and Campbell Black won a centenary air-race from England to Melbourne in the remarkable time of seventy-one hours. A commercial airline founded by Smith and Ulm in 1928 had failed because of the depression and a disastrous air crash; and Smith, who was knighted in 1932, was reduced for a time to giving joy-rides to earn a living. In 1935 he and a companion, J. T. Pethybridge, set out to attempt yet another England-Australia record and their aircraft disappeared near Singapore. Meanwhile several internal airlines had been established and John Flynn had greatly expanded his Flying Doctor service. In 1934 Qantas linked with Imperial Airways to share an England-Australia air-mail service and four years later the same company introduced flying boats over the same route.

Australia's great sporting idol of the early 1930s was a four-legged one called Phar Lap, who won the Melbourne Cup of 1930. Later he went to the United States and when news came through that he had died soon after his first race there the nation went virtually into mourning. His mounted figure may still be seen in a Melbourne museum. Relations between Australia and the mother country were temporarily strained in 1932 when England's cricket captain, D. R. Jardine, introduced 'bodyline' bowling. Even the great Don Bradman was not immune and one newspaper announced his dismissal for a 'duck' with a succinct poster which simply read 'DON'. But Bradman's failures were rare and through the 1930s he dominated cricket as no player

Far left 'The Don', otherwise Don Bradman, the greatest batsman of them all.

Left Jack Crawford, winner of the Wimbledon singles in 1933.

Right Before the fighting started. Members of the Australian 6th Division leaving the Church of the Holy Sepulchre during a sight-seeing tour of Jerusalem.

Below Australian assault troops taking an Old Vickers position on Bobdubi Ridge, New Guinea, as seen by artist Ivor Hele.

ever had. Among other great sporting heroes of the time were Jack Crawford, who won the Wimbledon singles in 1933, and Walter Lindrum who reduced billiards to such an exact science that new rules had to be introduced to curb his astronomical breaks. Australians were only moderately successful in the Olympics of 1932 (Los Angeles) and 1936 (Berlin) but they did much better against less formidable opposition in the Empire Games of 1938, which were held in Sydney.

However, beneath the surface gaiety of the post-depression years was a growing realization that Australia would soon be required to face her greatest test as an emerging nation. The rise of Hitler in Germany, Mussolini's invasion of Abyssinia and the Spanish Civil War were signs that could not be ignored. The Munich pact of 1938 came as a disillusioning shock and the country suddenly became aware of the pitiful inadequacy of its defences. Ill and overworked, Lyons cracked under the strain and died in April 1939, and when war came on 3 September the main burden fell on his successor, Robert Gordon Menzies.

Recruiting for the three services began at once and the response was keen. Compulsory military service was reintroduced, with the proviso that

Above left Australian mechanized cavalry advance in battle formation during the attack on Bardia on 3 January 1941.

Above centre Australians advancing into the Tobruk defences on 21 January 1941.

Below far left 'Journey's End', a painting by Frank Norton of HMAS *Waterhen* which was sunk while taking supplies to the besieged Australian garrison at Tobruk.

Below left Australian sentry on guard at the El Adam road approach during the defence of Tobruk.

Above Italians surrendering to an Australian during the desert campaign.

Below HMAS *Sydney* during the action off the Calabrian coast on 19 July 1940 in which she sank the Italian cruiser *Bartolomeo Colleoni*. Painting by Frank Norton.

conscripts would be required to serve only in Australia and its territories. Naval vessels in reserve were recommissioned and work began on building others. Efforts were made to supplement from abroad Australia's 164 combat aircraft, most of which were already obsolete and Air Force volunteers were sent to Canada to take part in an Empire air training scheme. Two AIF divisions, the 6th and 7th, were formed under Lieutenant-General Sir Thomas Blamey and sent to Palestine to complete their training. They were meant for service on the western front but by June 1940 France, Belgium, Holland, Denmark and Norway had been overrun and no western front remained. However, their future was automatically settled when Italy came in on Germany's side and began a major offensive in North Africa aimed against Egypt and the Suez Canal. The Allied counter-attack, launched in December, was spearheaded by Australian and New Zealand troops. By late February Bardia, Tobruk, Derna and Benghazi had fallen, many thousands of prisoners had been taken and the Italians were in full retreat. Meanwhile Australian warships had been active with the British fleet in the Mediterranean. The *Sydney* had sunk the Italian cruiser *Bartolomeo Colleoni*, and Australian ships had been

Above left Australian troops relaxing on a transport on their way from Egypt to Greece.

Above John Curtin, wartime Prime Minister of Australia, from October 1941 to his death on 6 July 1945.

Below left Australian troops in action at Parit Sulong during their fighting retreat in Malaya in December 1941. The artist is V. M. Griffin.

conspicuous in the battles of Taranto and Matapan.

The arrival of strong German forces with powerful air support transformed the situation in North Africa, and the Allies began a fighting retreat. In March 1941 the Australian 6th Division was relieved by the newly-arrived 7th and 9th and moved to Greece, where a German invasion was imminent. It came, in overwhelming strength, during April. By the end of the month Greece had fallen and Allied troops had withdrawn to Crete. In turn Crete fell to an airborne invasion and by early June the surviving Australians were back in Egypt. With hardly time to rest or regroup they went into action in Syria and Lebanon against the Vichy French, who were beaten in a five-weeks' campaign. Meanwhile Benghazi and Derna had fallen to Rommel's Afrika Corps; Tobruk, garrisoned by Australian (9th Division) and British troops, was under siege; and Egypt was threatened.

In Australia the Menzies government had narrowly survived a general election in October 1940. The following August Menzies was supplanted by A. W. Fadden (Country Party); and two months later the government was defeated and Labour took over with John Curtin as Prime Minister.

Hitler's invasion of Russia in August 1941 radically changed the situation in Europe; and the

Above left Within half a mile of the enemy Australian troops in New Guinea take time off to vote in the Federal elections of September 1943.

Above A study by William Dobell of a barrowman at work on the Captain Cook Graving Dock, Sydney. Civilian labour was conscripted by the Allied Works Council as part of Australia's all-out war effort.

Below left A house in Darwin after the disastrous Japanese air-raid of 19 February 1942, in which about 240 civilians, seamen and troops were killed.

whole pattern of the war was reshaped on 7 December when Japanese aircraft devastated a United States fleet at Pearl Harbour and massive Japanese forces invaded South-East Asia. The myth of Singapore's impregnability was shattered three days later when the British battleships *Repulse* and *Prince of Wales* were sunk off Malaya; and bitter jungle fighting followed as the Australian 8th Division and other Allied troops opposed the enemy's advance down the Malayan peninsula. Once Singapore was in Japanese hands Australia would be seriously threatened and Curtin readily agreed to Winston Churchill's suggestion that the 6th and 7th Divisions should be transferred from Africa to the Dutch East Indies. But the sheer pace of the enemy advance ruled this out. Singapore fell on 15 February 1942 and for most Australian survivors the next three and a half years meant Changi prison or slave-labour on the Burma railway. On 19 February Japanese carrier-based bombers attacked Darwin, sank eight ships and killed 240 seamen, troops and civilians. The war was coming uncomfortably close. On 23 February, against a strong protest from Winston Churchill, Curtin ordered the returning troops to be diverted to their own country. Ten days later Japanese aircraft raided Broome,

Left Infantry and Australian-manned General Stuart tanks attack Japanese pillboxes in the final assault on Buna in February 1943.

Below left Australians wading across the Song River, New Guinea, before attacking Japanese positions.

Above right Australian commandoes returning after a patrol in the Ramu River area, New Guinea.

Above far right Hundreds of lives were saved by the selfless devotion of native stretcher-bearers during the New Guinea campaign.

Below right The aircrew of an RAAF Beaufighter squadron in New Guinea.

Right At a clearing station in New Guinea a wounded Australian helps his mate to a light.

Below The Cenotaph in Martin Place, Sydney, a memorial to the Australian dead of two world wars.

Far right General Douglas MacArthur, supreme commander in the South Pacific, with a group of American officers.

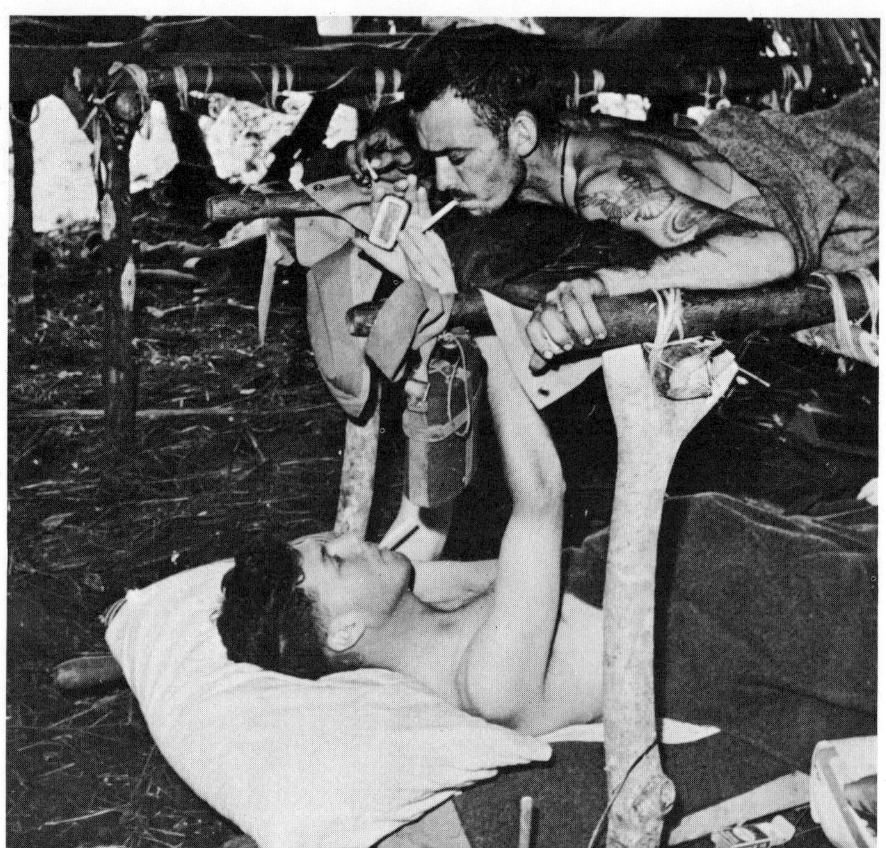

destroyed several combat aircraft and eight flying boats which were bringing civilian refugees from Java and killed about seventy people.

Australia's position was critical. Her fighting strength comprised 46,000 veterans of the 6th and 7th Divisions, 63,000 AIF who had not been out of the country and 280,000 militia. All were poorly equipped; there were practically no tanks, no aircraft and few fighting ships. Curtin faced the situation with a realism that won him many admirers. 'Without inhibitions of any kind,' he declared, 'I make it quite clear that (from now on) Australia looks to America, free of any pangs as to our traditional links or kinship with the United Kingdom.' On orders from Washington General Douglas Macarthur flew in from the Philippines as supreme commander, South-West Pacific Area. In his wake followed an American fleet and thousands of troops, with equipment, munitions and aircraft. Australia went on to a full wartime footing. Civilian labour was directed to where it could be most useful – in munitions factories, in building airfields and a strategic north-south road through the continent's heart, on the docks. Food, clothing, petrol and all luxuries were rationed. Taxes were heavily increased and the Commonwealth government took over all income taxation.

By now the enemy had moved into New Guinea and the Solomon Islands and invasion seemed imminent. Then came a dramatic change. On 7 and 8 May a Japanese fleet was intercepted and badly mauled in the Coral Sea; and early in June the enemy suffered a crushing defeat off Midway Island, losing four carriers, a cruiser and a destroyer. In between these battles, which were to prove crucial, two Japanese midget submarines penetrated Sydney harbour on the night of 31 May but succeeded only in torpedoing a ferry used as a depot ship before they were destroyed by depth-charges.

In the western desert the position remained critical. In June Tobruk fell after an heroic defence of fourteen months and the Afrika Corps reached to within sixty miles of Alexandria. The Australian 9th Division was moved from Syria to reinforce the Allies; and in October they played a vital part in General Montgomery's decisive break-through at El Alamein, which was to culminate seven months later in the surrender of all Axis troops in North Africa.

Through the second half of 1942 Japanese aggression in the south-west Pacific gradually waned in the face of stiffening Allied resistance. Guadalcanal, in the Solomons, became a major battle-ground; an enemy assault on Milne Bay, at the south-east tip of New Guinea, was repulsed with heavy losses; the

threat to Port Moresby was removed when Australian troops drove the Japanese back over the Kokoda trail; and fierce fighting followed in the Buna-Gona area on the north coast of New Guinea. In a naval engagement off Guadalcanal one of four Allied cruisers sunk was HMAS *Canberra*. In the early months of 1943 there was a lull as both sides reorganized and built up their forces. During August and September Lae, Salamaua and Finschhafen fell to the Allies and in the following month a strong Japanese counter-attack was defeated. By mid-1944 Japanese resistance in New Guinea had collapsed and in August Macarthur was able to move his headquarters north from Brisbane to Hollandia, in Dutch New Guinea. Then began the slow but inexorable process of flushing the Japanese out of the many islands they had occupied.

Although much desperate fighting was still to come in both the European and Pacific theatres there was little real doubt now about the eventual outcome. On 1 May 1945 Russian troops entered the ruins of Berlin and six days later the Germans surrendered unconditionally. Against what were by this time overwhelming odds the Japanese held out for another three months but they would have been wiser to accept the inevitable. Early in August a new and horrifying element was introduced when atomic bombs obliterated Hiroshima and Nagasaki and on 15 August on orders from the Emperor, Japan surrendered and the war was over. Because of the different character of the fighting Australian losses had been only about a third of those of the First World War – 21,000 dead and 58,000 other casualties. But psychologically the effect had been much more profound. Australia had emerged from dependent adolescence and was now, in her own right, an adult nation.

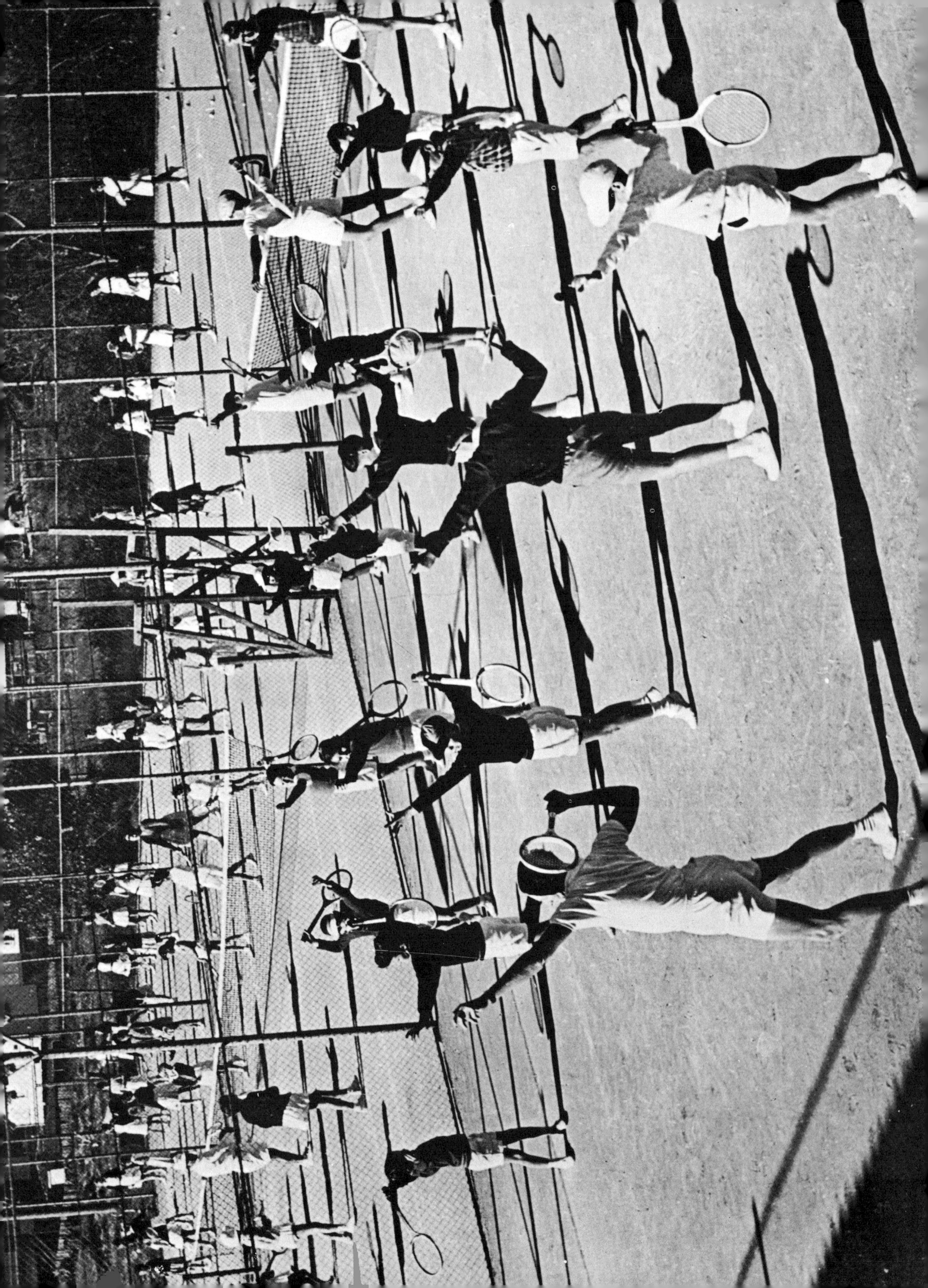

14 Coming of Age

The war had wrought many changes in Australia. Some were physical – new airfields, new ports, new roads, new factories – but the greatest change was in the outlook of the people themselves. Events had proved that they could no longer depend on Britain's armed might or their own physical isolation to protect them in time of war. Europe, once the centre of the world in their eyes, now seemed remote and its problems almost irrelevant. Geographically, they realized, Australia was an extention of South-East Asia and for good or ill it was here and in the Pacific that the future of their country lay. Even those for whom the ties of kinship were still strong had to admit that Australia's natural and most dependable ally was no longer Britain but the United States; and while it was reassuring that the United States was now the world's strongest single power her protection was clearly not something to be relied upon. To survive another war Australia must be strong in her own right and only she could make herself so. Her great and urgent needs were to expand industrially, to exploit and develop her natural resources, to create new markets and new political and economic alliances. To do these things she needed more people – millions more.

Prime Minister Curtin had died in office – his country's most notable war casualty – in July 1945, a few weeks before the capitulation of Japan. But his clear vision of Australia's future was shared by his colleague and successor, Joseph Benedict Chifley. In June 1945 Australia had taken a prominent part in the foundation of the United Nations Organization, created 'to save succeeding generations from the scourge of war'. In the following year she was one of the first to ratify the constitution of the United Nations Educational, Scientific and Cultural Organization (UNESCO); she was a member of the security council in 1946 and 1947; in 1946 she accepted trusteeship of the former mandated Territory of New Guinea and undertook to

Left A tennis nursery in Brisbane. It is the ambition of many Australian boys and girls to be a Wimbledon champion.

Right Joseph Benedict (Ben) Chifley, Labour Prime Minister of Australia from 1945 to 1949. He died in June 1951.

Top Hobart, capital of Tasmania, by night. Sullivan Cove, the original site of settlement in 1804, is at right.

Left The River Yarra and Prince's Bridge, Melbourne, capital of Victoria.

Above Australia's former Prime Minister, Sir Robert Menzies.

work towards its eventual independence; in 1948 an Australian, Dr H. V. Evatt, was elected president of the third general assembly.

On the domestic front Chifley coped well enough with the many problems of postwar reconstruction and launched several important developmental projects including the great Snowy Mountains hydro-electric scheme. However, not all his measures were approved by a majority of the electors. Many thought that his eagerness to turn Australia into a welfare state was premature. In 1946 he flouted public opinion by securing the appointment of W. J. McKell, Labour Premier of New South Wales, as Governor-General in succession to the Duke of Gloucester; and in 1949 he antagonized many of his own supporters when he broke a coal strike by putting troops to work in surface mines. But the rock on which he finally crashed was his determination to nationalize banking. This became a major political issue and in a general election of December 1949 Labour was ousted by a government led by Menzies and A. W. Fadden (Country Party). At that time few could have predicted that within another two years Chifley, the political idealist, would be dead and that Menzies, the political realist, would continue as Prime Minister for a record sixteen years and then retire undefeated, helped first by the ineptness of Chifley's successor, Evatt, and then by a schism within the Labour Party. Menzies was for free enterprise as opposed to socialization and he had a strong sentimental attachment to Britain and the Crown. Otherwise his foreign and domestic policies differed little in essentials from Labour's. The same was true of his successor, Harold Holt, who was to die tragically by drowning in December 1967 after less than two years in office; and it is true of the present Prime Minister, John Gorton.

The pattern of Australia's post-war foreign policy is consistent and clear. In 1947 she was a founder-member of the South Pacific Commission, which

Above Mock-Tudor buildings in London Court, a pleasant shopping precinct in Perth.

Below Asian students, in Australia under the Colombo Plan, outside Winthrop Hall, University of Western Australia, Perth.

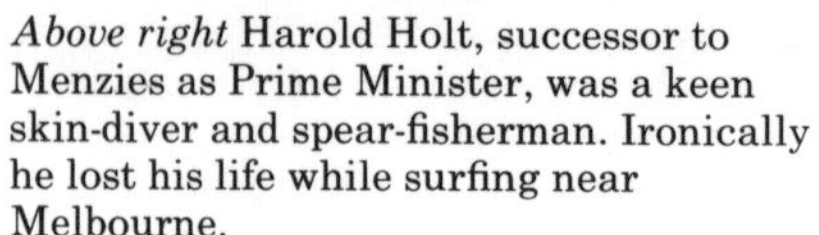

Above right Harold Holt, successor to Menzies as Prime Minister, was a keen skin-diver and spear-fisherman. Ironically he lost his life while surfing near Melbourne.

aims to improve the health and economic and social conditions of the 3,000,000 Pacific Islanders. Three years later she was prominent in the launching of the Colombo Plan, a programme of economic aid for the underdeveloped countries of South and South-East Asia and as part of her contribution an increasing number of Asian students of agriculture, economics and medicine were awarded scholarships to Australian universities. In 1950 Australia, New Zealand and the United States signed the Anzus Pact, a treaty to govern their mutual defence in the Pacific; three years later she was one of eight founder members of the South-East Asia Treaty Organization (SEATO), which sought to deter military (i.e. Communist) aggression in the area and to provide mutual economic, technical and cultural aid; and in 1966 she was one of nine founders of the Asian and Pacific Co-operation Council (ASPAC). Throughout his term in office Menzies was implacably anti-Communist; indeed, in 1950 he tried and failed to outlaw the Communist party in Australia, and in 1954 he was able to make much political capital from the defection of Vladimir Petrov, a Soviet diplomat and self-confessed spy. Large contingents of Australians fought in the Korean war of 1950-52; there were Australian units in Malaya during the troubles of the late 1950s; and

Above John Grey Gorton, former Senator, and now Prime Minister of Australia.

Above right Statue of Colonel Light, founder of Adelaide, South Australia, looks down from Montefiore Hill on to the city he created.

Below The national capital, Canberra, from the air. Arrows show the site of the new Federal Parliament House, on the shore of Lake Burley Griffin.

Left Immigrants from Italy arrive in Australia. The net gain from immigration since 1945 is about 2,000,000.

Below At the Holt memorial service in Melbourne. Front row: Prince Charles, Lord Casey (Governor-General), Lady Casey. Second row: President Johnson (USA), President Park (Korea), President Marcos (Philippines).

Right Troops of the 1st Battalion, Royal Australian Regiment, race into a helicopter on a search-and-destroy mission in Vietnam.

Below right The P & O liner *Oriana* (42,000 tons) leaves the overseas shipping terminal at Circular Quay, Sydney. Here less than 200 years ago was founded the first British settlement in Australia.

Australian troops are now heavily engaged in Vietnam. In 1963 Australia agreed to the establishment of an American naval communications base at North-West Cape, Western Australia; and she has promised increased technical and military aid to affected countries when Britain withdraws from Singapore in 1971. It is significant that of twenty leaders of state who attended the Holt memorial service only seven were from Commonwealth countries. Twelve were leaders of Asian nations and the twentieth was President Johnson of the United States. Europe sent no head of state.

Within Australia there has been extraordinary development in every sphere since the war. The census of 1947 revealed a population of a little over 7,500,000. In April 1968 the total passed 12,000,000, and statisticians predict that it will have reached 19,000,000 in another twenty years. Since the war about 2,000,000 migrants, most of them government-assisted, have settled in Australia. They are preponderantly British but there have also been many Greeks, Italians and Yugoslavs. On the Snowy Mountains scheme alone men of more than forty nations have been employed. At first they were housed separately and there was much bad feeling and many fights. Since this policy was abandoned

the harmony has been remarkable. New arrivals tend to cling together in national communities but this breaks down as their children grow up. Many a teen-age Papadopolous or Rikhjovic now speaks with a broad Australian accent. Socially the influence of these new arrivals has been immense. Its most obvious manifestation is in the Italian, Greek, French, Scandinavian and Asian restaurants which have proliferated in the cities and large towns and in the growing partiality of Australians to wines; but of course it goes much deeper. More than four in five of Australia's population now live in cities and towns; about 1,300,000 are employed in more than 60,000 factories. Sydney, with a population of 2,600,000, is now the twenty-eighth city in the world; Melbourne (2,300,000) the thirty-seventh.

Economic growth has more than kept pace with the rise in population. Australia no longer depends as she did on rural production. Wool is still the most important single export but price fluctuations – varying from a record 144d lb in 1951 to about 49d in 1968 – no longer vitally affect the economy. The livestock population and the acreage under grain are now far in excess of prewar levels; but although rural production is at a record figure of about $A2,500,000,000 a year this represents only a quarter of the country's total production.

Left T.1 power station, one of several in the Snowy Mountains hydro-electric scheme. It is 1,200 ft underground, and is reached by tunnel.

Below left Aerial view of Brisbane, Queensland's capital city. The city is undergoing extensive rebuilding.

Below Tumut Pond dam, part of the great Snowy Mountains complex.

Below right The SEDCO 135-E oil drilling rig in the Otway basin of Bass Strait. There have been several rich offshore gas and oil strikes in the same vicinity.

Below An iron-ore train at the new port of Dampier, W.A., named for the first Englishman who explored the area.

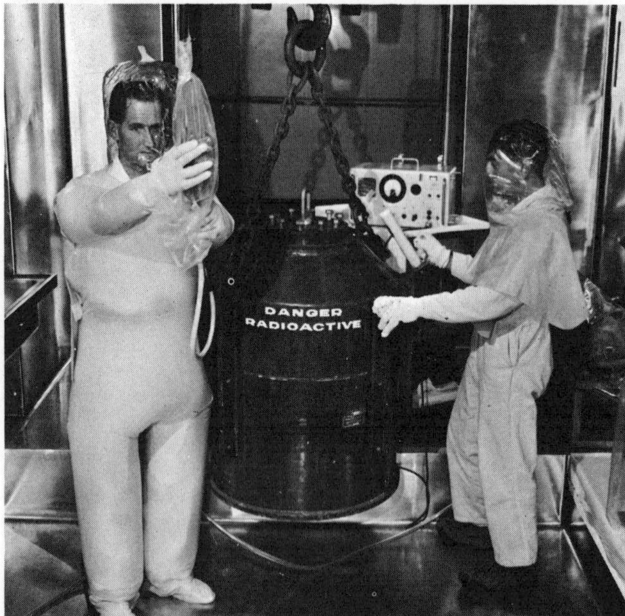

By far the most dramatic development in recent years, however, has been in the discovery and initial exploitation of what appear to be almost unlimited mineral resources. In fact the mining boom began as far back as 1949 when rich uranium was found at Rum Jungle, Northern Territory, but intense exploitation had heavily depleted the reserves by 1963. Since then there have been rich new finds at Mary Kathleen in Central Queensland. Australia is already one of the world's leading producers of lead, refined metal, zinc and mineral sands; her iron-ore reserves are tremendous and her reserves of bauxite (the source of aluminium) are easily the largest known in the world; and she produces sizeable export surpluses of barite, cadmium, black coal, copper, gold, gypsum, manganese ore, opal, silver, tin and tungsten. Within the last few years there have been exciting and extensive discoveries of nickel, manganese, phosphate rock, oil and natural gas. The value of mineral production has increased ten times over since the war and as yet many immense known sources have barely been tapped. Ten years ago Australia was paying £150,000,000 a year for imported oil. When they are in full production in the early 1970s already proved oilfields at Moonie (Queensland), Barrow Island (Western Australia) and Bass Strait (off the Victorian coast) will cut this bill by more than half and experts are confident that by 1980 Australia will be self-sufficient in oil.

Inevitably the general economic picture has been greatly affected by Australia's postwar political alliances. Imports from and exports to the United States have soared. Japan, a generation ago Australia's mortal enemy, is now her third best

Left Old terraces such as this one in Union Street, Paddington, once almost derelict, are now much sought-after by Sydney people.

Centre left At the atomic research establishment at Lucas Heights, near Sydney, technicians handle a shielded isopope transport container.

Below left Anti-Vietnam demonstrators throw themselves in front of President Johnson's car on his arrival in Sydney in 1966.

Right Cane-cutter at work on a Queensland sugar plantation.

Below The Academy of Science, Canberra.

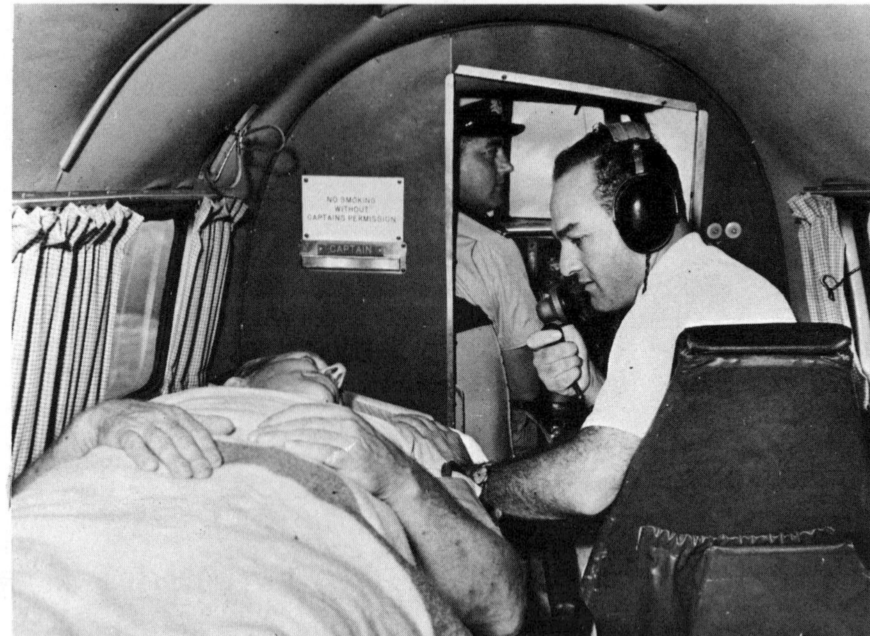

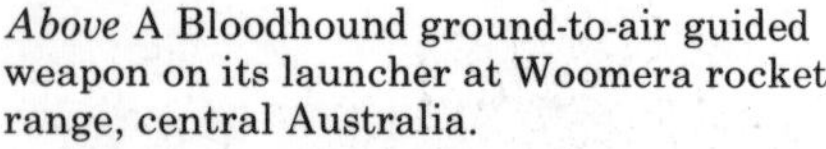

Above A Bloodhound ground-to-air guided weapon on its launcher at Woomera rocket range, central Australia.

Above right Inside a Flying Doctor aircraft. A doctor bringing in a patient calls his base at Charleville, Queensland, asking for an ambulance to stand by.

Centre right Jindivik Mark I pilotless target plane in flight over Woomera. It has a speed approaching that of sound and a ceiling of 50,000 feet.

Right Radio telescopes at Parkes. They are exceptionally accurate in pin-pointing radio sources in distant space.

customer. Britain is still her best but only just. The actual volume of trade between the two countries is higher than ever but in terms of percentages it has dropped very considerably. In 1938-39 more than forty per cent of goods which entered Australia were British. The figure is now about twenty-five per cent. In the same period Australia's exports to Britain have dropped from fifty-four to seventeen per cent, which makes her that much less dependent on the British market. American capital investment in Australia now exceeds British by about $A50,000,000 a year.

Australia's development in science has been equally spectacular. Much valuable work has been done by the Commonwealth Scientific and Industrial Research Organization (CSIRO) since its creation in 1949 in such varied fields as entomology, animal health, biochemistry, food preservation and transport, fisheries, meteorology, radiophysics, industrial chemistry, building research and irrigation. Perhaps its most dramatic single success was the introduction in 1950 of the virus disease myxomatosis, which in three years reduced the country's rabbit population by about eighty per cent and restored to profitable production hundreds of thousands of square miles of grazing and agricultural land. Within a few years the rabbits had developed a high degree of

Above right The late Albert Namatjira, a noted landscape painter, with his wife Rubina at Haast's Bluff, central Australia.

Right Surf boats battle against huge seas off a Sydney beach.

immunity necessitating a search for other methods of eradication. Meanwhile, they are no longer the pest they were.

In 1947, in conjunction with the British government, a rocket range was established in South Australia for the testing of long-range weapons and the launching of guided missiles. Appropriately it was called Woomera, the Aboriginal word for a spear-throwing stick. In the years since then much valuable and original rocketry research has been carried out, in some projects with French and German co-operation. One interesting offshoot has been the development by the Commonwealth aircraft factory of the Jindivik, a pilotless target aircraft, which is much in demand in the United States. In 1952 an atomic research station was established at Lucas Heights, near Sydney. More recent scientific developments include the construction of radio-telescopes at Parkes and Hoskinstown, N.S.W. and a deep space tracking station at Tidbinbilla, near Canberra. Agreement has now been reached between Britain and Australia to build at Coonabarabran, N.S.W. a 150-inch optical telescope, which will be the largest in the southern hemisphere with a capacity to probe 1,000 light years into space.

Above far left Aboriginal Lionel Rose, world bantamweight boxing champion.

Above centre left Evonne Goolagong, Aboriginal teen-age tennis star, tipped by experts as a future champion.

Above centre A contender for the America's Cup in a trial run.

Far left England's bid to regain the Ashes fails at Sydney in 1963. The English captain Cowdrey is caught by Benaud – bowled Davidson. Other Australian players to be seen are Simpson and Grout.

Left Flashback to 1956. John Landy, mile world record holder, is running a close second in a three-mile race to an eighteen-year-old unknown named Ron Clarke.

Right Australian Rules football has a huge following in all states but N.S.W. and Queensland. Picture shows an incident during a Melbourne grand final between Richmond and Geelong.

One of the most significant postwar industrial developments has been the mass-production by General Motors-Holden of a car to suit Australian conditions. The first Holden came off the assembly line in November 1948 and it was such an instant success that in the first seven years alone 250,000 were produced. Many thousands of Holdens are now exported every year. In general, Australian heavy industry continues to be dominated by Broken Hill Proprietary Ltd. In recent years the steelworks at Newcastle and Port Kembla have been greatly expanded and in 1965 a third was opened at Whyalla, South Australia. In the same year launched a 49,000-ton bulk ore carrier, the *Darling River*, at its Whyalla shipyards. It is generally agreed that Australian industry and industrial exports have benefited greatly from the country's change to a dollar-cent decimal currency in 1966, and a proposal to change to metric weights and measures has had wide support.

Inevitably in such a booming country wages and general living standards are high. Proportionately more people in Australia own their own homes than in any other country and the ratio of motor vehicles to people is exceeded only in the United States. It is almost literally true that no-one able and willing to work need be unemployed. A national forty-hour, five-day working week was introduced by the Commonwealth government as far back as 1947. In most states all employees are legally entitled to three weeks' annual leave; in New South Wales since 1964 government employees have received four. There are still strikes but most are settled by compulsory arbitration before they can greatly harm the economy. The general industrial unrest which shadowed Australian history for more than half a century no longer exists. In the face of prosperity and security most Australians now realize they have nothing to fear from cheap, imported, coloured labour; and that the old White Australia policy, apart from giving offence to near neighbours, is no longer justifiable or valid. The presence of some thousands of Asian students in Australia has done much to break down this prejudice. In 1966 some restrictions on the entry of non-Europeans were relaxed and no doubt the law will be further liberalized.

In particular, if belatedly, there has been a marked change in the attitude of most Australians towards their own Aborigines. In 1960 Aborigines became eligible for social services benefits; two years later the Commonwealth and Western Australia gave them the vote. In 1964 the legislative council of the Northern Territory removed all legal discrimination against them and this was followed by the gazettal of minimum housing, food standards and wages for Aboriginal workers, many of whom are employed on the large cattle properties of the area. A national referendum held in April 1967 showed that ninety per cent of adult Australians favour full citizenship for Aborigines by removing from the constitution all wording which discriminates in any way against them. When the artist Albert Namatjira and the actor Robert Tudawali died many white Australians felt a sense of personal loss and some a sense of personal responsibility. Charles Perkins found himself almost a national hero when he became the first Aboriginal to graduate from an Australian university. An Aboriginal, Lional Rose, is not only the present bantamweight boxing champion of the world but also an M.B.E. Evonne Goolagong is Australia's teen-age tennis star and is already tipped as a future winner of the women's singles at Wimbledon.

It is not surprising that most Australians continue to expend much of their leisure energy on sport. Surfing and swimming have lost none of their popularity and there has been a great growth of interest in other aquatic sports such as yachting, sailing, water-skiing and skin-diving. The annual Sydney-Hobart race, inaugurated in 1945, is already one of

Above left A magnificent victory for Australian Ralph Doubell in the 800 metres at the Mexico Olympics, 1968. His time equalled the world record.

Below left Dawn Fraser (centre) after winning the 100 metres freestyle at the Tokyo Olympics of 1964. She had won the same event at Melbourne (1956) and Rome (1960).

Above The new National Library of Australia at Canberra. Its proportions are based on those of the Parthenon at Athens.

Below Rod Laver, winner of the first Open Wimbledon in 1968 and one of the tennis greats of all time.

the world's classic yachting events. Australia has challenged unsuccessfully for the America's Cup and Australian yachtsmen have won Olympic and other international events. Cricket has yet to produce another Bradman but Australian teams more than hold their own in Tests against England, the West Indies, South Africa, India, Pakistan and New Zealand. Names which spring easily to mind include Hassett, Lindwall, Miller, Harvey, Benaud and Simpson. Australia's domination of world tennis, amateur and professional, has become almost complete. Except in 1954 when she was beaten in the challenge round by the United States she held the Davis Cup continuously from 1950 to 1968, when she again lost it to the United States. Postwar Wimbledon singles winners have included Sedgman, Hoad, Laver, Fraser, Emerson, Newcombe and Margaret Smith. The first open Wimbledon in 1968 was won by Rod Laver. Australian squash players have won world titles; Australian golfers of the calibre of Thompson and Devlin have won many open tournaments around the world. In athletics one thinks of the distance runners Landy, Elliott and Clarke; in swimming of many world-record breakers including Dawn Fraser, an Olympic gold-medallist at Melbourne (1956), Rome (1960) and Tokyo (1964). It is demonstrable that in ratio to population Australia is today the world's leading sporting nation. Whether this is a good or a bad thing is, of course, arguable; but certainly it is a source of considerable pride to most Australians.

Australian achievement in what may be termed the international artistic field has not been nearly so spectacular. This is a cause of regret to many but it

Left Sydney, 1969, from the north shore. On the far horizon is Botany Bay which Captain Cook visited in 1770.

Above Melba's successor, Joan Sutherland, in one of her many triumphant operatic roles.

Right Buckjumping event at Warwick rodeo, Queensland. Aborigines are among the best horsemen in the world.

Above eft Prince Charles at Timbertop, part of Geelong Grammar, with his room-mate Stewart McGregor and another pupil, John Seow Kwang Min, of Singapore.

Left The Queen and the Duke of Edinburgh at a corroboree held in Darwin during their 1963 visit to Australia.

Above centre 'Boy with a lizard', by Russell Drysdale, whose paintings of the outback have won him international renown.

is not surprising in a country barely out of adolescence and still unsure of its own identity. A professional theatre and a professional film industry hardly exist, despite spasmodic and not particularly efficient attempts to encourage them. Far too much of Australian television is still given over to lightweight programmes from the United States, in spite of a growing home service. The over-publicized Sydney Opera House, although impressive architecturally, shows every sign of becoming a white elephant. Melbourne's new 'arts centre', less ambitious in conception, may well prove more practical in operation. Adelaide's Festival of the Arts, held every second year, began excitingly but has now settled into what many regard as dull conformity. Classical music has a big but perhaps a not very critical following. So has ballet. No-one is willing to pay the sort of subsidy that would make opera practicable on the scale of Covent Garden or La Scala. Surprisingly Australians buy more books per head than the people of any other country but an indigenous literature has hardly yet emerged. Australians also buy paintings and pay generously for them but too often, one suspects, as an investment. Even so, it is not difficult to think of Australians who have made or are making a perceptible

Right Australia's foremost portrait-painter, Sir William Dobell, at work in his studio.

Below Late afternoon on an Australian beach.

mark outside their own country. The Melba tradition has been carried on since the war by Sylvia Fisher, Joan Hammond, and – more recently – Marie Collier and Joan Sutherland. Malcolm Williamson has achieved some note as a composer, Charles Mackerras as a conductor, Sir Robert Helpmann as a ballet dancer and choreographer. Peter Finch, Leo McKern and Keith Michell are familiar names in the theatre and cinema; Zoe Caldwell won the 1968 New York critics' award for the best actress of the year; Rod Taylor is an established Hollywood film star. Russell Drysdale, Sir William Dobell and Sydney Nolan are painters of international repute and Patrick White's stature as a novelist is equally high. Undoubtedly the list will continue to grow.

Almost every Australian believes fervently and enthusiastically in his country's future. But what shape that future will take remains to some extent an open question. Politically the country is remarkably stable. Even if the present government were to be defeated the overall policy of its successor would be no more than marginally different. Australians have seen that free enterprise works and few want anything else. Saving a major disaster such as another world war the present economic boom seems likely to continue into the foreseeable future. The rural economy is stable; industrial output and mineral production will surely continue to increase at their present dramatic rate. So will population. There are bound to be other developmental projects comparable in magnitude to the Snowy Mountains scheme and perhaps these will help to fill the far north, where there are still only 0·07 people to the square mile. If any one state has a brighter individual future than the others it is surely Western Australia, the one-time Cinderella. She is already Australia's biggest wheat producer, with an annual harvest approaching 110,000,000 bushels. Much of the country's mineral wealth lies beneath her soil and she has other untapped resources.

Australia's political, economic and social relations with most of the countries of South-East Asia are already good and are bound to improve further. She and her nearest and potentially most powerful neighbour, Indonesia, have never been more friendly. Australians and Americans have much in common as people and American influence is strong and becoming stronger. British influence, on the other hand, has declined considerably in the last quarter of a century but to what extent this trend will continue is uncertain. A very large majority are still British by birth or origin and sentimental feeling remains strong. Although few native-born Australians nowadays refer nostalgically to Britain as 'home', hundreds of thousands still go there every year and many remain to work there. Most Australians still prefer to buy British goods but only if the quality is right. On her two visits to Australia since her accession Queen Elizabeth II has been rapturously received and if she goes again – as seems possible in 1970 – it is unlikely that her welcome will be any less warm. The Queen Mother and Prince Philip have been more frequent and equally welcome visitors; and most Australians were delighted and flattered that Prince Charles was able to spend two terms as a schoolboy in their country.

It is generally accepted by Australians and without marked regret that the British Commonwealth, as at present constituted, is unlikely to survive much longer. But no-one talks of the possibility that this could lead to a complete break with Britain. To an overwhelming majority of Australians this would be quite unthinkable.

Index

Acknowledgments

Agent-General for New South Wales
Agent-General for Queensland
Agent-General for South Australia
Agent-General for Tasmania
Agent-General for Victoria
Agent-General for Western Australia
Art Gallery of New South Wales
Australian National Library
Australian News & Information Bureau
Australian Tourist Commission
Australian War Memorial
Douglass Baglin Pty. Ltd.
Barnaby's Picture Library
Roy Birks
The Trustees of the British Museum, London
Camera Press
The late Mrs H. Drake-Brockman
John Fairfax Feature Service
Flight International
Geelong Art Gallery, Victoria
Keystone Press Agency Ltd.
La Trobe Library, Melbourne
The Leicester Galleries
London Express News & Feature Service
Mansell Collection
David Mist
Mitchell Library, Sydney
Nan Kivell Collection of the National Library of Australia, Canberra
National Gallery of South Australia
National Gallery of Western Australia
National Gallery of Victoria
National Maritime Museum, Greenwich
National Portrait Gallery, London
Naval Museum, Madrid
New South Wales Government Printer
New South Wales Public Library
New South Wales Railways
P & O Shipping Co.
Axel Poignant
Popperfoto
Radio Times Hulton Picture Library
Royal Commonwealth Society
Sports & General Press Agency
State Library, Victoria
Tate Gallery, London
Topix
Universal Pictorial Press

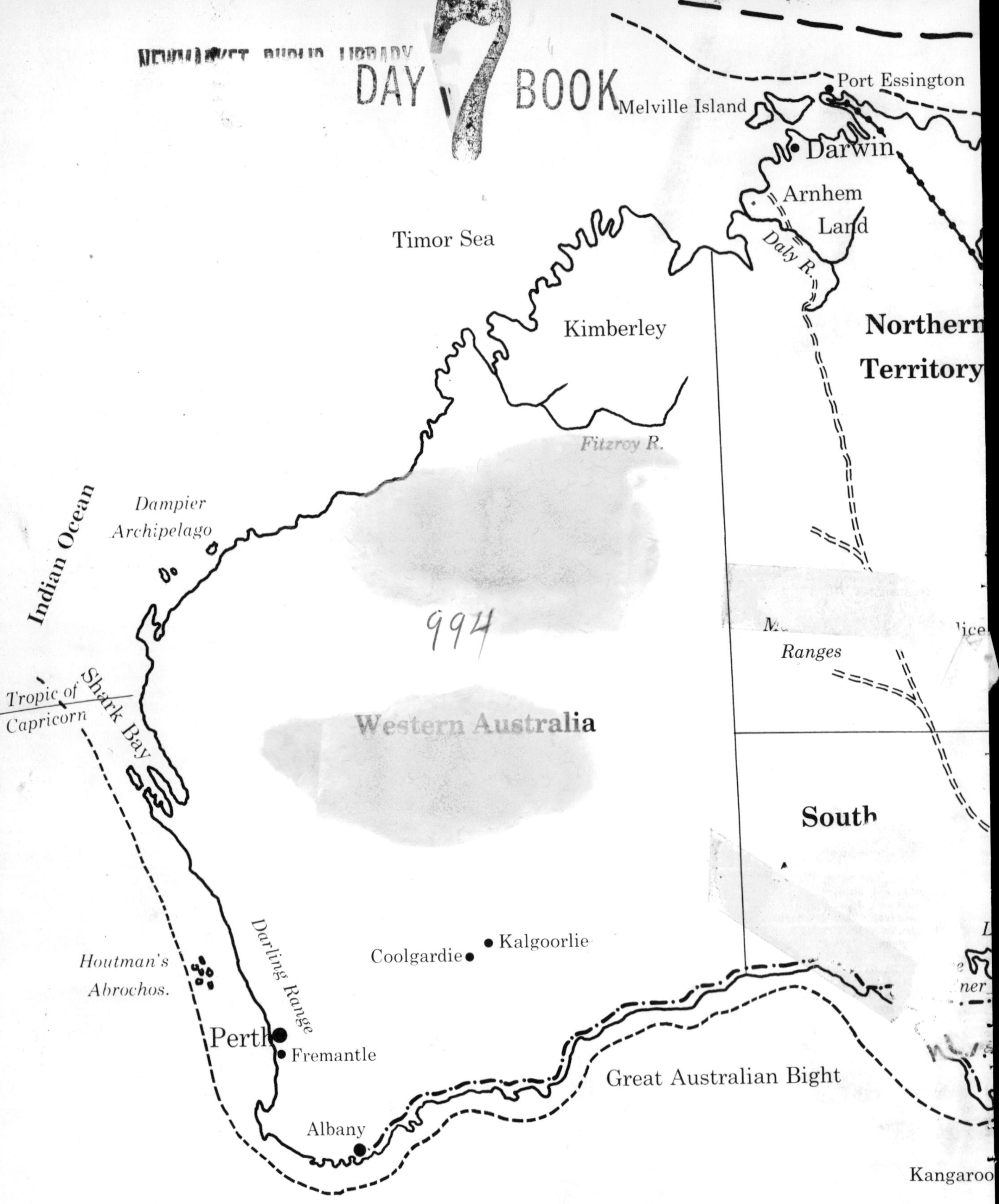
Port Essington
Melville Island
Darwin
Arnhem
Land
Daly R.
Timor Sea
Kimberley
Northern
Territory
Fitzroy R.
Dampier
Archipelago
Indian Ocean
Ranges
Tropic of
Capricorn
Shark Bay
Western Australia
South
Darling Range
Kalgoorlie
Coolgardie
Houtman's
Abrochos.
Perth
Fremantle
Great Australian Bight
Albany
Kangaroo